HARVARD JUDAIC MONOGRAPHS

4

Isadore Twersky, Editor

Hispano-Jewish Culture in Transition

The Career and Controversies of Ramah

Bernard Septimus

HARVARD UNIVERSITY PRESS

*Cambridge, Massachusetts
and London, England
1982*

Library of Congress Cataloging in Publication Data

Septimus, Bernard, 1943–
    Hispano-Jewish culture in transition.

    (Harvard Judaic monographs; 4)
    Includes index.
    1. Abulafia, Meir, 1180 (ca.)–1244.   2. Rabbis—
Spain—Toledo—Biography.   3. Resurrection (Jewish
theology)—History of doctrines.   4. Maimonides, Moses,
1134–1204—Theology.   5. Toledo (Spain)—Biography.
I. Title.   II. Series.
BM755.A29S46   296.3′092′4[B]   81-13275
ISBN 0-674-39230-2   AACR2

To

my father and mother

Preface

To trumpet cultural transition may seem banal; are not all living cultures "in transition"? But if change is a constant, its depth and pace are variable. Hispano-Jewish culture during the lifetime of Ramah (circa 1165–1244) was in rapid and profound transition in response to a radical change: Spanish Jewry had just transferred from the Arabic world to Christian Europe, and no aspect of its culture could remain untouched by this shift in historical environment and the new lines of communication that it opened. But to talk of Hispano-Jewish culture in transition is also to imply a coherent and self-conscious cultural tradition that survived the transfer. Transition thus has as its countertheme (or, better, complementary theme) the tenacious continuities of an old tradition perpetuating itself in a new cultural environment. Besides, continuity and change are not contradictory historical categories: in a changing context, the old can play new roles while the new assumes old ones.

Continuity and change in the wake of Spain's entry into Europe, the major background theme of this book, never strays too far from its primary subject—Ramah. Ramah has remained a relatively obscure figure in Hispano-Jewish history; but, once assembled, his curriculum vitae is impressive. Ramah was the leading talmudist in Spain at the beginning of the thirteenth century and the initiator of European polemic over Maimonidean rationalism. He was also an accomplished poet, a very important Masoretic scholar, an influential communal leader, and a man at home in the Andalusian literary-philosophical tradition. In a few remaining writings one can even catch a fleeting glimpse of an arresting personality of conservative sensibility, aristocratic refinement, and understated humor.

Ramah's obscurity apparently stems from the fragmentary and historiographically unpromising character of the surviving sources. They cannot sustain even a flimsy biographical framework, nor are they readily conducive to systematic reconstruction of Ramah's thought. It was in response to this problem that the theme of "Hispano-Jewish

culture in transition" originally suggested itself. It provided an inte-
grating perspective to impose structure and significance on sources
otherwise resistant to synthesis and to retrieve something of the living
context of Ramah's career. At the same time this perspective provided
an opportunity to use Ramah's career as a vehicle for broader explora-
tion of Hispano-Jewish developments and, on occasion, their Provençal
and northern French repercussions.

Ramah's scholarly career is sketched in the first two chapters against
the backdrop of the transfer to Christian Spain. The first chapter fo-
cuses on Spanish developments, while the second stresses the new lines
of scholarly communication and cultural influence between Spain and
European communities to the north. Throughout the book frequent use
is made of Ramah's halakic writings. The first two chapters in particular
place Ramah's career as a talmudist within the overall Hispano-Jewish
picture of continuity and change. But the technical exposition that a full
study of Ramah's halakah would have required seemed inconsistent
with the synthetic style aimed for by this study and best left for separate treatment. I wish to stress, therefore, that the space allotted in this
book to Ramah's halakah is not proportional to its historical significance. I hope to return to this subject in the context of a more general
study of early thirteenth-century Spanish halakah.

The surviving biographical sources on Ramah tend to cluster around
two episodes of intercommunal controversy over Maimonidean rationalism—one at the very beginning of the thirteenth century, and a second during the 1230s. Although this distribution of documentation necessarily skews our picture of Ramah's career, there is no question that
these controversies and the questions that they raised were crucial to
contemporary Jewish culture. The third and fourth chapters of this
book sketch the course of Ramah's involvement in the two disputes,
while the final two chapters explore the nature of his anti-rationalism and its relation to the old Andalusian tradition, to French anti-
rationalism, and to the new Spanish kabbalah. Although the Maimonidean controversies have been discussed by Jewish historians for well
over a century, it is my hope that the particular foci of this study (Ramah and Spain's entry into Europe) will contribute fresh perspective.

The general medievalist who stumbles upon this book will undoubt-
edly be struck by some obvious similarities (as well as important differences) between the Maimonidean Controversy and the great faith and
reason controversy that came to a head in Latin Europe (though not in
Spain) somewhat later in the thirteenth century. Certain parallel ten-
sions were bound to arise when two biblical religions sharing the medieval European environment were confronted with roughly the same
version of Aristotelian naturalism in the intellectual wake of Spain's

incorporation into Europe. But if the Latin faith and reason controversy was important in European cultural history, the Maimonidean Controversy, in Jewish cultural history, was momentous. The Latin controversy took place within a relatively unified scholastic culture that had long been subject to *some* philosophical influence. The cultural types confronting each other in the Maimonidean Controversy ranged from Spanish intellectuals saturated with Greco-Arabic philosophy to northern French talmudists totally innocent of philosophical thought. In Latin Europe the content of "faith" was fairly clear; its definition was in the hands of an authoritative institution. Lacking any accepted contemporary source of theological authority, the disputants in the Maimonidean Controversy were debating the definition of faith itself. Finally, the Latin faith and reason controversy took place within the confines of clerical culture. The Maimonidean Controversy engulfed entire communities from top to bottom in cultural conflict that spilled over into the political. The Maimonidean Controversy thus provides the framework for a study of fundamental spiritual developments that is nevertheless firmly grounded in the historical landscape. My goal has been to write "intellectual history as a history not 'of thought' but of men thinking" (Joseph Levenson, *Confucian China and its Modern Fate* [Berkeley, 1958], I, 163).

An early stage of my research was aided by a doctoral fellowship from the National Foundation for Jewish Culture, and a final stage benefited from Yale University's generous Morse Fellowship. I should like to acknowledge my debt to my teachers, Isadore Twersky and Yosef Yerushalmi, for their training and advice; defects, to borrow a medieval formula, stem from the imperfections of the recipient. Professor Twersky, now a senior colleague, remains my teacher in more than one sphere. His help in bringing this book to completion is just one of many kindnesses for which I am deeply grateful. My wife, Chani, made valuable criticisms of the first draft and helped in innumerable other ways. For my parents, to whom this book is dedicated, my love and gratitude are boundless.

Contents

I. Islam to Christendom   1

II. New Northern Connections   26

III. The Resurrection Controversy   39

IV. The Maimonidean Controversy   61

V. Varieties of Anti-rationalism   75

VI. Anti-rationalism and Mysticism   104

Notes   117

Index   175

HISPANO-JEWISH CULTURE

IN TRANSITION

I

ISLAM TO CHRISTENDOM

THE TWELFTH CENTURY marks an important turning point in Jewish history. The Jewish communities under Islam suffered decline and destruction, while those in Europe, despite an increasingly hostile Christian environment, showed an upsurge of vitality and cultural creativity. This shift in the center of gravity of Jewish life altered the framework within which Jewish history would unfold. For better or for worse, it was now bound up with the fate of Europe.[1]

The Spanish Jewish community, the most prominent in the Arabic world, fits this general pattern in a particular way. Instead of simply dwindling or decaying, Spanish Jewry transferred from the Arabic world to Christian Europe—and it did so as a community, with its collective identity more or less intact. Two forces, themselves diametrically opposed, combined to bring this transfer about with remarkable rapidity. The first was the progress of the Christian Reconquest of Spain; the second was the invasion of Muslim Spain by Berber tribes from North Africa. The Christian Reconquest steadily pushed the borders of the Muslim territories southward, bringing their Jewish populations under Christian control. The Berber invaders, on the other hand, though handing the Christian advance some serious setbacks, destroyed Jewish life in the south, forcing large numbers of refugees to flee to Christian territory.[2]

The transfer began in earnest in the last decades of the eleventh century. The Reconquest began to achieve significant successes, bringing important Jewish communities—most notably that of Toledo (1085)—under Christian control.[3] The first Berber invasion, that of the Almoravids—though temporarily stemming the Christian tide—weakened the political and economic base of Andalusian Jewry and encouraged emigration to Christian territory.[4] Nevertheless, the heart of Spanish Jewry remained in Andalusia. Cultural life was at its height with no creative

1

decline in sight when the end came, with brutal abruptness, in the middle of the twelfth century.[5] In response to fresh Christian successes, a
new and more fanatical Berber dynasty, the Almohades, invaded Muslim Spain in 1147 and proceeded to declare all religions other than
Islam illegal.[6] For Andalusian Jews, there was one alternative to death
or apostasy—flight. Most turned northward.

In his *Book of the Tradition*, the Andalusian exile Abraham ibn Daud
captures the agony and frenzy of the flight north and portrays the sense
of abrupt dislocation that it produced.[7] For Ibn Daud, Spanish Jewish
history—in fact, beginning in the eleventh century, all of significant
Jewish history—had been unfolding in Andalusia. Christian Spain was
a haven providentially prepared for the day when suddenly "the world
became desolate of academies of learning."[8] Ibn Daud's "world" com-
prised the noble and cultured communities of Andalusia, shattered and
scattered by the Almohade sword.[9] Within a few years, "all the nation
had finished passing over [from Muslim to Christian Spain]."[10]

Writing in Toledo in 1161, Ibn Daud was himself participating in an
attempt at reconstruction in Christian Spain. His history encourages the
hope that the political and cultural heritage of Andalusian Jewry will
somehow survive. On the political front, Judah ibn Ezra, who had
gained a position of influence at the court of Alfonso VII of Castile, was
aiding in the resettlement of refugees from the south. A son and a
nephew of Joseph ibn Megash (both named Meir) were attempting to
keep alive the talmudic tradition of the great academy at Lucena. Ibn
Daud was further developing the philosophical tradition of Muslim
Spain and writing in defense of the Jewish faith. But what could be sal-
vaged seemed meager indeed when compared to all that had been destroyed.[11]

By the beginning of the thirteenth century the Jewish communities of
Christian Spain were showing new strength. Seeds painfully planted
had taken root. They would soon flower into important achievement,
albeit in a form which no longer followed the lines of development that
had unfolded in Muslim Spain. Surveying the Jewish world of this period, the Hebrew poet Judah Alharizi is once again able to see in Spain
the height of Jewish cultural achievement. "Its air," he says, "is the life
of souls."[12] Alharizi's readers would easily recognize his playful inver-
sion of a familiar theme of Judah Halevi. Halevi, almost as if prophe-
sying the Almohade disaster, had rejected the political and cultural
order of Spain for the Land of Israel, whose "air" is the "life of souls."[13]
At the beginning of the thirteenth century Alharizi could, somewhat ir-
reverently, claim this very distinction for Spain.

After passing through "the lands of the Ishmaelites" the picaresque
hero of Alharizi's *Tahkemoni* enters "the lands of the uncircumcised
[Christians] in which the Israelites dwell." He arrives at Toledo, "the

royal city, clothed with the grace of majesty and having culture as her ornament, that the nations and princes may be shown her beauty." "For there," adds Alharizi, "have the tribes gone up, the tribes of the Lord."[14] Alharizi was probably alluding here to the role of Toledo as a refuge for the Jews fleeing northward from Muslim Spain.[15] But Alharizi has also, not inadvertently, borrowed a verse which in Psalms (122:4) refers to Jerusalem. Toledo possessed all the social and cultural achievements that Alharizi valued: aristocratic lineage, political power, literary and social grace, broad scientific and philosophical learning alongside a budding talmudic renaissance. If Spain could qualify as a surrogate Palestine, then Toledo was its Jerusalem.[16]

The most famous scholar in Alharizi's Toledo was the talmudist R. Meir ha-Levi Abulafia (circa 1165–1244). Abulafia has made his mark in medieval halakic literature as "Ramah" (רמ״ה), an acronym formed from the first letters of the name Rabbi Meir Halevi. Ramah was among the most brilliant and colorful figures on the Hispano-Jewish scene. Born of the old aristocracy of Andalusia and educated in the best tradition of its Judeo-Arabic paideia, he was the first major talmudist to appear in Spain since the Almohade invasion. Ramah combined the nobility, wealth, scholarly versatility, and literary finesse that Alharizi admired. And yet when Alharizi lists Toledo's most prominent men, Ramah receives a very mixed review: "Among their princes (nesi'im) is the Levite R. Meir b. Todros. None compare to him in wisdom. But he is haughty and his haughtiness lowers him."[17] Perhaps these are just the facts; but one man's insolence is often another's courage. Alharizi's condemnation of a man whose wisdom and station compelled admiration may be related to a crucial confrontation between the two: Ramah was only admired for his wisdom; but he had dared to criticize a man that Alharizi idolized—Maimonides. Criticism of Maimonides was, for many of his admirers, ipso facto an act of arrogance.[18]

Alharizi's terse appraisal yields two major foci of Ramah's career: profound scholarship and the controversy over Maimonidean rationalism. Both were of major historical significance. Ramah's "unrivaled wisdom" points to the recovery of Spanish Jewry from the Almohade disaster, for Ramah was the first major talmudic authority living in Spain in more than half a century and was at the same time at home in the literary and philosophical tradition that had been the special pride of Andalusian Jewry. Ramah's criticism of Maimonides, however, and his consequent condemnation by Alharizi represent a new historical turn. In Christian Spain, spiritual conflict would attain an intensity and centrality unknown in Andalusia. Ramah's criticism of Maimonidean rationalism initiated a controversy that had not yet ended when the last professing Jew left Spanish soil.

Ramah himself provides an interesting counterpoint to Alharizi's

glowing picture of a resurrected Sefarad. Following is a talmudic cata-
logue of evils that characterize "the generation in which [Messiah] the
son of David will come," together with Ramah's commentary (in
brackets):

> . . . the meeting house will be given over to harlotry [that is to say,
> people will be so unrestrained in their harlotry that they will set
> aside a public place in which to consort with harlots. And some
> say: the scholar's meeting house shall become a place of licen-
> tiousness.] And the parchment will be condemned. [This refers to
> the parchment of Torah scrolls; that is to say, it will be punished
> and wasted because its students have decreased] . . . And the wis-
> dom of scribes will become spoilt. And sin-fearing men will be
> despised [by the people]. The face of the generation will be [inso-
> lent] like the face of a dog. And truth will be wanting . . . And who-
> ever departs from evil makes himself ridiculous [that is to say, acts
> foolishly in men's eyes].[19]

Here, Ramah departs from his text with a dry aside: "And I wonder,
according to these signs why the Son of David does not come in this
generation of ours!"

Ramah's bit of pessimistic humor reflects an appraisal of Spanish
conditions quite different from that of Alharizi. But there is no real
contradiction, only a difference in focus. Alharizi's interest centered on
the life of the aristocracy—its nobility, power, and literate enlighten-
ment; Ramah's concern extended to the general level of morality, piety,
religious leadership, and scholarship. Alharizi's account quite correctly
communicates a sense of the new vigor of a recovered Spain. But
alongside renewed strength and cultural achievement, there existed
conditions that some found deeply disturbing. Ramah is but the first in
a long line of religious leaders sharply critical of social and religious
conditions in the Jewish communities of Christian Spain.[20] Ramah suggests that in his day "whoever departs from evil . . . acts foolishly in
men's eyes." His comment may be autobiographical. For as we shall
see, it was written when Ramah had just suffered severe censure for his
criticism of Maimonides (circa 1204). Ramah's "departure from evil"
may well be the "haughtiness" condemned by Alharizi.

According to a tradition current in Toledo in the fourteenth century,
Ramah was born in the north Castilian city of Burgos, while his literary
and teaching career was centered in Toledo:

> In [Maimonides'] last years there shone forth the brilliant star, the
> plate of the holy crown, the rock of assistance RaMaH—that is, R.
> Meir Halevi of blessed memory, the prince over the princes of the
> Levites, who was from the city of Burgos and came to the city of

Toledo, spread [knowledge of the] Torah there and raised up many disciples. He commented on many talmudic tractates with great precision and profound analysis and composed many works on the laws of the Torah. He died on Passover in the year 5004 [1244].[21]

All available evidence converges in support of this report on Ramah's origins.[22]

Ramah's father, the *nasi* R. Todros Halevi Abulafia, was a prominent statesman and leader of the Burgos community. A fine manuscript of the *Prophets* commissioned by R. Todros was completed in Burgos in 1207, five years before his death. The colophon describes R. Todros as "the first-born son of the great *nasi*, the fortress and citadel our master and teacher R. Meir Halevi."[23] Of this first R. Meir Halevi little is known beyond his apparent prominence. Nor can anything certain be said about the family's origins. The Arabic surname "Abu'l-'āfiyah" argues for a family originating in Muslim Spain.[24]

R. Meir Halevi's sons seem to have been men of some importance. We know the names of three of R. Todros' younger brothers: Judah, Zerahyah, and Joseph. Judah married a daughter of the Provençal *nasi*, R. Kalonymous and apparently took up residence close by his father-in-law.[25] Zerahyah, we may gather from Ramah's eulogistic remarks, was an extremely important and devoted communal leader and states-man who on occasion was able to use his influence to save Jewish lives.[26] We know nothing of the activities of R. Todros' third brother, Joseph; but he can be located in Toledo about 1195.[27]

Ramah's mother belonged to one of the outstanding families of the Spanish Jewish aristocracy. R. Aaron b. Meshullam of Lunel refers to "the glory of [Ramah's] mother's family."[28] In a letter written about 1232, Ramah's brother, Joseph b. Todros, reminds his Provençal corre-spondents that "if the Oral Law is the inheritance of the Congregation of Jacob, the tribes of my mother's father have already taken possession of one portion more than their brethren in that inheritance. Please in-quire in the *Book of Tradition* written by the great scholar R. Abraham b. David . . . and it will instruct you."[29] Unfortunately we can only guess at the particular family.[30]

R. Todros was apparently a patron of literature. Two contemporary poets are known to have dedicated works to him. In 1208 Judah ibn Shabbetai dedicated his *Offering of Judah the Misogynist* to Ramah's brother-in-law Abraham Alfakar. A young poet known only by the name Isaac composed *Women's Aid* in rebuttal and dedicated it to R. Todros in 1210.[31]

Poetic debate over women was lighthearted literary sport reflecting more the taste than the ideology of its patrons. Perhaps more revealing is the *Debate between Wisdom and Wealth* dedicated to R. Todros by Ibn Shabbetai. R. Todros, possessing both, is chosen arbitrator and declares a draw.[32] This work contains a rare description of R. Todros:

> God filled him with spirit in wisdom, understanding, knowledge and all areas of endeavor. All he lacks is kingship. God has abundantly provided him with wealth, property and honor. He is the wonder of the generation and its glory, the man whom the king delights to honor. And the nations walk by his light. By his speech the righteous is saved and by the breath of his lips he slays the wicked. Righteousness is the girding of his loins and faithfulness the girding of his hips. He is the man who was raised on high as a savior and redeemer during the third month after the Exodus of the Children of Israel, to sound the great *shofar* of our freedom at the time of the Revelation of our Torah, and to repair every breach until the coming of the Teacher of Righteousness. The princes and rulers also participated in his elevation. For He saw the affliction of His people living in unfortified cities. Their cries reached Him. He listened to their voices and sent them a savior and contender to deliver them: our master and teacher Todros Halevi. May his honor increase and his majesty be exalted. May he overcome and roar against his enemies and may his head reach unto the clouds.[33]

Although one must make allowance for hyperbole, Ibn Shabbetai's panegyric affords a glimpse at R. Todros' otherwise unknown political and communal activities. He was clearly famed for his wealth and wisdom. The king who "delights to honor" R. Todros is probably Alfonso VIII of Castile. Ibn Shabbetai's use of quasi-Messianic language indicates that R. Todros had considerable political power and was an outstanding leader of the Jewish community.[34]

Ibn Shabbetai alludes to a particular event of significance. R. Todros was appointed to a high political office, strengthening his power and position in the community. This new elevation was supported by the aristocratic "princes" of the Jewish community. In his new position R. Todros was able to strengthen the vulnerable position of the Jews in the towns of Castile, who had apparently been subject to persecution. At about this time the bishop of Burgos complained to Rome about exemptions and privileges enjoyed by the Jews. Innocent III thought the matter serious enough to address a sharp rebuke to King Alfonso VIII in 1205.[35]

Ramah's eulogies written at R. Todros' death in 1213 confirm this picture. Ramah refers to his father as *ha-Rab*,[36] indicating some measure of talmudic scholarship. There is also definite reference to an official position (*rabbanut*) held by R. Todros.[37] A halakic fragment of Spanish provenance dating from about this period quotes the opinion of a certain R. Todros,[38] but no certain identification can be made. Like Ibn Shabbetai, Ramah stresses his father's wisdom, justice, and relief of the oppressed.[39]

Both Ibn Shabbetai and Ramah refer to R. Todros' punishment of wrongdoers. "He was," says Ramah, "the rod of faith that every morning visited the backs of men of oppression and iniquity."[40] So too Ibn Shabbetai, who writes that "by the breath of his lips he slays the wicked." They may be alluding, among other things, to R. Todros' role in suppressing Karaism in northern Castile. This action is proudly mentioned by his son Joseph b. Todros.[41]

The date of Ramah's birth is unknown. A fair estimate is 1165.[42] Nor do we know anything of Ramah's early years in Burgos. Though not famous as a center of scholarship, Burgos was at that time the second largest Jewish community in Castile.[43] R. Todros, at any rate, was certainly able to provide his children with a complete education. When Ramah appears on the historical scene, at a relatively young age, he is already a skilled poet and an expert talmudic scholar.

Burgos could not compare with Toledo as a cultural center, and it probably looked toward the larger and more learned Castilian capital for guidance and scholarship. There is evidence of cultural and social ties between the two cities. We hear, for example, of a leading Toledo halakist being consulted by the Burgos community, and on another occasion of his intervening in its communal affairs.[44] A contemporary halakic manual contains a sample bill of divorce dated Toledo, 1205, from "Reuben b. Ya'aqob called Khalfon from the city of Toledo on the river Tajo" to "Sarah b. Abraham called Jamilah from the city of Burgos situated on the river Durano."[45]

We do not know the date or circumstances of Ramah's transfer to Toledo. He may have been attracted by its scholarly resources. Perhaps it was after his marriage to a daughter of its most distinguished family that Ramah decided to settle in Toledo. One could hardly ask for a more prominent and well-situated father-in-law; Joseph ibn Shoshan was the treasurer of Alfonso VIII of Castile, extremely wealthy and highly esteemed as a leader and protector of his people.[46] By 1194, in any event, Ramah can be located in Toledo.[47] By the turn of the century he was already playing an active role in the life of its Jewish community.

It is not strange that Ramah should have preferred Toledo, with its superior cultural opportunities, to Burgos. R. Todros, however, seems to have remained in Burgos until his death in 1213. Joseph, Ramah's younger brother, can still be found in Burgos in the fourth decade of the thirteenth century.[48] Ramah too continued to maintain close personal and scholarly contacts with the city of his birth.[49]

When his sister, apparently also a Toledo resident, died (a few months before R. Todros), Ramah "wrote to his father informing him of . . . [his daughter's death] and comforting him in her words [as if she were speaking]":

> Bear, O clouds, the greetings of my grave, to my father
> . . . . .
> And with lips of silence reveal to him
> my silent fate.
> But take heed lest my distress pain him,
> Lest he be saddened at my grief.
> For what profit in his suffering at my anguish,
> and in his pain, will mine decrease?
> What good your tearing open his heart, on my account?
> I would only be sinning against my father
> Who made the wings of his kindness my couch,
> and his merciful neck, my chariot.
> . . . . .
> Leave me alone, how long will you cry out to me,
> know that God's hand has touched me
> And Death, from the chamber of the husband of my youth
> has suddenly, like a lion, torn me.
> . . . . .
> And my buriers have covered my face with dust
> upon which I trod, but yesterday!
> And I shall draw all mankind after me,
> friends and enemies alike will come to me.
> For God summons to the abode appointed for all living,
> so that both sinner and prophet must die
> Till He restores souls to their bodies,
> and then, when I return, will I see your faces again.[50]

This poetic letter allows us a glimpse at Ramah's filial feelings. So, in a different way, does his dispute with Rashi on the meaning of the talmudic rule that a son "not decide on his [father's] words":

> Rashi interpreted "If [his father] was disputing a question of halakah with someone, he should not say: 'so and so's view seems reasonable.'" But Ramah wrote: "This would be redundant, for it would be [covered by the previous rule that prohibits] contradicting his words. [Its interpretation is] rather that even if he finds his father's words reasonable, he should not say: 'father's words seem reasonable'; for he would then appear to render decision on his father's words. He should rather—if he has a response to make to those who dispute [his father]—[simply] respond.[51]

A brilliant son of a scholarly father, Ramah may have had the opportunity to put his interpretation into practice.

A fine poem of praise to one of the great princes of the Andalusian "Golden Age" concludes with the restatement of an old biblical and talmudic theme:

> And the star which has issued forth from you,
> may God make his name even greater than yours.[52]

R. Todros lived to see this blessing realized in his son. Ramah soon outstripped his father, at least in halakic scholarship. Some time after Ramah's removal to Toledo we find R. Todros sending a difficult legal problem south for his son's decision. That correspondence has not come down to us—Ramah merely mentions it in a later communication to Burgos. His reference there to "my response to *our* master and father of blessed memory" indicates that he was writing to a brother. This responsum may be Ramah's only surviving communication with his brother Joseph b. Todros.[53]

An interesting exchange between Ramah and the powerful Barcelona *nasi* Isaac Benveniste took place upon R. Todros' death in 1213. Ramah's grief was aggravated by events in Burgos following R. Todros' death. These events are not entirely clear, but it appears that an influential but (in Ramah's opinion) unworthy successor aspired to R. Todros' position. Isaac alludes to this situation in his poetic condolence:

> And you who bring tidings [of R. Todros' death], publish them not
> in the ears of seekers of evil and iniquity
>
> Lest lowly men take note, grow arrogant
> and seek to gain high position.[54]

Ramah's reply to Isaac Benveniste was written "when the one who took upon himself the *rabbanut* [the upstart] had already done so."[55] Ramah, feeling that his father's memory had been dishonored, minced no words:

> The fool's stench rises
> though his clothes drop myrrh and aloes.
>
> For how can the lowly despise his day of little things
> and presume to seek high position.
>
> The vulgar has donned precious vestments
> only to show his shame and uncover his nakedness.[56]

Nothing more is known about the incident. Abulafia leadership was, in any case, eventually restored in Burgos: twenty years later Ramah's brother Joseph b. Todros was powerful enough to expel an influential visitor from the city.[57]

The Toledo community, when Ramah arrived, had a long tradition. It had been a significant center of population and learning under Muslim rule. And with the Castilian conquest of Toledo in 1085 and its establishment as the royal capital, the community's importance increased. Prominent Andalusian families, escaping unsettled conditions in the south, established themselves in Toledo. Jews were active in its economy and at the Castilian court. When the refugees from the Almohade persecutions arrived in Toledo, they found an established communal framework and relatively favorable political and economic conditions.[58]

By the time of Ramah's arrival, the Jewish community of Toledo was probably the most populous in Europe. According to a fifteenth-century source, Ramah's friend Abraham ha-Yarhi estimated Toledo's Jewish population at over twelve thousand.[59] Modern historians have been justifiably skeptical of this report,[60] but even the eyewitness Alharizi writes that Toledo "contains of the holy seed a community adorned with uprightness. Myriads, like the plants of the field."[61] Located at the center of political power, in the midst of a booming Reconquista economy, the Toledo Jewish community was perhaps the wealthiest in the world. It is the only Jewish community whose architectural splendors seem to have evoked Alharizi's admiration: "Many a charming palace therein shames the luminaries by its splendour and grace; and many synagogues are found there of peerless beauty."[62] Prominent among Toledo's synagogues "of peerless beauty" was the famous synagogue constructed about 1200 by Ramah's father-in-law, R. Joseph ibn Shoshan.[63] Ramah, in the course of a complex legal discussion, makes reference to "tall or expensive buildings, artistic inscriptions and ornamental paneling which people generally do not construct in places unprotected by a wall."[64] His statement reflects well the realities of this stage of the Reconquista. Some Jews had fine palaces, but were not without a sense of the insecurity of their position. The palaces of Toledan Jewry were to be found in a walled quarter which "was virtually a city in itself."[65] Spanish Christendom provided refuge and even prosperity, but not affection or security.

The impact of the Reconquista on the position of the Jews was complex. Popular fanaticism engendered by holy warfare tended to increase anti-Jewish feeling. But the political and economic requirements of the period made the talents and services of the Jewish aristocracy extremely valuable to the monarchy. During Ramah's times, the king's political and economic considerations generally prevailed. But the situation was inherently unstable.[66] Influential political leaders served, at best, as a protective shield for the Jewish community, and the death of one of these men might signal new attacks. Ramah's lament on the death of Joseph ibn Shoshan in 1205 captures the political mood well:

Woe, for enemies pursue us,
and gone is the prince whose kind hands were our weapons.

He was like a warrior, without shield or buckler other than his epis-
tles,
and his pens were our mighty staff.

He was like a muzzle upon the mouths of our enemies
so that a child might play in his days, upon the vipers' nests.

He was like thorns in the sides of our enemies
now with his passing, they are again thorns in our side.[67]

Ibn Shoshan had succeeded Judah ibn Ezra, providential hero of the
great northern emigration, in Ibn Daud's *Book of the Tradition*. It has
been suggested that Ibn Daud's treatment of Hispano-Jewish history
served, in part, as a response to the challenge posed by Judah Halevi.
Halevi had brilliantly questioned the political and cultural ideology of
the Andalusian aristocracy and then, putting theory into practice,
abandoned Spain for the Land of Israel. Had not the Almohade disaster
proved him right? Ibn Daud reaffirms the viability of the transplanted
Andalusian political ideal—and Ibn Ezra serves as his shining example.[68] Ibn Ezra was, in a way, a perfect foil for Halevi. A recently discovered genizah document shows that Ibn Ezra had originally planned to
follow Halevi but changed his mind at the last minute. That decision,
not to abandon "enslavement to kings" (*'abdut melakim*), made it possible for Ibn Ezra to serve as his people's savior in their hour of crisis.[69]

The men around Ramah continued in Ibn Ezra's tradition, perform-
ing important administrative, financial, and ambassadorial functions
for the Castilian court. They were filling an important vacuum in
Christian society, while at the same time continuing their Andalusian
political tradition. And as in Andalusia, political position and communal leadership went hand in hand.[70] Power and leadership were concentrated in the hands of a few aristocratic families like Ibn Ezra, Alfakar, Ibn Sahl, and Ibn Shoshan. It was to this group that the Abulafia
family belonged. Marriage alliances made this an interlocking elite.[71]
Its most honored members bore—like Ramah—the proud title *nasi*.
Ramah's wealth, culture, connections, and family tradition would have
made some involvement with the royal court natural. Still, he may well
have desisted; doubtless he was aware of the difficulties of combining
scholarship and politics.[72]

The situation is similar in the economic sphere. The members of
Ramah's circle did not share the distaste of the Hispano-Christian nobility for (nonmilitary) economic activity. They were particularly valued by the crown as urban colonizers, building new cities and rebuild-
ing those destroyed by war.[73] But we do not know the extent of
Ramah's involvement in these activities. He certainly was not lacking in

capital; Aaron b. Meshullam of Lunel, himself no pauper, even compared Ramah to the fabulously wealthy R. El'azar b. Harsom of talmudic fame.[74] Ramah was of the opinion that the ideal scholar *should* engage in economic activity—but only to the extent necessary to cultivate financial independence.[75] And in Ramah's case that may not have been very much. His surviving business correspondence comes to a few lines written to a traveling friend. The latter's problem with a slippery partner, Ramah reports, is being handled by someone else. His own personal message: Please don't forget to bring back those books that I ordered![76]

Although Ramah's direct involvement in economic and political matters may have been limited, he was surely no cloistered scholar, withdrawn from the world of affairs. On the contrary, his indirect contribution to the economic and even political life of the Hispano-Jewish community was vital. For Ramah provided indispensable juridical guidance in a period of rapid expansion and change. Scholarship and nobility gave Ramah a twofold title to leadership. The state of our sources makes it impossible to reconstruct his communal career. But there is a brief hint that he could combine learning with bold and vigorous action: R. Jonah ibn Bahlul, after praising Ramah's superlative scholarship which illuminated the Spanish scene, adds: "And he was not fearful of donning the robes of sovereignty (*bigde ha-serad*)."[77]

Ramah's writings provide interesting examples of the impact of the Reconquista on halakic literature. The problem of cost allocation for the construction of protective walls is very briefly treated in halakic literature prior to Ramah. By contrast, Ramah's treatment, with its detailed geometrical and topographical considerations, is mammoth.[78] Immediately after Ramah, jurists and commentators seem once again to lose interest. We recall the walled Jewish quarters of the Reconquista period; interest seems to have gone hand in hand with actuality.

The political realities of the Reconquista brought Jews into close relationship with the monarchy. "We had to send a messenger to the king and asked you to rent us your horse,"[79] begins the claim of an anonymous Jewish community in civil litigation submitted to Ramah. The community's need for rapid, direct communication with the king is mentioned as a matter of course. Repercussions of this political development are detectable in Ramah's treatment of the subject of communal taxation.

One of the reasons that non-Jewish governments were willing to grant autonomy to the medieval Jewish community was that it served as an effective agent for the collection of taxes. The community was taxed a lump sum, which it then apportioned among its members.[80] Now according to talmudic law, the property of minor orphans is exempt from all communal taxes; the only exception is a tax levied to provide monies for defense.[81] The question naturally arose as to whether taxes paid by the community to non-Jewish rulers could be classified as defense expenditures and collected from the property of minor orphans.

The last great halakist of Muslim Spain, R. Joseph ibn Megash, argued that a tax imposed on the community by the non-Jewish government clearly has nothing to do with defense.[82] Ramah disagreed. "Paying taxes to the king," he writes, "is certainly no less [effective] than hiring horsemen and guards for defense. Quite to the contrary, the protection provided by the king is certainly more effective."[83] Ramah's opinion reflects nicely the close relationship between Jews and monarchy during the Reconquista. Christian legal theory might consider the Jews to be "slaves of the royal treasury," and Jewish taxes, profits generated by royal property;[84] but in the eyes of the Jews, royal taxes constituted a highly effective defense expenditure. True, Ramah and his contemporaries had occasion to learn that royal protection had its limitations.[85] But they were still relatively optimistic about its effectiveness.

With the completion of the bulk of the Reconquista at about the time of Ramah's death, conditions steadily deteriorated. In the beginning of the fourteenth century, R. Asher b. Yehiel—having escaped persecution in Germany and writing under changed conditions in Toledo—sounds a poignant note. He agrees with Ramah but offers a less sanguine explanation: "It seems to me that all types of taxes must be considered defense expenditures. For it is they that preserve us among the gentiles. For what purpose do some of the gentile nations find in preserving us and allowing us to live among them if not the benefit that they derive from Israel in that they collect taxes and extortions from them."[86]

When Ramah arrived in Toledo, the struggle between Christendom and Islam for control of the Iberian peninsula still hung in the balance. The Jewish community could hardly remain neutral. When the Almohades advanced into Castile and ravaged the district of Toledo in 1196, the Jews of Toledo, according to a later chronicle, "went out to meet [the Almohade caliph] and fought against him and killed many of *their* enemies."[87] It was not until the defeat of the Almohades at Las Navas de Tolosa in 1212 that the tide was decisively turned in favor of the Christians; only then did it become clear that Spanish Jewry would remain under the domination of Western Christendom. The years of Ramah's mature leadership in Toledo saw the rapid triumph of the Reconquista. Shortly after his death the Reconquista ground to a halt, with all but the southern kingdom of Granada in Christian hands.[88]

One doubts that Spanish Jewry mourned Islam's defeat. In their experience, "no nation ever persecuted Israel like Ishmael." Hence the conclusion—"better under Edom [Christendom] than under Ishmael [Islam]".[89] As the saying implies, Edom was but the lesser of two evils. Even at the moment of the decisive battle at Las Navas de Tolosa, Toledan Jewry found itself severely threatened by the crusading fervor of the great Christian army keyed up for its confrontation with the Almohades.[90] And with the eclipse of Ishmael, in the thirteenth century, Edom regains the role of Israel's primary captor in Hispano-Jewish biblical exegesis and liturgical poetry.[91] Already in the poetry of Ramah it is "the bloody man," Edom, who appears as Israel's arch-foe.[92] And in a poem composed for Purim, Ramah has Israel address her adversaries in the following lines:

> You preach vanity and lies
> And pronounce to me a name I know not.
> And proclaim glad tidings you never heard
> To my face, always.
>
> Why do you thus conceal deceitful counsel
> And offer up before me the wine of lies
> And put down the bread of falsehood
> Upon my table, always.[93]

Israel's adversaries are clearly no longer Moslems. One easily detects in these proud words allusion to the name of Christ, the Gospels, the wine and bread of the Mass—in a word, the new religious world challenging the Spanish Jew in Christian Spain.

In the early thirteenth century, the Jewish community of Toledo retained the variety of cultural life typical of the Muslim era, if not its brilliance. The direct stimulus of the new Christian environment seems small when compared with the impact of Arabic literature and philosophy in Andalusia. The rapid growth in Latin Christendom's knowledge of "the true sciences" noted by Ramah's Provençal friend, Samuel ibn Tibbon,[94] still had little impact in Spain. This Spanish "belatedness"[95] was partially offset, in Toledo, by an extensive translation movement and the presence of intellectually ambitious northerners in search of Arabic learning. Moreover, the very absence of Christian expertise in certain traditionally strong "Jewish" disciplines (languages, medicine, the sciences) assured a "market" that encouraged the perpetuation of these disciplines in the Jewish community. But the primary impetus to cultural life still seems to have been internal. The southern émigrés in Toledo had striven, with moderate success, to transplant the educational ideal of Andalusia. Ramah was at least conversant with virtually all areas of literary and intellectual activity pursued in Toledo.

In the following bit of rhymed prose, written in the 1230s, the young

Nahmanides is proposing the by then venerable Ramah as arbitrator of a sensitive dispute: "Let's go to the land of ma'arab, to the most excellent scholar (ge'on) of ['eber] and 'arab, R. Meir ha-rab.'"[96] Nahmanides' description of Ramah echoes a line of Judah Halevi, in his famous first letter to Moses ibn Ezra. Halevi, having traveled from Christian to Muslim Spain, addressed himself to "the light of the ma'arab (Andalusia), the scholar (hakam) of 'eber and 'arab (Hebrew and Arabic), R. Moshe ha-rab.'"[97] Nahmanides, from his Catalan vantage point, viewed Toledo as the new ma'arab.[98] And he admired Ramah not only as a consummate talmudist but as master of the rich and varied Andalusian tradition of Hebrew and Arabic learning.

Nahmanides' view of Toledo as heir of Andalusia reflects not just the prominence of descendants of Andalusian émigrés in its population or even their efforts to perpetuate the Andalusian heritage, but the whole Toledan environment. Though politically part of Christian Europe, New Castile—and Toledo in particular—was saturated with Muslim influence. The survival of Arabic in the thirteenth century was particularly significant; linguistic continuity provided an important, if gradually weakening, link with the cultural heritage of Muslim Spain.[99]

Though born in Christian Spain, Ramah probably spoke Arabic and was conversant with Arabic literature. He thus had easy and unmediated access to the entire range of the Spanish Jewish intellectual achievement and its Islamic background. When editing a collection of his own (Hebrew) letters, Ramah wrote the introduction and editorial notes in Arabic.[100] In his talmudic commentaries, Ramah frequently explains difficult Aramaic terms by giving their Arabic equivalents.[101] Toledan Jews certainly knew Spanish; even a century earlier their poets could turn an elegant Romance verse.[102] But despite the hundreds of Arabic words that appear in Ramah's works, there is not a single surviving Latin or Romance term. Jews continued to refer to their cities by Arabic names—Burghush (Burgos), Tulaytulah (Toledo). This living tradition of Arabic helped to keep even literary and scientific works relatively accessible to serious students. Ramah even tried his hand at verse translation of Arabic poetry into Hebrew; he is, in fact, the first known Hebrew translator of Hispano-Arabic poetry.[103]

The Spanish tradition of linguistic and biblical studies was alive, if no longer flourishing, in Toledo. Its chief representative was Jacob b. El'azar, whose Kitāb al-Kāmil was widely respected.[104] Scattered comments and interpretations in Ramah's talmudic commentaries attest to familiarity with this tradition and a lively interest in biblical exegesis in general.[105] Nevertheless, Ramah did not accept the view that biblical studies should be a major occupation of the mature scholar. The talmudic statement that study time should be split between Bible, Mishnah, and Talmud applies, he says, only "to the earlier generations whose minds were receptive, so that two thirds of their days sufficed for Mishnah and Talmud. But for us, youthful study should be devoted to Bible and would that the rest of our days be sufficient for Mishnah and Talmud."[106] Masoretic problems seem to have been a subject of interest in both Burgos and Toledo at the time. Ramah was particularly interested in this field, where halakah and biblical studies overlap. He communicated with the scholars of Burgos on Masoretic problems and later produced a classic work on the subject.[107]

The men who labored so assiduously to reconstruct the cultural life of the Muslim period could scarcely neglect what was perhaps its most typical activity: Hebrew poetry and letters. The recitation of poetry remained a major source of cultivated entertainment, and its occasional composition remained an essential skill of the gentleman-scholar. Spanish poetry never succeeded in regaining the heights of the Muslim era; but Ramah's circle did contain the leading patrons and poets of the age. Among the important poets of Toledo at the turn of the century were Judah Alharizi,[108] Jacob b. El'azar,[109] Judah ibn Shabbetai;[110] and Ramah himself.[111]

A major stimulus to Hebrew poetry in Andalusia had been a desire to match or even surpass, in the Holy Tongue, the achievements of Arabic poetry.[112] Though this motivation was still alive among the poets and patrons of early thirteenth century Toledo, Ramah's generation was perhaps the last in which it played a significant role.[113] European influence can already be felt: Jacob b. El'azar, for example, who explicitly defined his literary vocation as the defense of Hebrew's honor against the pretensions of Arabic, is already influenced by the troubadours and courtly love themes.[114] Another development in Ramah's circle was the emancipation from biblical classicism, which had been modeled after the strict classicism of Arabic poetry. As the hold of its Arabic model weakened, Hebrew poetry was opened to the riches of rabbinic Hebrew.[115] Ramah resisted these trends; stylistically and thematically he remained loyal to the poetic canons of Andalusia, much as they had been "codified" by Moses ibn Ezra.[116] In his prose, however, Ramah carefully cultivated a lucid and flexible style that put to good use his mastery of rabbinic literature.

Medieval Hebrew poets were, sociologically, of two types: the professional poet, dependent on the generosity of patrons, and the financially independent practitioner of the art.[117] Ramah, belonging to the latter category, was spared the expediency of dedicating poems to wealthy patrons and engaging in poetic flattery. But Ramah's poetry was not without "social function." If, in fact, the surviving selection is representative, few poems were composed merely "for poetry's sake";

most were called forth by special occasions in the lives of family, friends, or prominent members of Ramah's aristocratic circle. They include poems of friendship and of polemic, a poem in honor of a wedding, elegies, and messages of consolation.

Three early poems are typical. One refers to a conflict within the community: R. Joseph ibn Shoshan was apparently opposed by some prominent members of the community. Ramah composed a poem praising R. Joseph, denouncing his enemies and predicting his ultimate triumph. The poem, written as a personal message of support, perhaps also served as a bit of political propaganda.[118] Another poem was composed on the death of R. Joseph Alfakar in 1195. R. Joseph was a physician and statesman in the service of the Castilian court and had worked with R. Todros toward the suppression of the Karaites in northern Castile.[119] Ramah wrote an elegy praising his wisdom and charity, and mourning his passing.[120] A year earlier, Joseph's kinsman Abraham Alfakar, a prominent diplomat in the service of Alfonso VIII, married a daughter of R. Joseph ibn Shoshan. The occasion called forth a fine poem by Ramah in honor of his new brother-in-law.[121]

Alfakar typifies the Andalusian aristocratic heritage still alive in Toledo.[122] He continued the old tradition of political service based on loyalty, practical wisdom, and polished elegance. In fine Andalusian style he used his position and wealth to aid and defend his fellow Jews. In the words of Ramah's eulogy, written on Abraham's death thirty-one years later, he was "a tower of strength . . . a fortress for the needy." Poets and scholars enjoyed his patronage.[123]

Ramah, in eulogy, chose to play down his brother-in-law's political power. He was "A prince and ruler only of *musar*, all other dominion he despised."[124] *Musar*, as used here, is a "loan-translation" of the Arabic *adab*—the literary culture that was the mark of the well-trained gentleman.[125] Alfakar's pen "Spat myrrh, sped like lightning, ablaze with a flame of consuming fire."[126] No sample of Alfakar's Hebrew *adab* has survived, but some of his Arabic poetry has. It was good enough to compel the admiration of Moslem critics:

> Anyone with an understanding of the poetic craft who reads his poetry will scarcely believe that these poems, glorious and perfect in their beautiful and pleasant style proceeded from the harp of a Jew. How can it be that God granted a Jew the ability to compose such fine poetry in the language of the Prophet? But this demonstrates how successful the Jews have been with our holy language and the extent of its mastery among these wise men who have gained repute in all the sciences.[127]

In some ways, Alfakar belonged to a vanishing breed. The new realities of Christian Spain made the gradual decline of Arabic culture inevitable. A Toledo contemporary of Alfakar can already be seen urgently requesting the translation of an Arabic philosophical text.[128]

His Toledo career spanning half a century, Ramah witnessed the gradual passing of the powerful men who had dominated the scene on his arrival. In verse and rhymed prose (once even appended to a legal responsum), he would mourn their deaths. Alfakar's tombstone inscription, composed by Ramah in 1225, is the last such poem in the surviving fragments of his *dīwān*.[129] But Ramah survived his brother-in-law by almost two decades. During those years, Ramah shared the communal leadership of Toledo with another Alfakar—Judah, whose father, Joseph, he had eulogized in 1195. Like Ramah, Judah Alfakar combined wealth and lineage with a brilliant mastery of the literary-philosophical tradition of Andalusia. Together they would play an important role in determining the stance of the powerful Toledo community in the great spiritual and intercommunal struggles of the 1230s.[130]

Various philosophical traditions jostled in Ramah's Toledo. The classical Jewish philosophers of Muslim Spain were, of course, well known. So too was the older geonic tradition, typified by Saadya. But new ideas were in the ascendant. Aristotelianism had already become popular with Jewish thinkers before the Almohade disaster;[131] but its full triumph came only in Christian Spain. The first philosophical work by a Jewish Aristotelian was written in Toledo by Abraham ibn Daud about thirty years before Ramah's arrival.[132] Ibn Daud's *Exalted Faith* was soon to be overshadowed by the works of Maimonides. The *Guide of the Perplexed* was available in Toledo some time before Maimonides' death in 1204,[133] and its impact was, to say the least, considerable.[134]

These works were accessible to most Toledo intellectuals in their original Arabic, as was the full range of Greco-Arabic scientific and philosophical literature. By the turn of the century Averroës had become available in Toledo and quickly assumed a central role as a powerful and authoritative interpreter of the Aristotelian corpus. Alongside Judah Halevi's polemic against an incipient Jewish Aristotelianism, Toledo's intellectuals could follow the parallel clash of Ghazzali and Averroës.

In Ramah's day the impact of Christian thought was still small compared to that of the Greco-Arabic tradition. However, as the dominant and always beckoning religion, Christianity could hardly be ignored. Even an émigré like Ibn Daud may have been influenced by Christian scholasticism.[135] It is doubtful whether any Jews, at this stage, bothered to learn Latin; but there was ample opportunity for oral communication with the Christian translators, still active in Toledo.[136] Much of their work was done with Jewish collaboration—a Jew translating from Arabic to Romance and then a Christian, from Romance to Latin.[137]

Ramah's pupil Judah ibn Matka was, at the age of eighteen, engaged in mathematical correspondence with the Sicilian court of Fredrick II.[138] It was probably a foreign translator who made the introduction.

Sharply contrasting with the various shades of philosophical opinion found among Toledo's aristocratic Southern émigrés were the popular religious beliefs of the relatively uneducated native Jewish population of Christian Spain. The latter possessed neither the philosophical sophistication of the Andalusians nor any strong intellectual tradition of their own.[139] But by the turn of the century one could find at least one French scholar in Toledo, disciplined and confident in an intellectual tradition of his own, to whom the world of Spanish Jewish philosophy was quite alien.[140] During Ramah's formative years, Franco-German Jewish culture was barely known by the Spanish aristocracy. By his death, its influence was considerable.

Ramah steered his own course in this bewildering sea of theological opinion. It is clear that he was conversant with the works of the major Jewish philsophers. But because little closely reasoned philosophical argumentation has come down to us in Ramah's surviving writings, it is hard to determine how much he read in the Greco-Arabic literature. Nor can we easily gauge the extent of his personal commitment to serious philosophical study. Although philosophy was not, for him, the high road to salvation, a partially preserved "philosophical poem concerning [God's] unity" *does* open with an exhortation to the soul to know its Creator through philosophical study of the glories of His work. Ramah skillfully compresses a Saadyanic proof of Creation into a few verses. He then proceeds to touch on such topics as God's unity and incorporeality, reconciliation of Divine attributes with unity, God's transcendence of time and place, and the paradox of its compatibility with His closeness to those that know Him.[141]

Clearly Ramah was no antiphilosophical obscurantist. But viewed against the backdrop of early thirteenth century Jewish philosophy, his philosophical tastes appear quite conservative. At a time when Aristotelianism had already become dominant, he was still staunchly committed to the moderate balance between reason and tradition struck by Saadya Gaon three centuries earlier. It was Ramah's concern with the movement in the direction of a more radical rationalism that forms the background for some of the stormier episodes of his life.[142]

As the works of Maimonides and Averroës were digested in the early years of the thirteenth century, it must have become clear, even to conservatives like Ramah, that there was no returning to the philosophical past. Ibn Matka's encyclopedia, *Midrash Hokmah*, gives some sense of where the philosophical curriculum in Toledo was going. Despite the author's strong defense of tradition, pre-Maimonidean Jewish philosophy hardly figures. Ibn Matka's base is the full Aristotelian corpus (ex-

cepting the *Politics*) and its commentators down to Averroës.[143] An unexpected comment in the section on zoology suggests that Ramah too
read more broadly than his surviving—and probably fairly early—
writings testify. After reproducing Aristotle's list of animals without
gall, Ibn Matka adds: "And Aristotle neglected to mention one other
species that has no gall, namely the dove—as [the Sages] of blessed
memory mentioned in the Jerusalem Talmud. Thus I heard from my
master, R. Meir Halevi of blessed memory."[144] Ramah must have rel-
ished this opportunity of comparing talmudic and Aristotelian scientific knowledge at the latter's expense. But it is hard to see how he could
have communicated this sort of offhand tidbit to his students had he
not been giving Aristotle a reasonably careful reading.

Fourteen years after Ramah's death, R. Jonah ibn Bahlul of the Castilian
town of Molina lists him among the great post-talmudic scholars: "The
Toledan, R. Meir,[145] illuminated our exile with his understanding. In
his days, his equal was not seen among all the scholars of Spain, for he
penetrated the depths of wisdom."[146] "Our exile" may well refer to
"the exile of Jerusalem that is in Sefarad [Spain]."
     For more than half a century before Ramah's appearance, Spain was
mute in the field of halakah. The fourteenth-century Toledan Menahem b. Zerah writes that "in [Ramah's] time and prior to it, all that was
studied in this land [Spain] were the *Halakot* of R. Alfasi."[147] That is to
say, the Talmud was not even studied in the original but only in Alfasi's
abridgment. Ben Zerah perhaps exaggerates, but there is no gainsaying
the weakness of Spanish talmudic scholarship during the second half of
the twelfth century. At the turn of the century halakic study was just
beginning its recovery from the blow struck by the Almohades.
     To Ben Zerah, exclusive study of Alfasi's abridgment was a sorry
state of affairs. Some of Ramah's contemporaries would have disagreed.
Alharizi, for example, thought Alfasi's abridgment a boon precisely
because it allowed one to dispense with prolonged efforts expended in
following complex talmudic argumentation. Maimonides' *Mishneh
Torah*, he thought, could serve the purpose even more admirably.[148]
Alharizi apparently felt that the student could spend his time more
profitably than in protracted talmudic study. This view had strong roots
in the tradition of Muslim Spain. The great eleventh-century philoso-
pher-pietist Bahya ibn Paqudah, whose *Duties of the Heart* Ramah had
carefully read, eloquently berated devotees to the study of halakic minutiae.[149] The difficulties facing Spanish talmudic scholarship were
thus twofold: the task of replanting old "academies of learning" in the
north, and the struggle with rival disciplines for the loyalty of talented
students.
     There is little question as to where Ramah's loyalties lay. His literary

skills and general learning notwithstanding, Ramah doubtless thought of himself first and foremost as a halakist. Talmudic studies received the lion's share of his interest and literary activity. His other interests often emerge on the periphery of this primary orientation. Halakic problems not treated in the classical texts provided an impulse toward outward literary expansion, while the exegetical demands of non-hala-kic talmudic passages occasioned internal asides. Thus the composition of Ramah's classic Masoretic dictionary was oriented toward the hala-kic problem of correctly writing a Torah scroll.[150] On the other hand, Ramah's philosophical opinions are most accessible in the aggadic exegesis included in his talmudic commentaries.[151] But the bulk of Ramah's literary work was halakic, in the strict sense of the term. A recent bibliographical study has underscored the broad range of his commentarial activity.[152] Ramah wrote extensively on most of the tractates of the orders *Nashim* and *Neziqin*. Most of these commentaries are lost, known only through fragmentary quotations by later authors; only commentaries on *Sanhedrin* and *Baba Batra* have survived whole.[153] We recall Ramah's urgent request for books, sent to a friend traveling to the north. Though interested in obtaining Rashi's commentary on several tractates, Ramah attached first priority to a copy of the talmudic tractate, *Horayot*;[154] apparently no adequate copy was available in Toledo.[155] Ramah may have been eager to begin the study that led eventually to his *Horayot* commentary. The eighteenth-century bibliographer Azulai still had a copy of Ramah's "*Peratim* on *Horayot* and *Abot* in manuscript on old parchment. And it is written that he composed them in Iyyar and Sivan of the year 4967 [1207] and called them *Perate-Horayot* and *Perate-Abot*."[156] The rate of writing is impressive.

The title of Ramah's commentaries was, as Azulai reports, *Peratim* (literally "details"); other sources call it *Perate-Peratim* ("the minutest of details").[157] These works, in the words of Isaac de Lattes, combined "the method of commentary (*perush*) and juridical decision (*pesaq*)."[158]

Perate-Peratim seems a particularly appropriate title for Ramah's commentary on Baba Batra. Commentary on each talmudic chapter is divided into numbered paragraphs, each comprising a discrete juridical unit. Not a few paragraphs run the length of a short essay. Combining explanation, analysis of legal terms, and reconciliation of contradictions, Ramah seems bent upon extracting every ounce of juridical information that his text can yield. *Perate-Peratim* thus lavishes loving care on precisely the "minutiae" with which men like Alharizi showed such impatience. Ramah's title forcefully, almost defiantly, calls attention to his rejection of their view.

A few pages of Ramah's *Gittin* commentary, preserved in a later anonymous Spanish work,[159] indicate a structure similar to that of *Perate-Baba Batra*. Thus the following comment of the fourteenth-century Spanish scholar, Ribash: "All this, Ramah has written in his *Peratim* on the chapter 'Hitqabel' [in Gittin] in an extremely lengthy fashion, as was his custom."[160] Ribash, though all for thoroughness, seems somewhat irked by Ramah's wordiness. To illustrate statistically, Ramah could take essentially the same argument disposed of by the Tosafists in forty words and expound it in over four hundred.[161] That Ramah was not invariably long-winded, however, is amply demonstrated by the lucid economy of his style in the *Sanhedrin* commentary. Ramah's Spanish audience may account for the comparative wordiness of some of his works. Substantial training is generally necessary before a student can decipher and digest a difficult Tosafistic gloss; and among Ramah's intended readers were doubtless many who had not yet appropriated the methodology of close logical analysis of talmudic texts. Ramah may have therefore felt that a less elliptical and more leisurely presentation was in order.

Ramah's concentration on the orders of *Nashim* and *Neziqin* and the juridical orientation of his commentaries may reflect his role as the outstanding legal authority in a changing political and economic environment. A fairly large collection of Ramah's responsa once existed. Unfortunately, most are lost. The surviving collection (of sixty-nine) begins at number two hundred forty, and these responsa deal almost entirely with civil law. Few of the missing responsa can be retrieved.[162] Even the survivors have been historically "maimed" by the excision of legally irrelevant "names and addresses." We can identify responsa to Burgos, Cuenca, Tudela, Estella, and Gerona;[163] but the actual range of Ramah's Spanish correspondence was certainly broader. Moreover, the geographic bounds of Ramah's authority, though unclear, certainly extended beyond Spain.[164]

A passing remark on legal methodology seems to reveal the conservative temper that we have found characteristic of Ramah in other fields: "Although the simple meaning of the talmudic discussion supports the first interpretation, since it is also possible to interpret it according to this [second, contrary] opinion, one should not reject the opinion of the masters without proof."[165] In practice, this principle does not prove terribly constraining. So full of novelties are Ramah's works that his originality as a commentator and jurist is unmistakable.[166] At least part of Ramah's achievement has long been known to halakists. For although he has suffered the familiar fate of medieval authors who eschewed brevity, many of his opinions were preserved at the very center of the mainstream by a later Toledan, R. Jacob b. Asher. Through the latter's *Turim*, Ramah had a significant impact on the development of Jewish family and civil law.

Despite Ramah's respect for the "masters," literary convention did not require that he consistently quote them by name. The few that he does quote are almost never contemporaries or near contemporaries. Ramah's commentaries thus do little to illuminate the dark age of Spanish halakah (1150–1200) or even to reveal the immediate sources of his own learning. Clearly, though, Ramah's halakic achievement did not spring forth *ex nihilo*. From the middle of the twelfth century, attempts had been made to replant the Spanish halakic tradition in Toledo. The work was begun, it will be recalled, by the two Ibn Megash cousins. Ibn Daud's description of their activities gives the impression of valiant effort and limited success.[167] When Ramah arrived as a young man in Toledo, a second generation of talmudic scholars was already on the scene. One, Isaac b. Meir ibn Megash, is described by Alharizi as "the wellspring of wisdom and humility in whom every comely virtue [resides]."[168] He was probably the son of one of the two previously mentioned cousins (both named Meir). R. Isaac ibn Megash served on the Toledo *bet din*,[169] but unfortunately nothing further is known of his scholarly career. A second prominent Toledo scholar was Ramah's uncle, R. Joseph ibn Sahl. Alharizi's list of Toledo's notables refers to "the *dayyan* R. Joseph, the sea of wisdom and a man greatly beloved."[170] He was probably a descendant of the earlier Joseph ibn Sahl, a poet and *dayyan* of early twelfth-century Córdoba. Like his brother-in-law, R. Todros, he was the son-in-law of one of the prominent scholars of the previous generation.[171]

Ibn Sahl was a man of many qualities, "a prince whose deeds were lowly in his own eyes though his virtues were exalted above the heavens." Known also as "R. Joseph the physician," he was "a faithful healer of every sickness." Perhaps also a metaphysician, "his thoughts had access to the heavens, not through perception but through prophecy."[172]

A sixteenth-century halakic anthology quotes "the words of R. Isaac Alfasi . . . in a responsum translated from the Arabic by R. Joseph ibn Sahl."[173] This translator has been identified with the first Joseph ibn Sahl.[174] The identification is unlikely: the first Ibn Sahl (d. 1123) was almost contemporary with Alfasi (d. 1103) who responded in Arabic because it was more accessible than Hebrew, in the first place;[175] the second Joseph ibn Sahl (d. 1207) is more likely to have felt a need for Hebrew translation of Arabic halakic material.[176]

Ramah was in contact with both of these scholars. In the case of Isaac ibn Megash, we can point only to the occurrence of their signatures together on a document executed by the Toledo *bet din*.[177] But Ramah's poetry testifies to a very close relationship with his uncle, Joseph ibn Sahl. The latter's character and scholarship are treated with profound respect. In a poem written in 1196 in Ibn Sahl's honor, Ramah seems to be describing a student-teacher relationship. Ramah seeks to understand his uncle's generously dispensed teachings:

> But my thoughts are perplexed about them and immersed in the pit
> of their ignorance
> Until you proclaim release through your intelligence and from their
> ignorance redeem them.[178]

In any case, Ramah found in Toledo at least two prominent bearers of the Spanish halakic tradition.

Ramah put great stock in the collection and comparison of old manuscripts.[179] He was particularly impressed with the accuracy of the Spanish talmudic text tradition.[180] One especially valued prize was a copy of the Talmud that had once been in the library of the great eleventh-century statesman, scholar, and patron, Samuel ha-Nagid. At one time, according to Ramah, this copy had been in the possession of R. Joseph ibn Megash.[181] With these fixed points we can speculate on the 150-year odyssey of the Nagid's Talmud from Granada to Toledo.

Samuel ha-Nagid's library was inherited by his son and successor, Joseph ha-Nagid. When Joseph was killed in a pogrom in Granada, "his books and treasures were scattered all over the world."[182] Subsequently, much of the Nagid's library was recovered by the talmudist-statesman-astronomer, Isaac b. Baruk Albalia.[183] Perhaps with R. Isaac, the Nagid's Talmud wandered from Córdoba to Seville to Granada. After his father's death, Baruk b. Isaac Albalia became a devoted student of the great North African émigré, R. Isaac Alfasi, in whose home at Lucena he studied the entire Talmud.[184] Had he brought with him the Nagid's copy? Then perhaps it was from R. Baruk that this Talmud passed to the library of the Lucena academy presided over by Alfasi's brilliant successor (and R. Baruk's boyhood friend), R. Joseph ibn Megash.[185] Or could the route to Lucena have been more direct? Fleeing the massacre in Granada, Joseph ha-Nagid's young son, Azariah, found refuge in the home of R. Isaac ibn Giat.[186] Can he have escaped with his grandfather's Talmud? Upon Azariah's premature death, the Nagid's Talmud might then have passed to the Lucena academy, headed successively by Ibn Giat, Alfasi, and Ibn Megash.

When Lucena fell to the Almohades several years after the death of Joseph ibn Megash, his son and nephew escaped to Toledo[187] and apparently succeeded in bringing at least part of their priceless library with them. After their death, the Nagid's Talmud was perhaps owned by R. Isaac b. Meir ibn Megash. At the beginning of the thirteenth century it was available to Ramah in Toledo. There is something almost symbolic in this long journey from Granada to Toledo; for these possible routes traveled by the Nagid's Talmud are roughly those traveled by the Spanish halakic tradition itself.[188] With the appearance of Ramah in Toledo, that tradition began to enter upon a new phase.

The historical significance of Ramah's scholarly achievement is twofold: it represents both continuity and outward expansion in the Spanish halakic tradition. Stylistically and substantively, Ramah's works belong to the talmudic tradition of Muslim Spain. Ramah still writes in a somber and authoritative geonic Aramaic, while Spanish texts and authorities form the basis for his works. Ramah's revival of this tradition was in itself a significant achievement. He was the first scholar living in Spain since Joseph ibn Megash (d. 1141) to have any real impact on halakic literature. His appearance thus represents the recovery of Spanish halakic scholarship from the intellectual dislocation that accompanied the destruction and resettlement of the preceding half century. But beyond continuity and reconstruction, Ramah's work marks a new direction in Spanish halakah.

Ramah's devotion to old Spanish texts has already been mentioned. At the turn of the century we find him making some new additions to his well-stocked library. Ramah, we recall, in one of his few surviving letters, pleads with a friend traveling in Aragon to bring back a copy of Rashi's commentary on several tractates of the Talmud.[189] Like the fate of the Nagid's talmud, these new acquisitions too have symbolic significance. For it is with Ramah that Spanish halakah was, for the first time, opened to the achievements of the schools of northern and southern France. This broadening of scholarly horizons was, in turn, the result of a larger historical development: the movement of Spanish Jewry from the Islamic world into Christian Europe. It is to the implications of this important development that we now turn.

II

NEW NORTHERN CONNECTIONS

ABRAHAM IBN DAUD, we recall, perceived the Almohade invasion of Spain as a "global" disaster: "After the demise of R. Joseph ha-Levi . . . the world became desolate of academies of learning."[1] In the year 1300 the Perpignan scholar Menahem b. Solomon ha-Meiri introduced his commentary on *Abot* with a lengthy historical essay on the great scholars of the Oral Law. Following is his description of Spain after the Almohade invasion: "At that time, Spain became desolate of academies."[2] Ha-Meiri's historical information was drawn from various traditions and medieval chronicles at his disposal. This particular description, like most of the material on Muslim Spain, betrays its origins in Ibn Daud's *Book of Tradition*.[3]

Ha-Meiri apparently felt it necessary to revise Ibn Daud's formulation: not "the world," just Spain, became desolate of academies. To this proud adherent of the Provençal halakic tradition, at home in the achievements of several halakic schools, Ibn Daud's metaphoric identification of the world with Spain must have seemed rather provincial. As a matter of fact, at precisely the time that "Spain became desolate of academies," the schools of northern France and Provence were embarking on a period of intense creativity.[4] Ibn Daud had heard of these developments only as a distant rumor.[5]

Writing in Toledo only three decades before Ramah began his career, Ibn Daud serves to accentuate a major development of Ramah's generation: the breakdown of Spanish isolation from Europe. The movement of Spanish Jewry from the Islamic world into Christian Europe was, of course, the result of political transformations. But the new social and cultural ties that resulted were to have a profound impact on the future history of European Jewry. Ramah was not only familiar with the Provençal and northern French schools; he was the first scholar nurtured in the tradition of Muslim Spain to assimilate their achievements and to maintain personal contact with their major representatives.

The new European connections of Spanish Jewry brought an increased consciousness of community with the Jews of Europe. Ramah's pupil Judah ibn Matka experienced this personally. As a young prodigy, Ibn Matka carried on a mathematical correspondence with one of the royal scholars of Frederick II. That initial contact led, eventually, to a journey to Frederick's court. While still in Toledo, Ibn Matka had composed an encyclopedia of the sciences and philosophy in Arabic. When he arrived in Italy, Jewish acquaintances requested a Hebrew version. Ibn Matka obliged, translating his own work under the title *Midrash Hokmah*.[6] His European experience increased Ibn Matka's appreciation of the unifying role of the Hebrew language: "Ours is a single, uniform tongue so that we might all have one language. And as a result, peace and love might enter into our midst. But among the other languages of the nations you will find numerous variants in what is called one language. Thus, Romance (*la'az*) differs in Spain, France, and other places."[7] The sense of unity and continuity surviving in a sea of historical flux is expressed in a passing comment by the son of an Andalusian émigré, David Kimhi, who was actively spreading the Spanish heritage in Provence: "For all the nations have already been exiled and intermingled. And there is not today a distinctive people (*goy meyuhad*) save Israel alone."[8]

The straightest route from Toledo to Provence leads through the territory of Aragon. Its communities formed a link between Ramah's Toledo and the European communities to the north—hence that Toledan, traveling in Aragon, who received Ramah's impatient request for copies of Rashi's commentaries. Little is known of the cultural life of the Aragonese communities at the beginning of the thirteenth century. They were probably in fairly close contact with Toledo; partially preserved communication survives on some disputed halakic issues between Joseph ibn Shoshan and "the scholars of the territory (*hebel*) of Aragon"[9]—the latter apparently acting as a group. (During the Maimonidean Controversy of the 1230s the unified communities of "the territory (*hebel*) of Aragon" would be at odds with the Toledo aristocracy over more momentous issues.)[10] Ramah's commentaries were probably well known in Aragon: the earliest quotation from Ramah's *Peratim* appears among the surviving fragments of a work written by R. Meir ha-Kohen of Saragossa in 1235.[11]

Although Catalonia had been politically united with Aragon since 1137, its Jews maintained a separate communal and cultural identity. Arabic was still strong in the Aragonese communities. The major Catalan communities of Barcelona and Gerona had been under Christian rule since Carolingian times.[12] Their European ties were the strongest in Spain. A particularly close relationship had developed between the Jews of Catalonia and those in Provence; it was probably encouraged by Catalonia's strong political, cultural, and linguistic ties with southern France. Unlike Ibn Daud in Toledo, Barcelona scholars had been in contact with Provençal counterparts since at least the beginning of the twelfth century.[13] Toward the middle of the century Zerahyah Halevi of Gerona traveled north, became a pillar of Provençal halakah, and later returned home.[14] Rabad, the dominant figure in twelfth-century Provençal scholarship, probably visited Barcelona.[15] At the beginning of the thirteenth century an internal squabble in Barcelona could involve the Jewish communities of Narbonne, Lunel, Beziers, and Montpellier.[16]

The Jewish aristocracies of Toledo and Barcelona were apparently in close contact. We have, for example, evidence of a close relationship between Ramah's circle and the powerful Benveniste family of Barcelona. Three of Ramah's surviving poems and letters relate to a sad event in the history of that family. The most prominent member of the Benveniste family was the royal physician and bailiff, Sheshet ben Isaac. In about 1195, R. Sheshet lost the last of his three sons, Samuel. Ramah wrote to R. Sheshet, both in poetry and rhymed prose, mourning his son's passing and offering consolation. We also have a fine letter of consolation composed by Ramah for his uncle, Joseph b. Meir, to be sent to R. Sheshet.[17]

Ramah seems to have been on particularly close terms with R. Sheshet's nephew, R. Isaac Benveniste. R. Isaac was a distinguished statesman and scholar, and, according to Alharizi, a fine poet.[18] His three surviving poems, addressed to Ramah, were found in the latter's *dīwān*.[19] We shall have occasion to return to Ramah's relationship with R. Sheshet Benveniste.

Catalonian halakah, at the beginning of Ramah's career, seems to have been in a kind of incubation period; at any rate, we do not hear of outstanding scholars in this period. But by the beginning of the thirteenth century, some of the bright young men of Barcelona and Gerona were assiduously studying under Provençal and French masters.[20] As mature scholars they were destined to complete the renaissance of Spanish halakic scholarship begun by Ramah. Nahmanides, their most brilliant representative, was in contact with Ramah, whom he seems to have regarded as the senior representative of the Spanish halakic tradition. The fifteenth-century historian Abraham Zacuto reports that Ramah "wrote *responsa* to Nahmanides' inquiries." We know of two; in one case, Ramah was chosen to decide a halakic dispute between Nahmanides and his old friend, R. Solomon b. Abraham of Montpellier.[21]

Ramah appears here in the role of elder statesman to the up-and-coming scholars of the younger generation.

Directly north of Catalonia lay the communities and schools of Provence. The establishment of a close relationship between Spain and Provence was a major development of Ramah's period and one in which he played an important role. The Jews of Muslim Spain had not, of course, been totally isolated from their brethren to the north. An eleventh-century Cordoban, Moses ibn Chiquitilla, was familiar with cultural conditions in Provence and had even made a modest attempt at transmitting a bit of Spanish learning to Provençal acquaintances.[22] Contact may have been on the rise in the first half of the twelfth century: the poet and halakist Judah ibn Giat was, for a time, in Narbonne where he translated an Arabic halakic work of Alfasi;[23] and Judah Halevi was on close terms with one David b. Joseph of Narbonne.[24] At the same time the beginnings of scholarly exchange are in evidence between the talmudic academies of Narbonne and Lucena.[25]

Spanish-Provençal contact was accelerated by the Almohade invasions. Cultural influence moved northward from Spain to Provence as Spanish refugees fled the Almohade persecutions. The Spanish émigrés brought with them the achievements of Spanish halakah, philosophy, biblical exegesis, and letters, stimulating in Provence a period of intense creativity and cultural change.[26] But before Ramah, the main flow of ideas seems to have been unidirectional; in Ramah's generation we can already speak of vigorous interplay.

The scant surviving biographical information concerning Ramah points to important personal contacts in Provence. First of all, there were close family ties: Ramah's uncle, R. Judah b. Meir, was married to a daughter of R. Kalonymous b. Todros, the *nasi* of Narbonne. The Toledo branch of the Abulafia family remained in contact with R. Judah and his son Meir. Our knowledge of their relationship stems from a family tragedy: shortly after the death of R. Kalonymous, R. Meir b. Judah's wife died in childbirth, and the surviving letters of consolation, in poetry and rhymed prose, were composed by Ramah for his brother Samuel Abulafia.[27] Family connections in Narbonne may have led to broader contacts; we find, for example, the scholars of Narbonne turning to Ramah for guidance on a difficult halakic question.[28]

Ramah was in communication with some of the outstanding scholars of Provence. In addition to the scholars of Narbonne, he was in contact with members of the famous school of Lunel.[29] He was also on excellent terms with the translator Samuel ibn Tibbon, who lived in Marseilles.[30] Ibn Tibbon had traveled to Spain, ransacking the libraries of Barcelona and Toledo for accurate copies of Arabic scientific and philosophical works.[31] He was close enough to a Toledo resident, "R. Joseph son of the *hasid* R. Israel," to refer to "the perfect love that is between us."[32] It is thus likely that Ramah and Ibn Tibbon were personally acquainted.

A long poem of friendship addressed to a mysterious Abraham b. Moses of Carcassonne appears in Ramah's *dīwān*. It provides a disconcerting example (to the historian, at least) of the tendency toward universal categories in Spanish poems of praise. R. Abraham b. Moses was deeply admired by Ramah as one of the outstanding men of the generation; but after seventy-four lines of praise it is still difficult to say much about him that is specific.[33]

The new Spanish-Provençal contacts produced, and were in turn reinforced by, a tendency toward cultural convergence. Cultivation of new literary and philosophical studies brought the intellectual world of Provençal Jewry at the beginning of the thirteenth century closer to Spain than would have seemed imaginable a century earlier. Perhaps less obvious but also important was the adoption of elements of Spanish manners, style, and social convention.[34] Even liturgical poetry dropped its Franco-German character and took on the Spanish style beginning in the mid-twelfth century.[35] These developments helped to cement the new relationship between Spain and Provence that emerges in Ramah's generation.

Extra-talmudic interests imported from Spain were not the sole component of the new shared intellectual environment. Not long after Spanish philosophical ideas took root in Provence, the teachings of Provençal mystics began to move southward into Spain. Though the earliest center of Spanish kabbalah was in Catalonia,[36] we soon hear of kabbalistic debates in the streets of Burgos.[37] The name of "the *hasid*, R. Judah ibn Ziza" has come down to us as an early kabbalist of Ramah's Toledo.[38] By the end of the thirteenth century Ramah's name had been identified with kabbalah, though his surviving works lend little support to this claim.[39]

Spanish-Provençal interaction was most complex in the field of halakah. Both Spain and Provence had strong, independent halakic traditions prior to their encounter. Their confrontation in the middle of the twelfth century initiated a vigorous and fertile dialectical relationship.

The second half of the twelfth century defines the first stage of Spanish-Provençal halakic interaction. Along with the rest of the Spanish heritage, works and students of halakah begin to appear in Provence at the time of the Almohade persecutions. The ideas of Alfasi, Ibn Megash, Judah b. Barzilai, and, later in the century, Maimonides enriched native scholarship and inspired a generation of Provençal halakists to give the Spanish tradition a critical going-over.[40] All this time Spanish halakah itself was reeling at the blow struck by the Almohades.

The second stage of the Spanish-Provençal halakic dialectic begins with the recovery of Spain and its new contact with the communities and schools of Provence. When the renascent Spanish tradition came under the influence of Provençal halakah, the latter was at the end of its period of classical achievement. Not the least part of this achievement was a searching criticism of the very tradition that the Spanish scholars were working to revive. The impetus provided by new Provençal ideas and challenges contributed to the creative brilliance of thirteenth-century Spanish halakah. This new stage of Spanish-Provençal interaction emerges for the first time on the pages of Ramah's works.

Spanish scholarship had not been the only stimulant to twelfth-century Provençal halakah; the monumental accomplishments of Rashi and the Tosafistic school of northern France also had an important impact. By the turn of the twelfth century Provençal halakists were quite familiar with the work of northern schools.[41] It was probably through Provençal channels that Ramah became acquainted with northern French scholarship, and its influence on him was perhaps even greater than that of Provençal scholarship. Here, too, Ramah's work begins a new era in Spanish halakah.

The few names that appear in the *Peratim* reflect the new breadth that would characterize thirteenth-century Spanish halakah. For among the predecessors that Ramah quotes are not only geonic,[42] north African,[43] and Spanish[44] authorities but also representatives of the Provençal,[45] French,[46] and German[47] schools. Study of the anonymous portions of the *Peratim* yields evidence of influence far greater than the number of quotations would indicate.[48] Ramah stood at the intensely challenging and stimulating meeting point—sometimes collision point—of powerful intellectual traditions. Often he proudly maintains Spanish tradition against northern attack;[49] at other times we find him abandoning a long-standing Spanish position in favor of convincing arguments from the north.[50]

The new contacts with northern French halakah were not, as in the case of Provence, part of a more general cultural convergence. To the contrary, increased contact accentuated differences. To some, like Ramah, whose center of gravity lay in halakic scholarship, these differences were perhaps not crucial. But they were destined to play an important role in the religious controversies that emerged later in the century.[51]

It is difficult to determine the precise channels through which Provençal and French ideas reached Ramah. One naturally wonders whether he traveled to any of the great centers of scholarship outside of Toledo. Unfortunately, the only hint of travel occurs in a brief poem bemoaning "the fire of wandering."[52] More certain is the role of books, letters, and scholarly travelers in bringing Ramah abreast of talmudic learning north of Spain.

Only one of Ramah's Toledo contemporaries has found a permanent place in halakic literature; he was Ramah's senior colleague on the Toledo *bet din* at the turn of the century, R. Abraham b. Nathan ha-Yarhi.[53] The latter part of Ha-Yarhi's career forms an interesting episode in the early meeting of Spanish Jewry with the cultural heritage of the communities of northern and southern France.

We turn first to a source in which Ha-Yarhi is not mentioned. Judah Alharizi and Ha-Yarhi were together in Toledo at the beginning of the thirteenth century.[54] Ramah, we recall, received a mixed review in Alharizi's register of Toledo notables; Ha-Yarhi did not even rate mention. A man of no mean talent and achievement, his cultural and social credentials seemingly did not meet Alharizi's standard of excellence.

Ha-Yarhi's origins and education were far from those of the Toledo aristocracy and intelligentsia. He was born in Lunel and had studied in the great Provençal talmudic academies.[55] At a time when some of his countrymen were beginning to plunge into the world of Spanish philosophy and literature, Ha-Yarhi instead turned northward and studied under the scholars of northern France.[56] Ha-Yarhi's forte was talmudic scholarship. Talmud, it will be remembered, did not rate very high in Alharizi's curriculum. Poetry did. But Ha-Yarhi apparently could not manage a Hebrew poem, Spanish style.[57] Alharizi was at home in Arabic literary culture. Ha-Yarhi's thought world was dominated by traditional midrashic sources and the Provençal kabbalah.[58] One might almost say that these two contemporaries were situated in the nonoverlapping sections of newly intersecting cultural spheres.

Ha-Yarhi arrived in Toledo some time before the end of the twelfth century and became a taxpaying member of the community.[59] Halakic competence, essential to the management of an autonomous Jewish community, was at a premium in Castile. By 1195 Ha-Yarhi was exercising a degree of halakic authority in Toledo.[60] In fact, his influence was more than local, for he was also involved in the communal affairs of Burgos.[61] By the turn of the century he had mastered Arabic well enough to translate halakic material into Hebrew.[62] But even after his arrival in Toledo Ha-Yarhi continued, through frequent trips, to maintain contact with the scholars of Provence and northern France.[63]

Ha-Yarhi was apparently close to Ramah's father-in-law, Joseph ibn Shoshan, to whom he shows great deference as a leader and perhaps as a patron. Somewhat after the fashion of the local poets, he dedicated a brief and clearly written halakic manual to Ibn Shoshan and his two sons, Isaac and Solomon.[64] In this work, popularly known as *Sefer ha-Manhig*, Ha-Yarhi drew on his broad learning and experience, describing and comparing for the first time the customs of Jewish communities throughout Europe.[65] Ha-Yarhi's actual title, *Manhig Bene ha-'Olam*, uses *'olam* (the world) with considerably less hyperbole than Ibn Daud (although it is now a mostly European world in which Spain is located).

Though the *Manhig* showed him to be a remarkably "cosmopolitan" halakist, Ha-Yarhi also had occasion to serve as a staunch defender of local Toledo custom. Some of the scholars of Aragon had found fault with a beautiful Torah scroll prepared in Toledo, declared it unfit, and set out their arguments in a letter to Joseph ibn Shoshan. The affair seems to have aroused considerable local passion. The question was submitted by "our master and teacher, the prince of God, the leader of the generation R. Yehosef (may his resting place be in Eden) son of R. Shlomoh" to "me, one of his minor servants, Abraham b. Nathan Ha-Yarhi."[66] We may speculate that Ramah was not yet a mature scholar at the time. After consultation with local scholars, who brought certain geonic sources to his attention,[67] Ha-Yarhi, making full use of his French training, penned a sharp response stoutly defending the customs of Toledo and demolishing the Aragonese objections.[68] He added, for good measure, a critique of several customs prevalent in Aragon, broadly hinting that the Aragonese scholars would do better to concern themselves with setting things aright at home.[69] The tone of Ha-Yarhi's responsum reveals the intense pride and loyalty felt in Toledo toward local custom.[70]

Ha-Yarhi makes a strange appearance in Ramah's poetry. One would generally consider taxation to be a rather prosaic matter, but it seems to have "inspired" two poems that Ramah composed for his friend. In financial straits, Ha-Yarhi had applied to Joseph ibn Shoshan for a reduction in his communal tax assessment. The application was denied. Ha-Yarhi then asked Ramah to put the request in verse.[71] Social convention among the Toledo aristocracy was apparently such that a poetic petition had a better chance of success, for refusal of a request couched in elegant verse would border on poor form. The device may have proved effective; another poem, composed under similar circumstances, was addressed to Abraham Alfakar, who was probably in charge of communal taxes after Ibn Shoshan's death.[72]

Though Ha-Yarhi had occasion to appreciate poetic talent, his relationship with some Toledo poets was apparently less than cordial. In a commentary on the minor tractate *Kallah Rabbati*, designed generally to impart the exacting standards of sexual behavior of the northern schools,[73] Ha-Yarhi has some harsh words for certain unnamed poets. Basing himself on so unimpeachable a Spanish authority as Alfasi,[74] he condemns "those who sing . . . about things upon which it is forbidden to look, mirthfully and with levity like empty and impulsive fellows." Singled out for particular censure are those young fellows who have . . . written books on the love of women and their guiles . . . I have no part in them, neither their honey nor their sting. Their authors ought to suppress them . . . for they have appropriated biblical verses . . . and applied them to the shameful vices of women. Woe to them, their copyists and their readers. Not only do they neglect the study of the Torah because of them, but bring others to [similar] neglect . . . He who reads them . . . has no share in the World to Come.[75]

The reference is apparently to the playful poetic debates about women that were enjoying popularity in Ramah's aristocratic circle during this period.[76]

Two categories of secular poetry escape Ha-Yarhi's disapproval: wedding songs and eulogies. The latter may legitimately borrow biblical expressions, for "it is proper that a man eulogize the wise and upright, or the leaders of the generation who stand in the breach and those who provide lodging for the homeless and those who give charity."[77] In wedding songs Ha-Yarhi will countenance even the love motifs of "the poets of Spain" who are "accustomed to recite poetry about the groom and his bride in order to endear her to her husband, if he understands and appreciates poetry. And even if he doesn't understand, he glories in the recitation and she is more beloved in his eyes for it."[78] Whether a result of his halakic scruples, self-censorship, or the vagaries of literary survival, there is little in Ramah's extant poetry that would give serious offence to his French colleague.[79]

Ha-Yarhi, it would seem, played a significant if somewhat uneven role in the cultural and communal life of Toledo. Some of the local literati probably found little common cultural ground with him. Communal leaders like Ibn Shoshan may have valued his halakic competence. But to native talmudic scholars like Ramah, Ha-Yarhi's presence in Toledo must have seemed like a boon. Ha-Yarhi had studied at the greatest schools of Provence and France and was thus able to bring them up to date on the most recent achievements of French and Provençal halakah.

Even Ramah, however, must have had an occasional disagreement with Ha-Yarhi. Ramah, for example, belonged to the school of Spanish halakists that looked askance at interruption of the regular liturgy by *piyyut*. He nevertheless reports keeping tactfully silent—perhaps in his own father-in-law's synagogue—while his view is regularly flouted. As he wryly observed to a perplexed inquirer, "What you were told about my sitting among them, hearing and keeping my peace, was correctly reported to you . . . But what you were told about my having the power to protest, was not correctly reported."[80] Ramah's power to protest was certainly not helped any by the vigorous Franco-German defense of *piyyut* confidently presented in Ha-Yarhi's *Sefer ha-Manhig*.[81]

A somewhat similar response, this one to Nahmanides, illustrates the new southward flow of Franco-German custom and its mixed reception in Spain. Toward the end of the twelfth century, after a brilliant Provençal career, R. Zerahyah Halevi (not Ramah's uncle) had returned home to Gerona. With him he brought the custom of prefixing the phrase "God, the faithful King" to the *Shema*.[82] Nahmanides wanted to suppress this northern interpolation and turned to Ramah for support. Heartily agreeing with his younger correspondent, Ramah appears here as a defender of the purity of Spanish tradition against the inroads of Franco-German custom. His response, however, ends on a statesman-like note: "This custom is without basis. Whoever can abolish it without strife, but rather in a company that is of one mind, should do so. And one who cannot abolish it should himself desist."[83] Ramah's awareness of the need for tact perhaps stemmed from personal experience. Well before Ramah lent his support to the Spanish resistance in Gerona, Ha-Yarhi can be seen propagating this very Franco-German custom in Toledo.[84] On the other hand, the Spanish counterattack, led by Ramah and Nahmanides, apparently extended up into Provence itself. By mid-century a Narbonne halakist warns that "this custom should not be changed"[85]—always a sure sign that someone is trying.

Ha-Yarhi is especially interesting in his role as a transmitter of new ideas and values.[86] Personally, he exposed Toledo associates to the values and ideals of talmudic scholars to the north. His *Sefer ha-Manhig* presented to the princes of the Spanish aristocracy a popular exposition that included French and Provençal halakah, custom, midrash, and mysticism.[87] To the halakists of Toledo he brought detailed knowledge of rich new traditions that they were eagerly—though critically—beginning to assimilate.

The turn of the century saw Ramah involved in a struggle with Spanish rationalism. With few allies at home, he looked abroad for support. It should come as no surprise that we find Ha-Yarhi conveying at least part of Ramah's correspondence with the great scholars outside of Spain.[88]

By the first years of the thirteenth century, Ramah, still a fairly young man, had produced several major talmudic commentaries. In subsequent years, he became increasingly interested in Masoretic studies. In 1227, after what must have been years of careful research, Ramah published his bold and highly influential *Masoret Seyag la-Torah*, which attempted no less than the establishment of a definitive text of the Torah.[89]

As a halakist, Ramah's primary concern was the text of the Pentateuch. Theoretically, a Torah scroll that deviates by so much as one letter from the "norm" is unfit.[90] But, in fact, before Ramah no such norm existed. Ramah reports that orthography—especially in regard to defective and *plene* spelling—is in a state of chaos. Even the talmudic rabbis confessed uncertainty about defective and *plene* spelling:[91]

> . . . how much more so we, in whom has been fulfilled: " . . . and the wisdom of their wise men shall perish and the discernment of their discerning men shall be hid" (Is. 29:14). And should we seek to rely on the corrected scrolls in our possession—they too present numerous discrepancies. And were it not for the Masoretic notes which have become a fence around the Torah, a man could hardly find his hands and feet on account of these discrepancies. But even the Masoretic notes have not escaped the [ill] fortune of discrepancy; for they too differ in many places—though not as much as the scrolls. Should a man attempt to write a Torah scroll in accordance with halakah, he will be smitten with [orthographic] deficiencies and excesses and will thus grope like a blind man in the darkness of discrepancy without succeeding in reaching his goal. And should even a wise man seek to know—he will not succeed.[92]

About half a century earlier, Maimonides, in his introduction to *Mishneh Torah*, had quoted Isaiah 29:14 with regard to the more apparently chaotic state of the "oral Torah." Ramah was now applying it to the text of the "written Torah" itself. The bold self-consciousness with which Ramah ("I, Meir ha-Levi son of R. Todros ha-Levi, the Sefardi") announces, in his introduction, that he has confronted the problem is reminiscent of the similar announcement in the introduction to *Mishneh Torah*.[93]

Ramah made an assiduous search for Torah scrolls and manuscripts of the Masorah that, in his judgment, were old, reliable, and carefully copied and checked. He established his text in accordance with the testimony of the Masorah, when clear, and in case of discrepancies, he applied the halakic principle "incline after the majority" to the best texts.[94] A recent student judges Ramah to have succeeded admirably in restoring the original Tiberian Masoretic orthography and securing its almost universal acceptance.[95]

It is remarkable that so old and pressing a problem waited until 1227 for its solution. It took a rare combination of halakic authority, Masoretic expertise, textual acumen, and self-confidence to produce and secure acceptance for what was, after all, an eclectic text of the Torah—which corresponded to no existing text.[96] But Ramah also stood at the right historical juncture. The breakdown of Spain's relative isolation may have been as great a stimulus to Ramah's Masoretic achievement as it was to his halakah. It must have heightened awareness of the discrepancies between the various text traditions. But at the same time, it also made possible a solution to the problem; for only the accessibility of a variety of traditions made possible a nonparochial collation of texts to which the principle of majority rule could be reasonably applied. The almost universal acceptance of Ramah's project was also facilitated by Spanish Jewry's new connections. As recently as fifty years earlier it would have been difficult to conceive of *any* Sefardic innovation being accepted by all Ashkenazic Jewry—certainly not a revised text of the Torah!

Ramah's familiarity with the lexicographical tradition of Andalusia allowed him to arrange *Masoret Seyag la-Torah* by roots in a convenient dictionary form.[97] But he also prepared a Torah scroll incorporating his results, which involved further research on the very difficult problem of the "open" and "closed" paragraphs and the arrangement of "songs." From Ramah's scroll, authoritative codices were copied. One such codex, which also contained important colophons and a letter by Ramah, was brought by French exiles to Perpignan in the wake of the expulsion of 1306. There it came into the hands of Ha-Meiri, who passes on Ramah's testimony that he "took pains and sent to all the *yeshibot*, to *Erez he-Ma'arab* and to the rabbis of Germany (Ashkenaz)" requesting reliable manuscripts.[98] One does not, of course, send for precious old manuscripts without accompanying payment. Ramah's very healthy economic status was doubtless helpful in carrying out his great Masoretic project.

Ha-Meiri's paraphrase of Ramah's testimony, though unclear and perhaps incomplete, is of considerable interest. It provides our only information that Ramah's contacts extended as far as Germany. Six years after Ramah's death a very careful German scholar was in Toledo to procure a copy of the Torah text that Ramah had established, for use in "a far-off land, in France and Germany."[99] What is meant by "all the *yeshibot*" is unclear. "*Erez ha-Ma'arab*" would generally include Muslim Spain or North Africa, or both.[100] A Toledo resident writing toward the end of the twelfth century indicates that business trips to Muslim-controlled districts of Spain and to North Africa were a matter of course.[101] Similarly, diplomats like Abraham Alfakar moved between Toledo and the Maghreb. It is thus possible that lines of scholarly communication remained open. A recent suggestion has Ramah as the author of several responsa previously ascribed to R. Joseph ibn Megash,[102] one of which was sent to North Africa.[103] While the link with North Africa is not impossible, the argument for Ramah's authorship is a bit shaky.[104]

Another Masoretic work by Ramah, composed in response to a request from Burgos and no longer extant, dealt with the problem of identifying the open and closed paragraphs in the Torah. Ha-Meiri preserves the letter that accompanied this work to Burgos.[105] Here, instead of attempting the reconstruction of an eclectic text—a recent student concludes that no coherent Masoretic tradition on open and closed paragraphs emerges from the manuscripts[106]—Ramah relied on the enumeration copied by Maimonides from the famous Ben Asher codex. His major problem was in clearing up the corruptions and uncertainties in the texts of *Mishneh Torah*.

Ramah's letter to the scholars of Burgos ends with the following anguished lines: "And receive instruction from one so inflicted with the reproofs of instruction—not with whips but with scorpions—that he must make known his suffering to the many. Perhaps they will seek mercy for him from the All-Merciful." Ramah was perhaps referring to the death of his son, "R. Judah Halevi," in 1226, before the completion of his twenty-third year. Ramah, in the words of his editor, "spoke the words of a bereaved father":

> Leave off vain comforters, the bereaved father,
> leave off the tree whose branches Sheol consumed.[107]

Ramah's "vain comforters" perhaps sent poetic consolations using a conventional motif: the deceased was taken because the Heavenly Court longed after his excellent qualities. Ramah replied:

> If the angels have coveted his intellect,
> would O my friends that he had been a fool.[108]

Ramah had been his son's devoted teacher:

> A son that my soul toiled to make wise,
> would that it might have rejoiced in him when he attained wisdom.[109]

Rejecting the comfort of friends and unable to forget his grief, Ramah ends with the hope that:

> . . . God will be gracious and turn
> to comfort my soul as he has bereaved it.

> For it is He that has afflicted and He will bind,
> he has smitten and He will heal.[110]

Ramah would return to this last motif little more than a year later, upon completion of his *Masoret Seyag la-Torah*. One imagines a mournful father seeking refuge from his grief in the intricate world of Masoretic scholarship. The colophon to a manuscript of *Masoret Seyag la-Torah* preserves the author's acknowledgment of "the aid of He who decrees and [yet] sustains."[111]

III

THE RESURRECTION
CONTROVERSY

AT ABOUT THE TIME that Ramah was becoming acquainted with the work of the French schools, a literary event occurred that excited the halakists of Europe. One of Ramah's halakic discussions refers to a decision made by "the greatest scholar of the generation," and it can be shown that he was alluding to a statement in the newly arrived *Mishneh Torah*.[1] Maimonides' *Mishneh Torah* reached Europe shortly after 1193 and almost immediately became the object of admiration and scholarly criticism.[2]

It is perhaps symbolic of the increasing detachment of Spain from the Islamic world and its new attachment to Europe that the works of this great Spanish exile, living in Egypt, seem to have reached Spain through Provence. When Ramah wanted accurate readings of *Mishneh Torah*, he wrote to Samuel ibn Tibbon in the port city of Marseilles, who had a manuscript of *Mishneh Torah* that had been checked against Maimonides' autograph copy.[3] Conversely Maimonides, in a pessimistic letter written in his last years to R. Jonathan ha-Kohen of Lunel, saw the Provençal schools as the last hope for the survival of talmudic scholarship. He says nothing of the beginnings of revival in his native Spain.[4]

As a result of the animated discussions surrounding *Mishneh Torah*, the scholars of the famous school at Lunel submitted a number of questions to Maimonides. Within two or three years of the arrival of Maimonides' answers in Lunel, the entire correspondence was in Ramah's hands.[5] Ramah, as we shall see, soon had occasion to subject some of Maimonides' responses to searching criticism. On other less publicized occasions we find him following Maimonides' lead. Ramah, in a responsum, reports a conversation with "one of the great men of Provence." Ramah had originally followed Maimonides on a certain issue. In response to questioning by the scholars of Lunel, Maimonides reversed his position. When informed of this by his Provençal col-

league, Ramah too reversed his position.[6] Ramah is best known as a
Maimonidean critic; but—though certainly not an uncritical admirer—
Ramah had profound respect for Maimonides and his *Mishneh Torah*.[7]

The two areas of Europe on which *Mishneh Torah* had an immediate
and deep effect were Spain and Provence. But the nature of its impact in
these two areas differed sharply. The Provençal communities were
small, well-educated in halakah, and at the height of their creative
powers. The arrival of *Mishneh Torah* served as a further stimulus to
scholarly criticism and discussion.[8] Though scholars like Ramah parti-
cipated in the great scholarly debates surrounding *Mishneh Torah*, the
overall picture in Christian Spain was quite different from that of Provence. Ignorance was rampant; and even among the educated not everyone was talmudically adept. For the broad public as well as for some
scholars, *Mishneh Torah* served primarily as a basic textbook. Intellectuals and literati like Alharizi welcomed it as a short, clear, and authoritative code that allowed them to dispense with protracted and involved
talmudic study.[9] For the uneducated masses, Maimonides' lucid prose
and clear organization and presentation served as an effective educational instrument that introduced a previously ignorant public to the
study of halakah.[10]

The educational revolution brought about in Spain by *Mishneh Torah*
was not without elements of discord. Local judges and religious func-
tionaries whose authority had previously gone unchallenged now found
themselves confronted with a newly critical public, still unfamiliar with
primary talmudic sources but eager to check all decisions against the
statements of Maimonides.[11] Still greater potential for discord lay in the
first section of *Mishneh Torah, Sefer ha-Madda'*. The relatively strong
dose of philosophical rationalism included in *Sefer ha-Madda'*[12] had a
twofold impact. Among Spanish intellectuals, it put the considerable
force of Maimonides' presentation and authority behind an already
strong rationalist tendency. To its less educated readers, on the other
hand, *Sefer ha-Madda'* presented a new and sometimes disturbing
world. Here too, the ability of *Mishneh Torah* to serve as a popular textbook was of crucial importance. For these simple readers were now
confronted, for the first time, with a brief but clear and powerful presentation of rationalistic theology.

One aspect of Maimonidean rationalism that troubled the unsophisti-
cated Spanish readers of *Mishneh Torah* was its eschatology. The problem hinged on Maimonides' interpretation of *'olam ha-ba*—literally, "the
world to come"—a central concept in talmudic eschatology. Popular
conception had followed the simple meaning of the classical aggadic
texts, which picture the "world to come" as the historical period

ushered in by resurrection in which the righteous receive their ultimate reward and the wicked their ultimate punishment. Maimonides interpreted 'olam ha-ba as the immortal existence of the disembodied soul of the righteous man who has perfected his deeds and his intellect.[13] This purely spiritual conception of 'olam ha-ba, propounded by their new and authoritative textbook, shook the naive faith of certain students of Mishneh Torah. Their sense of disillusionment is graphically described by Ramah's friend Ha-Yarhi: "When I came to Spain I found people in a number of places who were saying on the basis of the words of Moses, may he rest in peace [that is, Maimonides] that their hope had turned to despair and their longing had been in vain, for they denied resurrection: 'For, lo, the master [Maimonides] has said that the dead will not live nor shall the shades arise. Only the souls will hover about the world and fly in the air like angels.' These were their words."[14]

Spanish intellectuals found less cause for concern in Maimonidean eschatology. True, the great founder of medieval Jewish philosophy, Saadya Gaon, had vigorously defended the traditional conception of 'olam ha-ba.[15] But Maimonides' interpretation was no daringly new philosophical departure. By 1200 a purely spiritual interpretation of 'olam ha-ba was apparent to the careful reader of classical Spanish works going back at least a hundred and fifty years.[16] The novelty of the Maimonidean presentation lay in its forceful clarity. Few Spanish scholars saw cause for alarm.

Ramah, however, felt differently. Unlike many Spanish contemporaries, he was a staunch advocate of the relatively conservative philosophical views of Saadya and his geonic successors. Ramah would probably have agreed with the following characterization of Saadya's views by a modern student:

> The idea of immortality . . . is subordinated to the idea of resurrection of the dead. After the soul's separation from the body, it remains in a kind of intermediate state until it is joined again with the body at the resurrection, when both will receive their proper reward in an eternal life. All this is in accordance with talmudic teaching . . . Saadiah's doctrine of retribution is thus deeply rooted in Jewish tradition, not a mere echo of certain Talmudic statements. The same holds true of the whole system. It adheres to the essential contents of traditional Jewish religious ideas.[17]

Ramah, though aware that Maimonides' opinion was no eccentric innovation, was nevertheless sufficiently alarmed by the eschatological rationalism of Sefer ha-Madda' to conclude that some action should be taken. For one thing, Maimonides' "codification" of the spiritual interpretation of 'olam ha-ba would place a seal of authoritative approval on what he felt was the denial of a cardinal principle: "I was zealous for belief in resurrection which was already lost among the majority of the people of our time. How much more so now that they have found fortified cities [that is, the authority of *Mishneh Torah*] in which to escape."[18] Secondly, as I have indicated, *Sefer ha-Madda'*, as opposed to earlier Spanish philosophical works, was accessible to and read by many simple non-philosophers in whose view death was no boon, nor bodily existence a tragedy. Ramah was concerned over the religious predicament of these people, who now found their hopes for ultimate triumph over death declared an illusion: "Behold they say: Who will heal us? Our hope is lost! We are cut off!"[19]

Ramah, apparently, had initial misgivings: "I said to myself: 'Come, let me taste of joy and abandon words of controversy and rebuke.' But my heart was consumed with the fire of zealousness. I was unable to contain myself; I simply could not."[20] Vainly, Ramah sought support among the members of his own circle: "I called upon all of my trusted friends to join me. And I looked, but there was no supporter. None of them would aid."[21]

Ramah then turned to Provence for support. It must have seemed like a natural move. Ramah's "trusted friends" had, after all, been brought up on Spanish philosophy. The great centers of traditional scholarship to the north might be expected to be more sympathetic to his position. In about 1202 Ramah addressed a fateful letter to "my masters, the scholars of Lunel and its men of piety . . . and at their head, the venerable elder who is a priest to God most high, R. Jonathan ha-Kohen."[22]

Ramah's choice of Lunel is not difficult to explain. The Lunel school, headed by R. Jonathan ha-Kohen, was perhaps the most prestigious in Provence.[23] Moreover, its scholars had played an important role in the European diffusion of *Mishneh Torah* and were thus indirectly responsible for the spread of its teachings. Since they had lines of communication with Maimonides, the Lunel scholars would be in a position to request clarification or even retraction. Ramah was held in high regard in Lunel and apparently expected a sympathetic hearing.[24]

Writing in a proud and ornate style, Ramah called upon the Lunel scholars to show zeal for tradition and the religious hopes of the people by rebuking Maimonides and asking him to retract his views: "Hear, now, Yehonathan the High Priest, you and your colleagues who sit before you . . . God . . . has appointed you commander over the House of the Lord, to pierce the heart of the perverse with the arrows of your chastisement and to catch feet that have strayed from the path in your net."[25] Perhaps aware that Maimonides' definition of *'olam ha-ba* had not gone unnoticed in Provence,[26] Ramah demanded: "Now, then, why have you not rebuked the man whose feet strayed from the decree of the King and his nobles?"[27] Ramah did not deny Maimonides' great stature: "Should you say: 'He is a great man and there is none in Israel like him'—granted, that it is as you say. Nevertheless, neither wisdom nor understanding [are accorded consideration] in the face of one who lops off a branch with an axe [that is, denies a cardinal principle of faith]."[28] Calling for vigorous action, Ramah left a somewhat vague opening for graceful retreat: "And so hasten to admonish him so that you may know well, the man and his speech. If little foxes have spoiled his vineyard,[29] he will surely catch them in his net. If, however, he has erred and failed to remove dross from silver, does there not exist a refining pot for silver and a furnace of intelligence? And if, God forbid, he should persist therein . . . the rod of chastisement has not departed your hand nor is his sentence unknown to you."[30]

Ramah felt confident that he had argued his case convincingly. But one thing troubled him: he had heard that the Lunel scholars had begun treating *Mishneh Torah* as an oracle of sorts.[31] By way of argument against any presumption of infallibility, Ramah appended to his letter a few well-reasoned refutations of Maimonidean halakic decisions.[32]

The halakic objections fall into two groups. One group seems a natural enough choice under the circumstances; it consists of refutations of six of Maimonides' celebrated responsa to Ramah's addressees, the scholars of Lunel.[33] A second group of halakic objections is a bit puzzling, for the topics of these objections seem unconnected and randomly chosen. But in fact, as will be shown later, they emerged quite naturally from Ramah's program of study.[34]

Halakic criticism was, in any case, peripheral to Ramah's primary theological concern.[35] Ramah merely wished to show that though *Mishneh Torah* indeed "gives goodly words . . . there is no grain without chaff."[36]

Ramah had misjudged the climate of opinion in Lunel. His letter failed, even backfired. Instead of support, he received severe reproach.

The reply from Lunel came not from R. Jonathan ha-Kohen, but from the wealthy and respected R. Aaron b. Meshullam.[37] Responding for the scholars of Lunel, R. Aaron lectured Ramah on his pride in presuming to attack Maimonides. Before proceeding with Aaron b. Meshullam's letter, we must ask why it was he that served as spokesman for the Lunel school. Ramah, after all, had addressed his letter to R. Jonathan ha-Kohen; why did the primary addressee fail to respond? In the absence of clear evidence, I offer the following conjecture: R. Jonathan ha-Kohen became acquainted with Maimonides' works late in his career. His training was in the Provençal tradition.[38] Since R. Jonathan was a disciple of Rabad, the dominant figure in twelfth-century Provençal halakah,[39] Ramah's challenge may have put him in an awkward predicament.

Rabad, as is well known, wrote the classic critique of *Mishneh*

Torah.[40] The celebrated queries put to Maimonides by Jonathan and the Lunel scholars had originally been raised in Rabad's *Hassagot.*[41] Ramah's rebuttal of Maimonides' responsa to Lunel, in effect, reaffirmed Rabad's positions. Moreover, Rabad, in a brief critical gloss, had anticipated Ramah's fuller and more urgent critique of the Maimonidean definition of *'olam ha-ba.*[42] Since a vigorous defense of Maimonides would have aligned R. Jonathan squarely against his deceased teacher, we can understand his reluctance to enter the fray.

R. Aaron b. Meshullam, in any case, felt no qualms about giving Maimonides his unequivocal support.[43] Aaron waxed eloquent in praising Maimonides and censuring the pride of Ramah for daring to attack him.[44] Dutifully, he produced a long reply to Ramah's halakic objections.[45] But Aaron's formulation and defense of Maimonides' position on *'olam ha-ba* are not very successful; for in attempting as he did to reconcile the mutually exclusive interpretations of Maimonides and Saadya, Aaron could not but seem forced.[46] Ramah felt that R. Aaron, instead of judging the issues with an open mind, "was intent on supporting him [Maimonides] by any means available, whether valid or invalid."[47] Ramah later admitted serious error in expecting the support of the Lunel school.[48] What exactly was the nature of his error?

Ramah may have underestimated the inroads of Spanish rationalistic eschatology in Provence. But the text of Aaron b. Meshullam's letter contains little to support this view; on the contrary, R. Aaron's attempt to identify the traditional Saadyanic *'olam ha-ba* with that of Maimonides indicates an imperfect appreciation of the latter.

R. Aaron himself suggests, in effect, that it was more the tone than the substance of Ramah's polemic that was objectionable: "Would that you had shown deliberation in expressing your wisdom, culture and understanding . . . Indeed, some of what you have said merits entry into the inner sanctum. But you have vaunted your wisdom with a haughtiness, pride, arrogance and contempt . . . that have spoiled your pleasant words."[49] We recall Alharizi's similar appraisal.[50] Accordingly, one might conclude that Ramah failed because of his brashness. Had he not, in the heat of controversy, violated the canons of modesty and scholarly etiquette, had he but kept within the bounds of polite scholarly debate, he would have received a more sympathetic hearing.

There is no denying the strong language of Ramah's letter.[51] But rough polemical rhetoric directed against scholarly peers was no rarity in those days,[52] and it cannot entirely explain the response that Ramah evoked. Crucial in Ramah's failure was not merely the tone of his argument but its target. The reader of R. Aaron's letter knows that no reasoning, no matter how polite, could have convinced him that Maimonides had denied a cardinal principle of the faith. Thus Ramah's failure was a foregone conclusion. The pride and severity of his attack merely compounded the offense.

Underlying the dispute between Aaron b. Meshullam and Ramah were two differing appraisals of Maimonides. Both were highly positive. There is no doubt that Ramah had an extremely high opinion of Maimonides; even in the heat of debate he was willing to concede that Maimonides was without peer among contemporary scholars.[53] But, for Ramah, he was at most *primus inter pares*—quite fallible and perfectly fair game for conventionally rough literary polemic. Ramah, while writing his first letter, already had indications that a rather different image of Maimonides prevailed in Lunel. In the mind of Aaron b. Meshullam, Maimonides was more than the finest contemporary scholar; he had already transcended the role of prominent contemporary and become a figure of heroic proportions, the symbolic manifestation of a cultural ideal. This, then, was Ramah's error: he had not grasped the nature and strength of the new Maimonidean image. It simply would not crumble under a few well-reasoned halakic refutations.

Against the conception implicit in Ramah's treatment of Maimonides, R. Aaron argues as follows:

> If your God has aided you and anointed you with the precious perfumer's oil of wisdom and honor above your fellows . . . why have your thoughts grown so proud . . . Perhaps you have smitten the inhabitants of your city, teacher and pupil alike, by your sword . . . so that you have proudly . . . taken counsel to strive against God by speaking contemptuously of Moses, the man of God. For one who contends with his master is as if he contends with the Shekinah. And he [Maimonides] is perforce your master and the master of your master and of all those dwelling round about you and in your midst. You were, therefore, quite guilty of childish waywardness when your haughtiness and pride enticed you . . . to multiply words against him. For in truth, his God sent him to His people as a source of life. He saw the weakness of their jurists, while the condition of the Children of Israel progressively worsened. And he [Maimonides] . . . stretched his mighty rod over the sea of the Talmud so that the Children of Israel could walk on dry land in the midst of the sea. And he extricated his people from the sea of ignorance . . . Behold it is written before me, I will not keep silence, that from the days of Rabina and R. Ashi, none has arisen in Israel like Moses who has been wonderful in counsel and excellent in wisdom. His deeds are greater than the deeds of R. Hiyya. For he has . . . established teaching in Israel which will not be forgotten by their seed.[54]

Aaron's letter, though hardly illuminating on the issue of resurrection, is a historical document of major significance. It marks the emergence of what was to become an important component of the cultural heritage of post-Maimonidean Spain, Provence, and Italy: the heroic image of Maimonides. In future controversies even anti-rationalists would tend increasingly to operate within its constraints.[55] R. Aaron's very imperfect understanding of Maimonides' 'olam ha-ba serves only to accentuate the extent to which the Maimonidean image could have a life and power quite independent of precise and technically accurate understanding of the master's thought.

Ramah was bitterly disappointed by the reply from Lunel.[56] Yet it could have been worse; Aaron b. Meshullam had been careful to balance reproach with respect for Ramah's scholarship and station.[57] Moreover, the interpretation that Aaron gave to the Maimonidean 'olam ha-ba was not terribly radical. It remained for another opponent to exhaust more fully the possibilities of personal attack and theological opposition. He was, ironically, a close friend of the family: the great Barcelona nasi, Sheshet b. Isaac Benveniste.

A few years earlier Ramah had referred to Sheshet Benveniste as "the singular [member] of our generation."[58] It was no idle compliment. The roster of his achievements is truly impressive; scattered sources attest to Sheshet's high political position, communal leadership, philanthropy, literary patronage, poetic skills, and medical prowess.[59] Moreover, he was known as a man of deep piety.[60] At the time of the Resurrection Controversy, though well advanced in years, he was at the height of his influence. Sheshet was, in short, a formidable opponent.

Aaron b. Meshullam's letter cushioned criticism with praise and generally tended to blur the theological issue. In contrast, Sheshet's polemic shows neither haziness nor moderation.[61] It is characterized by relentlessly biting personal attack and a vigorous and lucid statement of rationalistic spirituality that sharply defines the divergent positions on resurrection.

Sheshet was enraged by Ramah's polemical activity in Spain and his apparently open letter to Lunel. Previously friendly family relationships could not deter his indignant response. Certain that the Lunel scholars would put Ramah in his place, Sheshet nevertheless felt impelled to present his own rebuttal of Ramah to R. Jonathan ha-Kohen.[62] We do not know how Sheshet's letter was received in Lunel, but one thing is certain: it was not seen as the intervention of some remote Spanish aristocrat. The communities of Provence and Catalonia were by this period quite close. Sheshet Benveniste was on intimate terms with the leaders of Provençal Jewry and was regarded throughout Provence with profound respect.[63]

Sheshet's letter is unique among the polemical documents that have come down to us from the great medieval Jewish debates over rationalism, for he shows no trace of the defensive prudence of the religious philosopher under hostile traditionalist attack. The letter makes no attempt to obscure the full measure of his rationalism. If the Lunel scholars did not yet understand the kind of thinking that had alarmed Ramah, this defense of Maimonides must have enlightened them.

After putting down Ramah as an arrogant young fool,[64] Sheshet proceeds to argue passionately for a purely spiritual interpretation of resurrection.[65] In brief, his position is that Maimonides has, in fact, denied physical resurrection and that he is absolutely correct! *Tehiyyat ha-metim* (literally, the coming to life of the dead) refers to the eternal life of the wise and pure soul that begins with bodily death. All talmudic statements to the contrary, Sheshet insists, were written for the benefit of the masses, who cannot grasp anything that is not physical.[66] Sheshet's letter ends with the suggestion that criticism of *Mishneh Torah* by Ramah and other Castilian jurists is motivated by jealousy; for the educational impact of *Mishneh Torah* has shaken their unquestioned authority in the eyes of the previously ignorant masses.[67]

Ramah, we recall, was a rather well connected man. By attacking him so severely, Sheshet would seem to have risked alienating the leaders of the powerful Castilian aristocracy. A bit of information preserved in Abraham Zacuto's *Sefer Yuhasin* affords a remarkable glimpse at the strategy followed by this skillful old diplomat: "And our master Sheshet, son of the great *nasi* Ben Venist,[68] composed a poem of one hundred forty-two lines in the year 4963 [1202 or 1203]. He was at the time seventy-two years old. In it, he praised R. Joseph and his son and lieutenant R. Shlomo ibn Shoshan of Toledo."[69] If Zacuto's chronology is accurate, Sheshet was engaged in lavish praise of his opponent's close relatives at the very height of their conflict! By following denunciation of Ramah with praise for his powerful relatives, Sheshet may have hoped to isolate his opponent, appease old friends, and prevent the controversy from stirring up a family feud.

Ramah's two literary opponents were certainly not of one cloth. Ramah would seem to have more in common with each of his opponents than the latter had with each other. With Aaron b. Meshullam, Ramah shared a commitment to intensive talmudic study; with Sheshet Benveniste, he shared the common cultural heritage of the Spanish aristocracy. The dissimilarity of Ramah's two opponents makes it easy to isolate the common ground of their opposition. The very different responses of Aaron and Sheshet converge on one crucial point: the heroic image of Maimonides. Sheshet certainly argues the substantive theological issues with greater lucidity and conviction than his Provençal counterpart. But for both, the crucial issue—the thing that aroused passion and demanded refutation—was Ramah's "desecration" of the Maimonidean image.

Sheshet and Aaron did not, of course, draw identical portraits of Maimonides. Each accentuated different features: Sheshet stressed Maimonides' realization of the ideal of pure intellectual-spiritual worship and his fame among non-Jewish intellectuals,[70] while Aaron stressed Maimonides' superlative halakic achievements. But even wider variations in the Maimonidean image persisted throughout the Middle Ages.[71] Both Aaron and Sheshet could subscribe to an image of Maimonides that made any serious attack totally unacceptable. This new heroic conception of Maimonides was a central factor in the Resurrection Controversy and much subsequent cultural history as well.

Ramah composed a long, point-by-point rebuttal of Aaron b. Meshullam's letter.[72] But by this time he realized that he was not going to win Aaron over by argumentation. Once again, Ramah tells us, he considered abandoning the field of battle, but nevertheless resolved to persevere: "For I was angered by a tumultuous voice . . . a voice striking terror into the hearts, a voice that weakens the warriors . . . uprooting mountains and shattering rocks, a voice that rends innocent souls . . . a voice that says, 'Cry out . . . "All flesh is grass and all its goodness is as the flower of the field" ' [that is, the body will perish, its good deeds unrewarded]."[73] Ramah was probably referring to the "voice" of Sheshet Benveniste.[74] Sternly rebuked by Aaron in Provence and scathingly denounced by Sheshet in Spain, Ramah found himself beleaguered and isolated: "Woe is me, for I am like the last of the summer fruit . . . like corn blasted before it is grown up, like the gleaning grapes when the vintage is done . . . Why is my pain perpetual and my wound incurable? I fled the iron weapons and the sharpened sword, and the brass bow struck me through. The godly man is perished out of the earth . . . the upright man is no more."[75]

With "godly men" of sufficient influence in short supply in Spain and Provence, Ramah turned to the scholars of northern France. Exactly how Ramah first made contact with them is not clear; perhaps Ha-Yarhi served as his intermediary. But whatever the channels of communication were, Ramah's letter to the French Tosafists represents a new development. For the first time northern French scholars were invited to participate in an inter-European religious controversy. Moreover, the ensuing correspondence is the earliest surviving written exchange of any kind between the Jews of Spain and those of northern France.[76]

Ramah's letter cannot be dated precisely. It was likely written no earlier than 1203, for the French reply was composed after Maimonides' death in 1204. Ramah addressed himself to "our masters the most excellent rabbis of the land of Zarfat," specifically naming the seven scholars who stand "at their head . . . the lions of the company."[77] Of the seven, only four are known to us from other sources. The brothers, Samson b. Abraham of Sens and Isaac b. Abraham of Dampierre, were recognized as the outstanding Tosafists of their generation.[78] A third addressee, R. Solomon b. Judah of Dreux, had studied with Samson and Isaac at the celebrated school of Isaac b. Samuel at Dampierre.[79] The work of a fourth addressee, Eliezer b. Aaron of Bourgogne, is quoted by Aaron ha-Kohen of Lunel in his *Orhot Hayyim*.[80] The remaining three, Samson of Corbeil, David of Chateau Thierry,[81] and Abraham of Toques, though unknown to us, doubtless enjoyed high regard in their day.

Ramah was asking men with whom his ties were at best tenuous to intervene in a controversy outside their geographical "sphere of influence." But ideologically, at least, the northern French scholars were natural allies. The Tosafists were completely untouched by the Spanish rationalism that had been making inroads in Provence. Ramah could thus be confident that his addressees would have little sympathy for the rationalistic interpretation of *'olam ha-ba*. Nor did the image of Maimonides loom so large in northern France. Even the halakic portions of *Mishneh Torah* had relatively little influence among French Tosafists. Its author certainly never became the cultural symbol that he was in the south.[82]

Ramah knew that the position taken by the Tosafists would be of considerable importance. Some of the local Spanish intellectuals might sneer at the French talmudists, with their circumscribed education and unpolished style;[83] but for anyone seriously committed to talmudic scholarship, the dazzling achievements of the twelfth-century Tosafists demanded a healthy measure of respect. Had not the Lunel scholars themselves sought guidance to the north?[84]

Ramah submitted a copy of his correspondence with Aaron to the French scholars, requesting that they set Aaron and his colleagues straight. Passionately, he exhorted them to lead the battle in defense of the principle of resurrection: "And now O kings . . . prepare for battle; don the armor of wisdom . . . rouse up the heroes, let all the warriors come forward . . . and let them smash like a hammer, the rock of arrogance."[85] The letter must have been widely circulated, for it reached as far as Germany where it was discussed by R. Eliezer Rokeah and his circle of pietists.[86] French Tosafists and German pietists alike agreed that Ramah's points were quite well taken; but no one had the least intention of "preparing for battle."

The French reply to Ramah's letter was written by R. Samson b. Abraham. Using a bit of imagery from the Book of Daniel,[87] Samson begins his letter with a vivid description of the debate, and of the French consensus:

"I saw the ram pushing westward, northward, and southward so that no beast could stand before him . . . but he did according to his will and magnified himself"—this refers to R. Moses ibn Maimon. "And as I was considering, behold a he-goat came from the west across the face of the whole earth . . ."—this refers to R. Meir Halevi. "And it came to the ram that had two horns . . . and ran at him in the fury of his power . . . and it was enraged against him and smote the ram and broke his two horns"—this refers to R. Moses b. Maimon and to R. Aaron B. Meshullam who came to his aid. "And the ram had no power to stand before him"—this refers to Rambam of blessed memory. "And he cast him down to the ground and trampled upon him"—this refers to Ramah. "And there was none to deliver the ram out of his hand"—this refers to the French who have put the issue to a vote and concluded that both body and soul are present in 'olam ha-ba.[88]

At first glance, Samson seems to be describing the controversy as a fateful, almost earthshaking confrontation. But Samson's talmudically knowledgeable reader, recognizing that his little "midrash" was borrowed whole from an early rabbinic source, would catch its true import. For this literary device was originally used, perhaps humorously, to describe a Tanaitic dispute over an abstruse point of halakah.[89] Samson seems to be hinting that the current controversy as well, for all its sound and fury, is a perfectly legitimate and not terribly major scholarly debate.

Samson's opening sets the tone for the remainder of his very businesslike reply. The corporeality of 'olam ha-ba is treated as just another talmudic problem—of the same order as Ramah's halakic points. The Tosafists agree that Maimonides' conception of 'olam ha-ba is erroneous;[90] but the assumption implicit in Ramah's letter—that this error constitutes a major theological calamity and must, therefore, be stamped out—is simply ignored.

The relatively mild reaction of the Tosafists calls for an explanation. They were certainly further removed from the world of philosophical rationalism than Ramah. Indeed, thirty years hence their disciples would lead a vigorous attack against Maimonidean philosophy.[91] Why, then, did they stand aside now?[92]

Close reading of the correspondence suggests a surprisingly simple explanation. The Tosafists did not share Ramah's concern because they simply did not see the controversy as a conflict over philosophical rationalism. R. Samson treated the resurrection issue as just another talmudic debate because that is precisely the way it appeared to him.[93] There is no evidence that he in any way connected this dispute over the correct definition of 'olam ha-ba with the study of philosophy. In fact, the Tosafists were probably not yet sufficiently acquainted with Spanish rationalism to have adopted a consciously anti-rationalist posture at all. They were as yet only potential anti-rationalists. Thirty years later the scholars of northern France became convinced that certain addicts to the study of "Greek wisdom" were reinterpreting traditional religious terms while rejecting their simple meanings; they lost no time in joining battle.

Ramah knew perfectly well that what was at issue in the Resurrection Controversy was the philosophical reinterpretation of traditional eschatological concepts.[94] But, perhaps because he was not entirely opposed to philosophical study himself, he chose not to say so explicitly.[95] Instead, he marshaled biblical and talmudic proof texts in support of his definition of 'olam ha-ba. This cautious formulation may have cost him French support. Samson, unfamiliar with the broader cultural and religious background of the debate, probably took the correspondence at face value and concluded that Ramah was unduly alarmed.

Other factors may have further encouraged moderation in the French reply. Samson's letter was written shortly after news of Maimonides' death reached Europe; he was understandably sensitive about "arguing against the great lion after his death."[96] Moreover, the Tosafists may have gotten wind of the fact that their stance was no longer quite so relevant. By the time Samson put down his reply, the major combatants had backed away from their earlier confrontation. To see how and why this happened, let us pick up where we left off in Toledo, and follow the controversy to its conclusion.

We know very little about events within Toledo during the controversy. Ramah indicates that he had little local support, but says nothing more. We can, however, guess at the identity of one of his local opponents. Consider the following facts about Judah Alharizi: he was in Toledo at about the time of the controversy,[97] had no patience with critics of *Mishneh Torah*, admired the spirituality of Sheshet Benveniste,[98] quite possibly accepted Sheshet's interpretation of resurrection,[99] and thought Ramah arrogant.[100] Alharizi seems a likely member of Ramah's Toledo opposition.

Little more can be said about local events. The surviving documents illuminate only the "international" side of the debate; local controversy was probably carried on orally. One small literary effort, however, was probably aimed at an audience closer to home. Soon after the dispatch of his letter to northern France, Ramah published an edition of his polemical correspondence entitled *The Book of Letters* (*Kitāb al-Rasā'il*). It contained his exchange with Aaron b. Meshullam, his letter to the northern French Tosafists, and a brief introduction describing the cir-

cumstances under which these letters were written. The title and introduction of Ramah's *Book of Letters* were written in Arabic.[101] Its intended
audience was thus the old Spanish intelligentsia, still at home in Arabic.
Ramah may have wished to set the record straight in the face of local
criticism.

The publication of *Kitāb al-Rasā'il* is the last bit of polemical activity
that we can ascribe to Ramah. Shortly thereafter the Resurrection Controversy ended; more precisely, it shifted from the arena of strident intercommunal debate back to the literary and oral channels through
which religious and intellectual issues were regularly argued. What
happened—did the intercommunal polemic simply peter out in the face
of a weary stalemate? Or did some particular event bring it to an end?
To anticipate the conclusion of the forthcoming chronological considerations, it seems likely that the controversy *was* ended by a particular
event: the publication of Samuel ibn Tibbon's translation of Maimonides' *Treatise on Resurrection.*[102]

Unbeknown to the European participants in the Resurrection Controversy, Maimonides had already clarified and defended his position
in the face of similar attacks by Eastern critics.[103] His *Treatise on Resurrection,* written in Arabic in 1191, explicitly affirms physical resurrection. This *tehiyyat ha-metim,* however, is to be followed by a second bodily death and eternal life of the soul in a purely spiritual *'olam ha-ba.*

Maimonides' *Treatise on Resurrection* was at some point translated into
Hebrew by Samuel ibn Tibbon. The date of this translation is, as
Steinschneider long ago pointed out, unfortunately not known.[104] It is,
however, possible to establish fairly narrow limits within which the
translation must have appeared.

The Resurrection Controversy itself provides a *terminus a quo* for the
appearance of Ibn Tibbon's translation. For had Maimonides' *Treatise
on Resurrection* been known in Europe, the whole controversy could not
have occurred. Ramah would not have alleged Maimonides' denial of
physical resurrection; Sheshet Benveniste certainly would not have defended such a denial; and Aaron b. Meshullam would not have explained Maimonides in terms of a Saadyanic position rejected in the
Treatise.[105] The last document in which one of the above-mentioned
combatants affirms his position is Ramah's letter to northern France. I
have already indicated that this letter was probably written no earlier
than 1203; therefore this date is a likely *terminus a quo* for Ibn Tibbon's
translation.

When Ibn Tibbon's translation of the *Treatise* did become available,
Ramah had a change of heart. His revised position found expression in
his commentary on the talmudic tractate *Sanhedrin.* Ramah's treatment
of Maimonides' *'olam ha-ba* is now one of polite scholarly disagreement

rather than censure and polemic.[106] Ramah indicates that his earlier communication to Lunel reflected a misunderstanding now clarified by Maimonides' Treatise.[107] Perfectly at home in Arabic, Ramah would have preferred using Maimonides' original text. Apparently, however, it was unavailable: "And the translator [Ibn Tibbon] translated his Arabic into an extremely difficult Hebrew. Nevertheless, I will reproduce that portion of his language that seems clear to me while changing other parts so as to make clear the notions that the author intended to convey, to the best of my ability."[108]

A *terminus ad quem* for the Ibn Tibbon translation would clearly be provided if we could date Ramah's *Sanhedrin* commentary. Such dating is fairly straightforward and yields a surprising result. Maimonides is referred to as living in most of the *Sanhedrin* commentary, including its discussion of resurrection.[109] The Ibn Tibbon translation of the *Treatise on Resurrection* thus predates the death of Maimonides. The *Treatise*, still unavailable when Ramah wrote to northern France, must have become available soon thereafter. Ramah had a chance to study the *Treatise*, reconsider, and put his new position in writing all before news of Maimonides' death reached Toledo in 1205.

Having established that the *Sanhedrin* commentary was in preparation at the time of the Resurrection Controversy, we are finally in a position to solve the puzzle of the six seemingly random halakic criticisms of *Mishneh Torah* that Ramah had included in his letter to Lunel. All six are related to passages in *Sanhedrin*.[110] They probably arose quite naturally in the course of Ramah's preparation of the *Sanhedrin* commentary.

Three facts about the Ibn Tibbon translation emerge from the *Sanhedrin* commentary: it was available in Toledo before Maimonides' death; the Arabic original was unavailable; and there was dissatisfaction with Ibn Tibbon's Hebrew. Taken together, these facts serve to corroborate at least part of the report given by Judah Alharizi in the introduction to his rival translation of Maimonides' *Treatise on Resurrection*.[111]

Alharizi's rival version reflects a standing dispute with Ibn Tibbon. The latter stuck closely to his Arabic originals, sacrificing ease and style for accuracy and technical precision. Alharizi, on the other hand, felt that translation should be clear, elegant, and not slavishly literal. Ibn Tibbon considered Alharizi incompetent at philosophical translation. Like Ramah, Alharizi thought Ibn Tibbon's translation graceless and at times hardly comprehensible.[112] Alharizi tells a very strange story about his version of Maimonides' *Treatise*: it is, he claims, a translation of a translation of a translation! Ibn Tibbon's inelegant Hebrew translation was translated back into a fine literary Arabic by one Joseph b. Joel; and Alharizi, in turn, translated this Arabic version into civilized Hebrew. So, at least, Alharizi would have it.

Alharizi quotes what purports to be a letter of the translator, Joseph b. Joel:

> This treatise did not reach me in Arabic. True, my utmost desire was to see it in its author's language. But the wise and honorable scholar, R. Samuel ibn Tibbon, our faithful friend who is learned in every science, translated it into Hebrew upon receiving it from the master [Maimonides] and sent it to me in accordance with the latter's command. And it reached me only in his [Ibn Tibbon's] translation. Now the vast vocabulary of Arabic cannot be matched by Hebrew for we possess but a small remnant of the latter.[113] Accordingly, this translation was quite obscure . . . Therefore a beloved friend, a member of the cultured class, requested that I restore it to its original state, to Arabic.[114]

Some think Alharizi's story so strange as to be incredible.[115] But at least as regards the publication and reception of Ibn Tibbon's translation of the *Treatise*, it tallies nicely with what we know from Ramah's *Sanhedrin* commentary.[116]

Alharizi's introduction, however, adds a very significant detail. Not only was Ibn Tibbon's translation done during Maimonides' lifetime, but Maimonides himself sent his *Treatise* to Ibn Tibbon with instructions for its distribution.[117] The fact that Maimonides had Ibn Tibbon translate and distribute his *Treatise* at the very time it was needed to end the Resurrection Controversy invites the following, admittedly conjectural, reconstruction of the events that brought that controversy to its conclusion.

By the time of the Resurrection Controversy the Lunel scholars had already established lines of communication with Maimonides. Faced with the disturbing charges brought by Ramah and the perhaps equally disturbing defense of Sheshet Benveniste, it was quite natural for them to submit the matter to Maimonides. Having already clarified and defended his position in his *Treatise on Resurrection*, Maimonides sent a copy to Samuel ibn Tibbon with instructions that it be translated and published. Maimonides himself thus brought the controversy to a close.

Publication of Ibn Tibbon's translation of the *Treatise* probably brought about a rapid and somewhat embarrassed truce; for the major protagonists now found themselves contradicted by Maimonides himself. Ramah, as we have seen, quickly put his modified position in writing. The sixteenth-century historian Azariah de Rossi makes a tantalizingly obscure reference to "the last letter of R. Meir b. Todros Halevi to the scholars of Lunel concerning Rambam's apologia for his treatment of this principle."[118] Perhaps de Rossi still had a letter in which Ramah had communicated his modified position to Lunel.

The change wrought by publication of Maimonides' *Treatise* was heightened by the events of 1205, "a year of disaster, a year of wrath and a time of sorrow." Locally it witnessed the death of the *nasi* Joseph ibn Shoshan. Only "a month or two" earlier, the sobering news of Maimonides' death had reached Toledo.[119] Criticism was suspended; it was a time for tribute. In a moving poem full of implied analogy to the biblical Moses, Ramah mourned Israel's loss and praised Maimonides' peerless achievements.[120]

Alluding to *Mishneh Torah*, Ramah rhetorically addresses the deceased master:

Awake! See all the scholars of the day knocking like beggars at the door of your understanding

They meditate upon your teachings and daily reap therefrom a double portion of wisdom (*mishneh te'udot*), purified like gold.[121]

Ramah could have maintained a benign silence about Maimonides' philosophical enterprise. It is significant that instead he expresses high praise for the recently arrived *Guide of the Perplexed*:

They [the scholars of the day] perceive in the *Guide of the Perplexed*, swords of intellect flashing lightning in the darkness.[122]

There, they see swords of perplexity sharpened for the innocent, smoothed by the oil of discernment.[123]

Words like apples, cast from the gold of wisdom, set in filigrees of understanding.[124]

Through them, the lost of the generation gained understanding while the neglectful were strengthened in the fear of their Creator.[125]

Obviously impressed with at least part of Maimonides' philosophical defense of the faith, Ramah asks: "Who now, will split open, in the rocks, springs of wisdom, and by whom will the bitter waters be sweetened."[126] Ramah was probably alluding to the "bitter waters" of Aristotelian philosophy.[127]

Ramah, in eulogy, acknowledges a personal debt to Maimonides' scholarship.

Would that I were like a swallow I would fly to his grave . . .

And water its dust with my tears, just as the springs of his teaching quenched my soul.[128]

When Ha-Yarhi, returning to Toledo from one of his frequent trips to France, finally delivered R. Samson's belated reply,[129] Ramah ignored the French pronouncements on '*olam ha-ba*. Instead, he took the opportunity to engage his French correspondent in further discussion of the halakic issues raised in the letter.[130] The Resurrection Controversy was closed.

Ramah's feelings at the close of the controversy are difficult to gauge. During the controversy he had suffered isolation and harsh denunciation. Publication of Maimonides' *Treatise* probably brought both further discomfort and partial vindication. On the one hand, the *Treatise*, by implication, characterized Ramah as one of those "who chose to speak falsely about us and attribute to us an opinion that we do not believe ... to be judged like any (wicked) man who suspects the innocent."[131] On the other hand, the *Treatise* partially vindicated Ramah in his battle with Spanish rationalists of Sheshet's persuasion; for it did put the weight of Maimonidean authority behind physical resurrection.

Ramah, as we have seen, quickly revised his position toward Maimonides. His eulogy expresses sentiments worthy of Maimonides' most faithful admirers. But Ramah was far from satisfied with the *Treatise's* reaffirmation of an incorporeal *'olam ha-ba*. One subtly ambiguous verse perhaps indicates a certain ambivalence. Ramah, in mourning, rhetorically asks: "Have the sins of the waters of Meriva been remembered today, do they yet pursue us?"[132] The reference is, of course, to the biblical waters of Meriva (contention), responsible for Moses' premature death. This recurrence of Ramah's Moses-Maimonides motif immediately suggests an association of biblical and contemporary *meriva*.[133] Sins of "contention" have now brought about the death of the second Moses as they did the first. Who was responsible for the tragedy of Meriva? Ramah's readers knew of two contradictory answers:

> And they [the Israelites] angered Him at the
> waters of Meriva so that it went ill with
> Moses for their sakes.[134]

> For you [Moses] rebelled against My commandment ...
> in the contention of the congregation,
> [failing] to sanctify Me ... before their eyes.[135]

Which of the two did Ramah have in mind? Perhaps both.

It would, in any case, be quite wrong to characterize Ramah's attitude at the close of the controversy as one of humble contrition. Ramah felt that he had been seriously wronged. Years later the wounds inflicted by his opponents still rankled:

> Well over thirty years ago when *Mishneh Torah* reached this land
> [Spain] ... I became zealous for the Rock of Israel ... and the
> principle of [divine] justice, having seen that belief in resurrection
> had long been lost in this land ... And so I wrote a letter of zeal-
> ousness to the rabbis, the scholars of Lunel of those days calling
> upon them to show zeal for the honor of God and His Torah ... I

waited for their words, listened for their wisdom; but none would stand fast with me to repair the breach in my people. Instead, one of their scholars arose to ride in the chariot of the *mishneh* [*Mishneh Torah;* also, one (who ought rank) second to the (divine) King] rather than calling himself after the Holy One of Israel . . . And the lot and recompense of God's servant was that bitter things were written and false statements made about him.[136]

When Ramah wrote these words, Jewish communities all over Europe were engaged in a great battle over philosophical rationalism.[137] Compared to that battle, the Resurrection Controversy seems a minor skirmish. Nevertheless, it anticipated, in miniature, important aspects of the later controversy. It was the Resurrection Controversy that introduced intercommunal polemic over rationalism to the European scene. And, as in the Resurrection Controversy, the image of Maimonides would play a central role. There was anticipation, too, in the fundamental issues underlying the debate. True, the Resurrection Controversy as it unfolds in *Kitāb al-Rasā'il* is ostensibly about the correct interpretation of talmudic eschatological terminology. But the letter of Sheshet Benveniste goes to the heart of the matter; and so too does the discussion in *Perate-Sanhedrin*, written at the close of the controversy.[138]

Even the overtly exegetical argumentation in *Kitāb al-Rasā'il* can be seen to anticipate an important issue in the controversy over rationalism. Since medieval Jewish thought often takes the form of commentary (in the broadest sense of the term) on the biblical-talmudic tradition, theological debate almost invariably has an exegetical side, with proponents of each position claiming support in the classical sources. On crucial points, rationalists tend toward nonliteral interpretation; and so exegetical methodology itself becomes a central issue of controversy. Thus in his letter to Ramah, Aaron b. Meshullam had rhetorically wondered: "How have you taken things literally and interpreted the verses at face value, going forth to prosecute like an accuser [or Satan]?"[139] Ramah's reply was as follows: "Is it really an affirmative *mizvah* to interpret without reason, against the plain meaning of verses and talmudic teachings . . . to defame all that will be and was? Surely the burden of proof rests on the claimant [that is, the nonliteral exegete]!"[140]

But should that burden of proof be successfully shouldered, Ramah was perfectly ready to concede the legitimacy, even the necessity, of nonliteral interpretation. The circumstances justifying such departure from the literal had long since been delimited by Saadya.[141] Ramah, who claimed quite correctly to be in complete accord with Saadya, was certainly no literalist. Not so R. Samson b. Abraham, representative of the French Tosafists. "How," he incredulously asks, "could anyone possibly think that we ought not take aggadah literally?"[142] R. Samson denies the legitimacy of nonliteral exegesis of aggadah under any circumstances. Having failed to grasp what was at stake in the Resurrection Controversy, R. Samson did not match Ramah's sense of urgency or indignation. But substantively, his exegetical conservatism far exceeded Ramah's.

In an introductory paragraph to his discussion of 'olam ha-ba in Perate-Sanhedrin, Ramah defined his exegetical position somewhat more sharply. At issue, he implies, is an attempt to impose philosophical doctrine on the classical texts by willful misinterpretation:

> We must interpret . . . in accordance with what we have received from our fathers and teachers and the tradition spread throughout Israel and also according to the plain meaning of the mishnaic and talmudic teachings and not employ insidious circumvention nor seek after [knowledge of] great things and disparage the tradition of our fathers and innovate, following after our lowly and small minds, seeking after secret things that belong to the Lord our God and are none of our concern to know their what and their wherefore.[143]

The sin of insidious misreading thus goes hand in hand with that of "seeking after secret things that are none of our concern." The perpetrator of the latter, for Ramah, is doubtless the overweening metaphysician.

Ramah identifies two sources of philosophical dissatisfaction with the traditional doctrine of resurrection. First is a rationalistic spirituality based on a sharp body-soul dualism: the soul (that is, intellect) is what really counts; the body is an impure impediment to perfection. Second is a tendency to extend the domain of natural causation at the expense of divine intervention or even omnipotence. These factors underlie rejection of the miracle of permanent bodily resurrection in favor of natural immortality of the soul, along the lines of the philosophers.[144]

The following is probably Ramah's response to the sharp and passionately spiritualistic body-soul dualism expressed in the letter of Sheshet Benveniste: "In what way is the soul of the righteous man superior to his body . . . ? If it be . . . the [alleged] intrinsic dignity of the soul, that it is purer and cleaner than the body—*have they [body and soul] not one Father, has not one God created them?* Moreover both . . . [body and soul] have an equal hand in their righteousness as well as their wickedness. Why then should the soul merit more than the body?"[145] So vigorous and straightforward a defense of the dignity and eschatological centrality of the physical body is hard to find among later anti-rationalists.

In attacking the naturalistic reinterpretation of traditional eschatology, Ramah seeks to unveil its accompanying axiological assumptions. The following blunt exposé is meant to show that the philosopher's immortality postulates a view that is elitist, unjust, antinomian, and, to boot, negates the value of (nonphilosophical) study of Torah:

> He who attaches greater importance to the soul than to the body in [the final] judgment is, it would seem, of the opinion that reward and punishment in 'olam ha-ba are not in accordance with men's deeds and the requirements of justice but rather in accordance with nature; for in this view the soul which is by nature immortal remains in existence while the body which is by nature mortal ceases to exist . . . and the soul of the righteous and wicked, according to this view, are judged not according to their deeds, but according to their intellects. For the soul that knows its Creator through philosophical proof is immortal by reason of its knowledge which is everlasting. But the soul that does not know its Creator by way of philosophical proof shall be cut off—though it be possessed of Torah and good deeds. The upshot is that there is no lasting benefit to Torah and good deeds since the matter is determined by nature.[146]

Ramah, it is clear, saw the resurrection problem as a particular manifestation of far-reaching and fundamental challenges to traditional belief. In the debate of the 1230s these more fundamental challenges would move to the foreground. A final anticipation may be noted. Of the participants in the polemic over resurrection known to us, two wrote in support of Maimonides and two in opposition. But they represent not two but four very different positions: the radical rationalism of Sheshet Benveniste bears little resemblance to Aaron b. Meshullam's attempted reconciliation of Maimonides and Saadya; and, as we have seen, Ramah's philosophically knowledgeable anti-rationalism is quite different from R. Samson's textualism. We will discover a similar lack of homogeneity in both the rationalist and anti-rationalist sides of the Maimonidean Controversy of the 1230s.

By that time, however, one important characteristic of the earlier dispute will be gone. The quality of straightforward innocence that characterizes the main spokesmen in the Resurrection Controversy—each in his own way—is no longer present in the 1230s. Provençal scholars continue to emphasize the continuity of Maimonidean rationalism with the geonic tradition; but none could, like Aaron b. Meshullam, simply assert its complete consistency with conservative Saadyanic positions. Northern French Tosafists could no longer, like R. Samson b. Abraham, fail to notice the fundamental challenge posed by philosophical rationalism to Franco-German talmudic culture. No Spanish rationalist could, like Sheshet Benveniste, argue so radical a position in an open letter to an eminent talmudist—and then expect his wholehearted support to boot. And finally, no sensible Spanish anti-rationalist could, like Ramah, appeal to public support without taking into account the heroic image of Maimonides.

IV

THE MAIMONIDEAN
CONTROVERSY

IN THE FOURTH DECADE of the thirteenth century, a great controversy over philosophical rationalism erupted among the Jewish communities of Europe.[1] Ramah, by now a venerable scholar and communal leader, played an important though restrained role in this controversy. In order to put his position in perspective, it is useful to sketch a rough periodization of medieval Jewish anti-rationalism.

Dispute over philosophical rationalism seems coterminous with the medieval rationalist tradition itself. Among the earliest documents announcing the arrival of philosophical reasoning at the heart of rabbinic Judaism is Saadya Gaon's *Book of Doctrines and Beliefs.*[2] Saadya's relatively conservative brand of rationalism was designed "to establish the principles of the Torah in our hearts by way of proofs and refutation of our opponents."[3] Nevertheless, in this work we find Saadya already constrained to reply to the criticism of anonymous Jewish anti-rationalists.[4]

Similarly in Spain, dispute over philosophical rationalism appears as an immediate response to the first Hispano-Jewish philosopher, Solomon ibn Gabirol (d. circa, 1052–1055).[5] We have no way of knowing whether Ibn Gabirol's anonymous critics really deserved the elegant disdain to which they are treated in his verse. They need not have been obscurantists. Ibn Gabirol's Saragossan contemporary, the physician, logician, and philologist Jonah ibn Janah, might well represent the type. Himself irked by the curricular narrowness that led certain talmudists to disparage philology, Ibn Janah nevertheless thought physics and metaphysics destructive of faith and a presumptuous exercise in futility.[6] Ibn Janah's criticism may reflect an abandonment by eleventh-century Neoplatonists, like Ibn Gabirol, of important aspects of Saadya's traditionalism.[7] But the complete eclipse of Saadya's system and a pervasive consciousness of powerful tension between philosophy and religion are not apparent until the twelfth century.[8]

61

The publication of Judah Halevi's *Kuzari*, in the fourth decade of the twelfth century, opens a new chapter in the dispute; for it marks the emergence of an articulate and philosophically sophisticated anti-rationalism. Halevi's anti-rationalism has been seen as but one side of a highly individual rebellion against Andalusian Jewish culture: at once, he rejected both the political program and the philosophical ideal that had characterized the Spanish Jewish aristocracy.[9] Perhaps; but the elegant symmetry of this formulation should not obscure the complexity of Halevi's anti-rationalism.[10] Rather than a wholesale rejection of the Spanish philosophical tradition, it is perhaps better described as a response, *within* that tradition, to new challenges.[11]

Halevi cannot be categorized with the opponents of Saadyanic rationalism—to the contrary. So long as Saadya's balance of rationalism and tradition remained viable, a crucial stimulus to the development of *philosophical* anti-rationalism was missing. It was only the collapse of the Saadyanic balance that set the stage for Halevi's thought.

Saadya's conservative brand of rationalism remained influential in Jewish philosophical circles until about the end of the eleventh century. Bahya ibn Paquda and Judah b. Barzilai, for example, still seem to consider Saadya philosophically quite adequate.[12] But by the twelfth century the ascendancy, in Spain, of Aristotelian *falsafa* had changed the picture decisively.[13] A more powerful and radical rationalism was now in vogue. Its adherents dismissed Saadya's *kalām* methodology as mere apologetic, not philosophy.[14] But acceptance of the new rationalism was fraught with tension. For, as even its adherents recognized, some of the opinions of the Aristotelian philosophers "ruin the foundations of the Law."[15]

Two types of response to this challenge emerge among philosophically trained Spanish Jews in the twelfth century. One, represented by Abraham ibn Daud and Maimonides, "clings to the assertions of the *falāsifa*," albeit selectively.[16] A second, represented by Halevi, decisively rejects Aristotelian rationalism. In Ramah's Castile, many of the outstanding leaders of the old Spanish aristocracy were representative of this latter, philosophically knowledgeable anti-rationalism;[17] they include Judah Alfakar, Joseph b. Todros Abulafia, Judah ibn Matka, and of course Ramah himself. But by this time, the debate over rationalism was entering yet another phase.

Before the thirteenth century the controversy seems to have been confined to the standard literary and oral channels of religious and intellectual discussion. In the thirteenth century this situation changes drastically. The Resurrection Controversy, at the beginning of the century, was but a small foretaste of things to come. In the 1230s, controversy reached the combustion point and exploded into local and inter-

communal battle characterized by a scramble for allies, polemical propaganda letters, excommunications, and finally even charges of illegitimacy and informing.

This explosive change of atmosphere in the old debate over rationalism coincides with a shift in arena. Previously, the controversy had
been carried on solely within the confines of Judeo-Arabic culture.
Now, with Spain's entry into Europe, the talmudic culture of Franco-
German Jewry became aware, for the first time, of Spanish philosophical rationalism. Two sharply contrasting interpretations of Judaism
were brought into abrupt confrontation, with the result that controversy over rationalism took a more vehement turn.

The new Spanish ideas scored their greatest triumphs in Provence. In
many circles, traditional talmudic-midrashic education and thought
underwent remarkably swift reorientation in the direction of Andalusian philosophical culture. Such rapid transformation of long-cherished
cultural patterns could not but call forth sharp resistance.[18] It is no
wonder, then, that the great Maimonidean Controversy of the 1230s
erupted in Provence.

A leading critic of the new Provençal rationalism was Ramah's one-
time correspondent, R. Solomon b. Abraham of Montpellier.[19] Together with his pupils, R. Solomon engaged in vigorous debate with the
proponents of philosophical learning. One of these pupils was Nahmanides' cousin, R. Jonah b. Abraham of Gerona, who had gone off to
study under the talmudic masters of Provence and northern France.[20] R.
Solomon and his opponents have differing versions as to who first
broke the rules of polite scholarly disagreement. But at some point,
more or less controlled debate escalated into harsh polemic.[21]

Maimonides and his works played a central role in their debates. For
one thing, Sefer ha-Madda' and the Guide of the Perplexed were basic textbooks of the emerging Provençal rationalism. Equally important was
the heroic image of Maimonides. Already full-blown in the mind of
Aaron b. Meshullam at the turn of the century, this Maimonidean
image served to personify the new Provençal cultural ideal. Under these
circumstances, R. Solomon could hardly have avoided some criticism of
Maimonidean positions in the course of his anti-rationalist campaign.
His opponents report with a pious shudder that R. Solomon has pro-
faned the master's honor.[22] What exactly that means and whether it is
true are hard to say. But the power of the Maimonidean image is nowhere more apparent than in R. Solomon's heated denial that he has
spoken ill of "the master."[23]

Whether out of desperation (as R. Solomon would have it) or out of
zeal (his opponents' version), Solomon's circle turned for support to the

Tosafist schools of northern France. It would seem that R. Jonah, a former student at the French academies, personally brought the case before his old teachers.[24] R. Jonah doubtless made clear what Ramah,
thirty years earlier, had obscured: that Spanish rationalism represented
a fundamental challenge to the theological presuppositions and educational ideals of Franco-German talmudic culture. French reaction was
now, understandably, quite different. This chapter of the Maimonidean
Controversy remains most obscure; but recent manuscript discoveries
by Joseph Shatzmiller have shown conclusively that at least some of
the Tosafists responded with sharp condemnation of Provençal rationalism and its cherished textbooks, *Sefer ha-Madda'* and the *Guide to the
Perplexed*.[25] The Provençal Maimonideans were furious. Their reaction
to this intervention by "the men of Zarfat" is highly instructive.

In the first half of the twelfth century the Barcelonan Abraham bar
Hiyya bemoaned the scientific ignorance of Jewish scholars in "the land
of Zarfat."[26] Spanish association of Zarfat with literary backwardness is
evident in Abraham ibn Ezra's well-known response to some verse by
the great Tosafist, R. Jacob b. Meir (Tam): "What's a Frenchman (*Zarfati*) doing in the House of Poetry?"[27] In the thirteenth century, this
geographical stereotype must have been widespread among Spanish
intellectuals. Ramah's brother, Joseph b. Todros, more than once felt
obliged to rebuke those who spoke slightingly of the scholars of Zarfat.[28] But a generation later this sin was committed by a Toledan member of the Abulafia family—Todros b. Judah Abulafia. In his satirical
poem on "R. Moses the Frenchman (*Zarfati*)," the negative stereotype
of the *Zarfati* is assimilated to an older Spanish motif, that of "the
graceless talmudist," which goes back to the poetry of Samuel ha-
Nagid.[29]

When, early in the twelfth century, Bar Hiyya referred to the sorry
state of scientific studies in Zarfat, that place name would seem to include Provence.[30] But the increasing cultural differentiation of northern
and southern France during the twelfth and early thirteenth centuries
made such generalization less and less possible. The Maimonidean
Controversy of the 1230s provided powerful new impetus to the negative image of the *Zarfati*—now restricted, of course, to the northern
French scholar.[31] That this occurred among Spanish rationalists is quite
understandable. What is fascinating, though, is the vehemence with
which the communal leaders of Narbonne and Lunel now characterize
the "men of Zarfat" as unenlightened, superstitious, and impulsive.[32]
The Provençal Maimunists were judging their northern coreligionists
by newly acquired Andalusian standards—not only of learning but of
form.

As if to underline the source of its newly acquired standards, a Narbonnese circular—after an outraged exposé, in rhymed prose, of north-

ern French magic and superstition—appeals to the ideology of *Sefardi* aristocracy in arguing for the precedence of Maimonides over his *Zarfati* detractors.[33] This circular was, diplomatically enough, addressed to the Jewish communities of Spain.[34] It was part of a three-pronged counterattack launched by the rationalist leadership of Provence.

First, at home, the rationalists engaged in a vigorous campaign to isolate and excommunicate R. Solomon and his pupils. Brushing aside moderate counsel, like that of the respected *nasi* R. Meshullam b. Kalonymous (brother-in-law of Ramah's uncle), they pursued this objective with ruthless determination.[35] Second, in letters to the scholars of northern France, the rationalists defended Maimonides and his Provençal disciples in tones ranging from respectful protest[36] to proud defiance.[37] Finally, the Provençal communities turned southward for support. What more natural ally in the battle for Andalusian philosophical culture than Spain itself?

As emissary to the Spanish communities they chose the aged and respected R. David Kimhi,[38] whose scholarship epitomized the new synthesis of Andalusian and Provençal learning. His mission was to mobilize support for the *herem* against R. Solomon b. Abraham and his pupils. But Kimhi encountered unexpected opposition in Spain. The results of his mission were mixed: at most partial success in Catalonia, more complete success in Aragon, and but little success in Castile.

According to Kimhi, "all of the communities of . . . Catalonia and Aragon have excommunicated" R. Solomon's party.[39] Surviving documentation supports this contention only partially. A cautiously conditional *herem* (". . . *if* they have spoken against the master . . . or do so in the future") was issued by the Aragonese communities in 1232.[40] But in Barcelona and Gerona there are indications of strong sympathy for Solomon's cause. Contradictory testimony on the stance of the Catalonian communities probably reflects internal conflict within those communities.

The powerful *nesi'im* whose aristocratic rule had long held sway in Barcelona and its environs were solidly behind the Provençal rationalists. But at about this time aristocratic leadership was being vigorously challenged by men far less friendly to the rationalist cause. Prominent in this latter group, which combined impressive spiritual authority and politico-economic influence, were Nahmanides and the wealthy halakist Samuel ha-Sardi.[41] Both sought to protect Solomon and his supporters while urging moderation on all parties. Nahmanides—who had grasped and, to a certain extent, accepted the role of Maimonides as a culture hero—attempted to seize the initiative in resolving the dispute along moderately anti-rationalistic lines that would yet preserve the honor of Maimonides.[42]

But opposition was too sharp and conflict too bitter for compromise or reconciliation. At some point during Kimhi's journey, under circumstances not entirely clear, *Sefer ha-Madda'* and the *Guide of the Perplexed* were denounced to the Inquisition in Montpellier and publicly burned.[43] The spectacle of Maimonides' writings consigned to the flames may have dampened the zeal of some in Solomon's party;[44] but it only reinforced the angry determination of the rationalists to mete out exemplary punishment.[45] Their course met its strongest opposition from an apparently unexpected source: the aristocratic leadership of Castile.

Few in Castile could have been more strategically located than Ramah. Scholarship and station made him among the most influential men in Toledo, the most powerful Jewish community in Castile and likely in all of Europe. Both sides to the controversy sought his support. Both were disappointed, though the rationalists were much more so.

Ramah's sole surviving statement on the controversy was written in response to a now lost letter from Nahmanides. That letter apparently contained two requests: first, that Ramah seek to thwart acceptance of the Provençal *herem* in Castile; second, that he join with Nahmanides to (in Ramah's words) "make league with our *Zarfati* teachers—as they have agreed—for the glory of God, and to close up the breach in His people, making our words complete destruction overflowing with righteousness [that is, taking stern but just measures] so that we might remove stumbling block and pitfall from the path of His people."[46]

Opening his reply with lavish praise of Nahmanides, Ramah joins the former in lament "at the strife among the Children of Israel and their trying the Lord."[47] He then presents a brief critical formulation of the radical rationalist position.[48] Ramah's description of Solomon b. Abraham's lonely and heroic opposition dovetails with the latter's own version in his letter to R. Samuel ha-Sardi.[49] R. Solomon's accusers are, as Ramah sees it, guilty of slanderous distortion. Far be it from the men of "this land" (Castile) to be taken in by such one-sided misrepresentation. Surely, Ramah assures his correspondent, "the merit of their ancestors [the Andalusian forebears of the Castilian aristocracy]" will protect them from error.[50]

> But should there, Heaven forbid, be among them a rebellious group—that delights in deep faithlessness and takes pleasure in the foreign-born [that is, philosophy] clinging to contention, deriding the Torah of God and invoking the heights of the *Moreh* in the vale of agitation—I stand ready swiftly to dissociate myself from that group. Their lot on earth shall be accursed. But I and those joined with me who believe in life and all those who fearing God stand with me shall be innocent.[51]

Thus did Ramah declare his staunch opposition to the rationalist *herem*. But he would go no further; he declines Nahmanides' invitation to join a Franco-Spanish alliance that would suppress rationalist excesses. Experience had taught him the futility of such campaigns even on a local level: "Surely you know that I too, have briers and thorns with me and do sit upon scorpions." Rebuke and exhortation had failed to clear Toledo of its rationalistic thorns and Aristotelian scorpions. And so, concludes Ramah, "How can a man, powerless to reprove his own neighbors who dwell close by him . . . reprove numerous distant peoples?"[52] "Besides," he adds, "the words of our masters, the rabbis of Zarfat, are like words of the Torah, and require no buttressing."[53]

Ramah then recalls the bitter rewards of his own zeal won "well over thirty years ago" during the Resurrection Controversy:[54] "What hope is there, then, in a man sending his letters to far-off places [in an attempt] to close up breaches and reprove men for their faults and call them to account for their guilt? Is it not a great enough thing for him to reproach himself for his own faults?" Doomed as they are to failure, such calls to repentance ought to be avoided, "lest those who violate the faith continue to blaspheme and curse wherefore the Name of Heaven shall be desecrated."[55] Subsequent events show Ramah's judgment on this score to have been quite sound. Attempts at suppressing rationalism by proclamation and ban proved ineffective so long as the rationalist tradition itself maintained its vitality.[56]

Having politely dismissed Nahmanides' plan, Ramah adds that only if both parties to the controversy were to come together before him and submit their claims to adjudication could he contribute a solution. Ramah must have realized full well the unlikeliness of this eventuality; he had, after all, just finished prejudging the case! And so he ends his letter on a prayerful note: "May the Rock who maketh peace in His high places, spread over all His people the protection of His peace and do good to the good and upright at heart; and may He turn the heart of fathers to their sons and the heart of sons to their fathers."[57]

So much for the content of Ramah's letter. But our analysis is not yet finished; for the full import of this document becomes evident only upon consideration of its intended audience. Ostensibly, that audience was simply the letter's addressee, Nahmanides. Read as a private communication, the gist of its message is something like this:

My Dear Friend Nahmanides,
    Although I think very highly of you and personally am quite sympathetic to the anti-rationalist cause, I have become convinced, by bitter experience, that the battle is futile and plan to remain neutral. The limit of my involvement will be to work locally against acceptance of the Provençal *herem*. I can only pray that God bring peace among His people.

But Ramah's letter to Nahmanides—though in form a personal communication—was at the same time something more. Like other documents of the controversy, preserved by medieval editors, it was destined from the first for circulation. Surely, Ramah's solemn and ornate exposition on the corrosive effects of rationalism, Solomon b. Abraham's noble struggle, and the base attacks against him was not composed for Nahmanides' benefit. Its purpose was rather to put Ramah's prestige and spiritual authority behind the anti-rationalist position; and the pained protests of the rationalists testify to its effectiveness.[58] As a public statement, Ramah's letter conveys roughly the following message:

> To All Men of Understanding,
> My dear friend Nahmanides is one of the truly great men of our generation. I share his profound concern for the grave danger posed by rationalist philosophy. R. Solomon b. Abraham and his pupils have done lonely and heroic battle in defending our faith from philosophical perversion. Their persecutors have resorted to slander and deserve to be rebuffed. But any organized attempt to suppress philosophical study is doomed to failure and would only be counterproductive. May God bless us with peace.

Ramah and his confederates successfully frustrated the aims of Provençal propaganda in Castile. Kimhi failed to gain the crucial support of Toledo and Burgos, the two largest Castilian communities. Indeed, he was not even accorded the perfunctory courtesy of a polite hearing by their most powerful leaders. The Provençal rationalists seem perplexed and indignant at this setback handed them by "the traitors of Toledo":

> We had hoped to hear good tidings . . . but behold the thunderous shouting of princes . . . came from the north [sic] from the great city of Toledo. We had thought her a city which is a mother in Israel—in Torah and halakah, in understanding, knowledge and all manner of works. But behold she has suddenly turned corrupt. For her princes, Meir and Judah violated the boundaries of the Torah . . . And they discouraged the hearts of the nobles from coming to the aid of the Lord and His warriors. Worse still, they sallied forth to the aid of utterly wicked men, showing love for the accursed enemies of the Lord who ascribe—after the vanities of the gentiles—corporeality to God . . . and they have given a monument and a name to a sinful, guilty fool—they, the princes of the congregation, summoned to assembly, men of renown. We had assumed that they . . . would support justice and righteousness. But behold out of their mouths went burning torches . . . Who has ever heard of such scandal upon men of renown?[59]

The second "prince" of Toledo who, along with Ramah, incurred the wrath of the Provençal rationalists was Judah Alfakar. More than thirty-five years before, Ramah had mourned the passing of Judah's father, Joseph Alfakar, in elegant verse.[60] Now Judah was his partner in leading the Toledo community. The two apparently saw eye to eye on the question of rationalism.

Ramah, we have seen, was intent on limiting his involvement in polemic. Not so Alfakar. In an exchange of letters with Kimhi—who had requested his aid in obtaining Toledo's ratification of the Provençal *herem*—Alfakar forcefully argued the anti-rationalist case.[61] He succeeded in compressing into one of these letters an incisive critique of Maimonidean rationalism that "raised the controversy to a philosophical level."[62] With rhetorical art to match his philosophical skills, Alfakar was none too kind to Kimhi and his constituency. No wonder that he roused the ire of the Provençal rationalists.[63]

Somewhat more evenhanded is the approach of Ramah's brother, Joseph b. Todros of Burgos.[64] Certain Provençal supporters of R. Solomon had protested ratification of the *herem* by "some of our [Joseph's] neighbors."[65] Joseph responded in an open letter to the communities of Provence, setting forth his position at length. He criticizes the tactics and tone of Solomon's party, urging moderation on both sides.[66] But like his brother and Alfakar, Joseph emphatically rejects the excommunication of Solomon and warns of the dangers of unchecked rationalism.

Kimhi had little success in Burgos. Overcoming the opposition of local rationalists, Joseph and his father-in-law, R. Nathan, expelled him from the city.[67]

Judah Alfakar soon had some second thoughts about the tone of his letters to Kimhi. Writing to Joseph b. Todros—who had taken exception to the trenchancy of his polemic—Alfakar now voices regret at his blanket condemnation of the Provençal rationalists; henceforth, he will "lead on slowly by the waters of calmness."[68] This new approach seems to reflect some statesmanlike advice given Alfakar by the Provençal *nasi* R. Meshullam b. Kalonymous, one of the few contemporary figures who could speak in the same breath of "the great scholar R. David Kimhi" and "the great scholar R. Solomon."[69]

Alfakar's polemic, even at its most vigorous, had kept close to the issues. But certain rationalist propagandists did not shrink from *ad hominem* attacks of a most unpleasant sort: they charged that some of their opponents, including R. Jonah b. Abraham, were illegitimate. The charge apparently stemmed from Beziers. Nahmanides, personally involved because he was R. Jonah's cousin, wrote a strongly worded protest to the leading scholar of Beziers, R. Meshullam b. Mosheh.[70] Nahmanides offered to submit the issue to the decision of Ramah or the rabbis of northern France.[71] But it is unlikely that such adjudication actually took place; for it can be shown from a halakic discussion in R. Meshullam's *Sefer ha-Hashlamah* that he was in complete agreement with Nahmanides on the matter.[72]

The Provençal communities had sought Spanish ratification of their *herem* "in order that those wicked men [Solomon's party] be unable to find their hands and feet [that is, find sanctuary] in all the boundaries of Israel."[73] Their fear that the Montpellier anti-rationalists might escape punishment by fleeing south was well-founded; for that, it would seem, is precisely what happened.[74]

At some point in the 1230s R. Jonah and perhaps other members of Solomon's party turn up in Barcelona. That community, we recall, was in the throes of a power struggle between two groups which, among other things, differed sharply in their attitude toward Maimonidean rationalism. That Barcelona was now more hospitable than Montpellier to excommunicated anti-rationalists indicates that the party led by Nahmanides and Samuel ha-Sardi was, at least, holding its own. The leadership of this antiaristocratic party was joined by R. Jonah and perhaps others from Montpellier.[75] For the first time we can document the entwining of controversy over rationalism with sociocommunal struggle.

Both factors figure in a propaganda letter written by supporters of the *nesi'im.* Invoking aristocratic ideology, it condemns the usurpers as "slaves who have rebelled against their masters." But its harshest words are reserved for certain leaders of the antiaristocratic opposition. Charges of illegitimacy against R. Jonah and others are revived. Moreover, it is stressed that one of these men seduced the scholars of Zarfat to join in speaking against "God, Moses and his works." An aristocratic political ideology and strong rationalist sympathies thus appear side by side.[76] The letter, however, does not integrate the two. It is possible that anti-Maimunist activity, like illegitimacy, is mentioned only in an attempt to discredit the antiaristocratic leadership, not because it was intrinsic to the struggle.

Two prominent Barcelonans who bore the title *nasi* were the brothers Abraham and Judah ibn Hasdai. Their circular to "the communities of Castile and Aragon" has long been known as an important document of the Maimonidean Controversy.[77] But its full import becomes clear only if it is read in the context of the communal struggle then raging in Barcelona.

The Ibn Hasdai brothers rehash the old charges against the anti-Maimunists and call upon their Spanish compatriots to avenge the desecrated honor of Maimonides. It would seem that the controversy had, by this time, quieted down somewhat and receded from the forefront of public consciousness. The Ibn Hasdai circular stresses that the anti-Maimunists "have not repented their sins nor regretted their wickedness"; to the contrary, "the rod of their injustice still blossoms . . . and they have now begun to ravage and to destroy, and to dishonor the glorious throne. Their lips boast . . . and though they now speak . . . in a different language, they remain wicked as ever."[78]

These unrepentant anti-Maimunists were located in Barcelona, for the Ibn Hasdai brothers claim to be suffering at their hands: "We have borne their revilement; we have behaved toward them as those who hear themselves insulted but do not insult." Perhaps anticipating dismissal of their problems as a purely local affair, they argue that "we have learned from our experience . . . that the entire House of Israel will drink from our cup . . . and all over, little foxes will rise up as adversaries against us." It would appear that the Barcelona nesi'im sought to shore up their political position by reviving calls for punishment of their anti-rationalist rivals.[79]

The Ibn Hasdai brothers were not so naive as to expect a friendly reception for their circular in Toledo; but neither were they giving up entirely. Accompanying their circular to Toledo was a letter from Abraham ibn Hasdai to Judah Alfakar.[80] The letter seems more concerned with nobility than theology. After lauding Alfakar's pedigree—"men whom the royal scepter never departed"—Ibn Hasdai argues that nobility obligates Judah to rise to the defense of Maimonides against his base detractors. By allowing himself to be misled by men of "well-known origin and inferior station," Alfakar betrays his aristocratic heritage.[81]

The letter continues with an indirect message to Ramah:

> More perplexing still, we have seen the miracle of the generation and its wonder, the height of intelligence and its peak, the seat of glory and its throne . . . the great scholar, the Levite nasi, R. Meir son of R. Todros, causing his skies to thunder and sending forth his lightning bolts, bending his bows and aiming his rhetorical shafts. Now if, like the first time [the Resurrection Controversy?], it was for his peers and equals that he weighed, sought out and ordered parables and figures . . . and multiplied his armies, we would have said: "The Lord's hidden wisdom belongs to those who fear Him" [that is, Ramah and not us]. We would not have wondered at them [Ramah's figures and parables] nor questioned them. But now [that his addressee is of inferior station], seeing the desecration of . . . his glory, we have become exceedingly zealous for him, though he has foregone his honor.
>
> And despite all this our feet have not inclined nor our steps slipped from the path of his honour and his precious love. And we have not departed the path of perfect goodness, setting before him a table of greetings . . . diligently seeking the presence of his excel-

lency, going aside to enquire after the peace of his Torah. May the horn of his wisdom be forever elevated and may his kingship be exalted.[82]

The particular composition deemed so inappropriate by Ibn Hasdai was, it would seem, Ramah's letter to Nahmanides. It was not so much its anti-rationalist content; that alone he would have been able to suffer in silence, deferring to Ramah's superior wisdom and piety. It was rather the letter's addressee, a man of inferior station. Addressing a letter to Nahmanides violated Ramah's exalted rank, and that is what evokes Ibn Hasdai's zealous protest; or so he claims.

Why such resentment of a letter to Nahmanides—undeniably a gentleman (an occasional visitor at the royal Aragonese palace)[83] and a scholar? Even the Provençal rationalists, while fulminating at Ramah's treachery, spoke of "the *hasid* and great scholar, faithful with the Holy [God], our master R. Moses the son of R. Nahman of blessed memory." For was it not Nahmanides' eloquent letter than helped secure retraction of the northern French decrees against *Sefer ha-Madda'* and the *Guide?*[84] It is likely that Ibn Hasdai's special animus toward Nahmanides resulted from the latter's leadership of those Catalonian "slaves who broke away from their masters"; and Ramah's letter—among other things a glowing letter of recommendation of Nahmanides—must have served to neutralize the propaganda of the Barcelona *nesi'im.*[85]

Ibn Hasdai's appeal seems directed toward the sense of solidarity of the old Spanish aristocracy. But the events of the 1230s show that aristocracy split along spiritual lines stronger than any sense of class solidarity. Neither side conceived of itself as abandoning its cherished aristocratic heritage. Ibn Hasdai could argue that bearers of the Andalusian aristocratic tradition were duty-bound to punish anti-Maimunists; but Ramah and especially his brother Joseph could, with equal solemnity, invoke their noble forebears in favor of the opposite course.[86]

Defining the relationship of the old Spanish aristocracy to rationalism is a difficult and complex problem that still awaits adequate solution. Here we can only take note of the apparent geographical pattern exhibited by aristocractic opinion during the Maimonidean Controversy of the 1230s. Most of the aristocracy seems to have been aligned with rationalism in Aragon and Catalonia. But in Castile—precisely where the Andalusian cultural ideal remained strongest—noble "princes," staunchly and eloquently defending the anti-rationalist cause, were able to carry the day.[87]

Controversy over Maimonides and his works was twofold: theological and legal. In addition to criticism of Maimonidean rationalism, there was vigorous controversy over the individual decisions, general authority, and proper function of *Mishneh Torah* as a work of halakah. The relationship, if any, between the legal and theological Maimonidean controversies has long been the subject of speculation.[88] The first to posit a link between these controversies would seem to have been Sheshet Benveniste. In his polemical letter to Lunel, Sheshet, seeking to unmask the ideology of Castilian critics of *Mishneh Torah*, made the following assertions: first, *Mishneh Torah* is bringing about an educational revolution among the ignorant Spanish masses; second, many Spanish jurists oppose *Mishneh Torah* out of jealous anger, for it is destroying the ignorance upon which their authority feeds; and finally, Ramah is one of their ilk, whence his attack on *Mishneh Torah*.[89]

Sheshet's contentions are supported, in part, by Jonah ibn Bahlul's *Minhat Qena'ot* (literally, *Offering of Jealousy*). Ibn Bahlul's jealousy is for the honor of Maimonides' *Mishneh Torah*. Writing in 1258,[90] he seeks to preserve a record of the sorry state of affairs prevailing in Spain prior to the arrival of *Mishneh Torah*: "I shall begin to tell of the [ignorant] practices that prevailed . . . prior to the arrival of the fourteen books [of *Mishneh Torah*] . . . I will make them known to all the world, so that those ignorant practices, which were not brought to an end till the appearance, in this land of . . . *Mishneh Torah* not be concealed. No scholar or *gaon* other than he [Maimonides] can claim: 'I have composed a halakic code that has rescued Israel from error.' "[91] Like Sheshet, Ibn Bahlul tells of self-serving criticism of *Mishneh Torah* on the part of incompetent teachers, angered because its educational impact threatened their hegemony: "All this hatred resulted from rivalry and jealousy. For as a result of reading these books [of *Mishneh Torah*], there came to be knowledgeable men in every town . . . And the critics were irked to discover that the land was filled with knowledge . . . and so they gnashed their teeth to swallow him up [Maimonides] without [just] cause."[92]

We have no way of determining the identity, much less the true motivation, of these early Spanish critics of *Mishneh Torah*. But Sheshet's allegation concerning Ramah cannot withstand even a cursory study of Ramah's halakic writings. In refusing to abdicate juristic independence, Ramah was no different from any other major halakist contemporary to or succeeding Maimonides. But even though Ramah was a vigorous proponent of Maimonidean fallibility, no contemporary or near-contemporary halakist had authority for Ramah comparable to that of Maimonides. He is the only contemporary mentioned in Ramah's commentaries—once, simply, as "the greatest scholar of the generation." Ramah was quite conscious of the educational value of *Mishneh Torah* for non-talmudists. Thus, in a responsum, he says: "And whoever has not reached [the point] where he can understand the [talmudic] account . . . let him study the work of R. Moses of blessed memory, for he will find all this explained in *Sefer ha-Madda'*, chapter seven of the 'Laws concerning Study of the Torah.' "[93] In another responsum, Ramah accepts "the opinion of R. Isaac Alfasi and the opinion of R. Moses of blessed memory, author of the *hibbur* [*Mishneh Torah*]" on a disputed issue: "This is the law ... according to the opinion of these two great pillars. And they are worthy of being relied upon even when circumstances are not pressing."[94]

For Ramah, the questions of Maimonidean halakah and Maimonidean rationalism were essentially unrelated. In his letter to Lunel during the Resurrection Controversy—the one instance in which Ramah did connect the two—his intention appears to be the opposite of that posited by Sheshet Benveniste: halakic criticism serves to limit the authority of Maimonidean rationalism, rather than vice versa. Ramah's point is that *Mishneh Torah* is capable of error; nothing more.[95] He himself characterized the halakic discussion in *Kitāb al-Rasā'il* as extraneous to the controversy.[96]

Writing at the height of the controversy of the 1230s, Ramah claims that admiration for Maimonides' halakic achievement has muted his criticism of Maimonidean rationalism: "I have not allowed my mouth to sin against the great master who lightens my darkness, who has sown the light of his *Mishneh Torah* over the very edges of oblivion, planting therein trees of knowledge and wisdom."[97] Ibn Bahlul provides confirmation: in the very midst of his scathing denunciation of the early Spanish critics of *Mishneh Torah*, he could still engage in unqualified praise of Ramah.[98]

V

VARIETIES OF
ANTI-RATIONALISM

LIKE THEIR FATHERS a generation earlier, the scholars of Lunel in the 1230s were exceedingly zealous for the honor of Maimonides. They looked unkindly upon anyone who supported Solomon of Montpellier. Both Ramah and the scholars of northern France did just that; but the reactions that they evoked were very different.

The Lunel scholars were angered by what the French Tosafists had done; but they were not at a loss to explain it. What more, after all, could one expect of the impulsive, uncultured *Zarfati?*[1] To Ramah's opposition, however, the reaction was one of pained disbelief. The rationalists of Lunel had been confident of his support; when the opposite was forthcoming, they reacted like men who had been stabbed in the back. Ramah was denounced (along with Alfakar) with the bitterness reserved for a traitor. But it was a baffled bitterness; the Lunel scholars could still muster no motive—base or otherwise—to explain his apostasy.[2]

Their amazement requires explanation. For was Ramah, by any stretch of the imagination, a traitor to the cause of rationalism? Was he not, rather, an old enemy? Surely Lunel had not completely forgotten the Resurrection Controversy. Why, then, should they have expected Ramah to champion the rationalist cause in the 1230s, and why was there such bewilderment at his opposition? How could the scholars of Lunel have been guilty of such blundering misjudgment?[3] In fact, theirs was an intelligent error. In order to grasp the logic behind that error, to understand why the scholars of Lunel had reason to hope for Ramah's support, we must look carefully at his views on the issues under debate in the Provençal arena of the controversy. The best source for determining these views, however, is not Ramah's highly general expression of support for the French and Provençal anti-rationalists in his letter to Nahmanides.

It must be remembered that the parties to the Maimonidean Controversy did not form around jointly proclaimed declarations of theological principle. They were forged in the heat of a battle dominated from the first by attempts at intercommunal action and counteraction. Joining the controversy meant first and foremost aligning oneself in the real intercommunal struggle. Men whose positions were substantively quite different could find themselves allied in battle.

Fortunately, our sources for the reconstruction of Ramah's position include nonpolemical writings, which serve to put polemical statements into perspective. Consider the following passage from Ramah's letter to Nahmanides: "the words of our masters the rabbis of Zarfat are [like] words of Torah and require no buttressing."[4] This is an elegant bit of rhetoric: Ramah is expressing solidarity with his French allies while simultaneously declining to join in their planned offensive. But its apparent implication——that Ramah is in full agreement with the northern French position——must be taken with a grain of salt. For Ramah's comments on various aggadic texts in his talmudic commentaries allow us to compare his views with the northern French position; and there are differences significant enough to explain the misplaced hopes of the Lunel rationalists.

Ramah's aggadic exegesis touches on almost all the issues debated in the French arena of the Maimonidean Controversy; for most of these issues were closely connected to the question of the authority and interpretation of aggadah.

Medieval rationalists often found aggadah problematic. A Maimonidean aside captures this feeling nicely. Introducing an aggadic dictum in support of his position on divine attributes, Maimonides adds parenthetically: "Would that all dicta were like it."[5] But Ramah, too, could find aggadah problematic. On occasion he frankly confesses perplexity, as in his comment on the following aggadic dictum: "The [eschatological] row [of righteous men] which stands before the Holy One, blessed be He, is eighteen thousand parsangs long, as it is said (Ezek. 48:35): 'It shall be round about eighteen thousand; [and the name of the city from that day shall be, The Lord is there].' "[6] Ramah's comment is as follows:

> R. Solomon of blessed memory [Rashi] has written that this verse refers to the celestial Jerusalem. But we——in the poverty of our understanding——do not know where this celestial Jerusalem, mentioned in the Talmud, is nor where it will be. If it be in the heavens——is there really building in the heavens? And if it be the name of an elevation in the sky which is called Jerusalem, it follows that the righteous are to be seated in the sky. And it is quite a

bafflement how these bodies are to be seated in the sky if not by way of a miracle. And I find it difficult to lean on the miraculous where there is neither a clear proof from Scripture nor a tradition broadly accepted in the teachings of the Sages. But we have already discharged our obligation to truth by clarifying our doubts and the perplexity in which we find ourselves. And perhaps from above, God will illumine our eyes so that we may interpret the plain meaning of this dictum.[7]

Anxiety of this sort is foreign to the French anti-rationalists. Ramah is, on this score, more akin to his rationalistic opponents.[8] And this kinship extends further to include common approaches to the authority and interpretation of aggadah.

First, let us consider the question of the authority that attaches to aggadah. To the French anti-rationalists it was axiomatic that anyone who disagreed with an aggadah of the talmudic sages was an *epiqoros*.[9] The passage quoted above shows that Ramah could hardly have agreed. He expresses reluctance (admittedly not of Maimonidean proportions) "to lean on the miraculous." Just any aggadic affirmation would not suffice to overcome that reluctance; it would have to be "a tradition broadly accepted in the teachings of the Sages."[10] Apparently, *aggadot* not belonging to this category are without authority.

There is nothing anomalous about this, for Ramah was schooled in the Spanish talmudic tradition. Following in the footsteps of the geonim, Spanish talmudists had long distinguished halakah, which is binding, from aggadah, whose authority is limited.[11] This distinction provided rationalists an easy solution to the problem of aggadah: "One learns from these aggadic interpretations to the extent that they are acceptable to reason; as for the rest—one does not lean upon them."[12]

Ramah belonged to the more conservative wing of the Spanish school—thus his insistence on the authoritative character of *aggadot* that reflect a *qabbalah peshutah* (broadly accepted tradition) such as bodily resurrection.[13] Still, one wonders what Ramah's French allies would have thought of the following comment on a tannaitic aggadah, in *Perate Sanhedrin*: "The words of this *beraita* are not a tradition but mere opinion (*sebara be-'alma*) . . . [and since] it would seem that the words of the *tanna* stem from his own deduction one has a right to disagree with this *beraita*."[14]

Denying the authority of a difficult aggadah was, at best, a partial solution for the rationalist. It may have freed him from the obligation of accepting "the unreasonable"; but it left the text without adequate explanation and the honor of the sages without defense. Beginning about the twelfth century, there seems to be an increasing concern, in the Spanish school, with the explanation of aggadah. It is variously suggested that certain problematic *aggadot* represented dreams, visions,[15] a kind of poetry,[16] humorous relief from more weighty scholarly discussion,[17] or a necessary concession to popular religion.[18] But by far the most important method of explanation was nonliteral exegesis.[19] Like R. Samson thirty years earlier, the French anti-rationalists would have none of the latter. Their one surviving polemical letter equates nonliteral interpretation with rejection.[20]

From Provençal protests we learn that northern French scholars had condemned any interpretation of talmudic aggadah deviating from Rashi's.[21] We must, of embarrassing necessity, interpret this condemnation not quite literally; for never do the writings of the Tosafists give the slightest hint of abdicating interpretative independence in favor of Rashi. What the *Zarfati* scholars probably meant to condemn was deviation not from the substance of particular interpretations but rather from Rashi's *method* of interpretation in accordance with the plain sense of the text.

Ramah's commentary on *Sanhedrin* shows that he was quite conscious of practicing just this kind of deviation from Rashi. Indeed, he felt that Rashi's method of literal interpretation could yield results that were nothing short of scandalous. One aggadah, for example, tells how God made a secret tunnel through the heavens so that a repentant Manasseh could be smuggled up unnoticed by the Attribute of Justice.[22] According to Ramah, this is only a metaphoric way of saying that God graciously accepted Manasseh's repentance even though it ought not have been accepted by the standards of strict justice. But Ramah was aware of what seems to be a quite literal interpretation in the commentary ascribed by him to Rashi: "The Attribute of Justice was preventing the acceptance of Manasseh in repentance. And the Holy One Blessed Be He made a secret tunnel in the heaven and stretched forth His hand and received him without the knowledge of the Attribute of Justice."[23] Though tactfully avoiding explicit criticism of Rashi, Ramah's appraisal of this interpretation is quite clear: "We have seen another interpretation in accordance with its plain sense. But because it contains unfitting statements concerning Heaven and [because] it is not worthy, we have not quoted it."[24]

Another aggadic text identifies the one who, at the End of Days, will have "his hands on his loins, as a woman in travail" (Jer. 30:6) with "the one to whom all might belongs."[25] According to Ramah this means that "even the mightiest of the mighty among men will at that time have his hands on his loins like a childbearing woman along the lines of 'the stouthearted among the mighty will flee naked that day' (Amos 2:16). And the one who puts forth an interpretation other than this is destined to be called to account."[26] Ramah's last remark is directed against an interpretation that would take "the one to whom all might belongs" as a reference to God. This is, of course, the plain meaning of the phrase; and it is precisely the interpretation given by the commentary that Ramah ascribed to Rashi.

The thing that Ramah found objectionable in these explanations was their seeming attribution of human form and characteristics to God. Such explanations are not exceptional; northern French exegesis rarely departs from the literal sense of biblical and aggadic texts to avoid anthropomorphism. This does not *ipso facto* exclude the possibility that "the people perceived these [anthropomorphic] expressions in their metaphoric sense and in their naiveté saw no contradiction between the words and their content."[27] Ramah's protests indicate that he, at least, took literal interpretation literally. Moreover, several sources indicate that in the course of the Maimonidean Controversy northern French scholars condemned nonliteral interpretation of anthropomorphic verses and *aggadot.* In opposing anthropomorphism with some passion, in both aggadic and biblical exegesis, Ramah stands with the Provençal rationalists on an important issue of the Maimonidean Controversy.

Unfortunately, we must have recourse to the testimony of opponents in determining the position taken by the northern French scholars on anthropomorphism, since no explicit northern French statement on the subject survives. Outright condemnation of Spanish-style figurative interpretation of anthropomorphic passages can be documented only in a polemical tract by the contemporary German scholar R. Moses b. Hasdai.[28] It would perhaps be rash to assert that R. Moses was fully representative of mainstream Franco-German tradition.[29] But since not only rationalist polemicists but even an anti-rationalist like Nahmanides indicates that anthropomorphism played an important role in the condemnation of Maimonides' works,[30] it seems likely that the views of Moses b. Hasdai do approximate a significant body of Franco-German opinion.[31]

In his *Ktab Tamim* R. Moses offers—among many proof texts for anthropomorphism—the following aggadic explanation of the biblical injunction that a hanged criminal be buried before sunset:[32] "Says R. Meir, a parable has been told. To what is this compared? To two twins living in the same city. One was appointed king. And the other went out into brigandry. The king had him hanged. All who saw him said: 'The king is hanged.' [So] the king had him taken down."[33] Franco-German proponents of anthropomorphism would hardly have applauded Ramah's comment on this aggadah: "The basis of this saying is that it is written: 'Let Us make man in Our image' (Gen. 1:26). *And this refers to [man's specific] form [which is his power] of understanding.* And the Holy One, blessed be He, does not wish to degrade something created in His image."[34] Ramah not only rejects an anthropomorphic interpretation of Genesis 1:26, he adopts the substance and even the philosophical terminology of Maimonides' interpretation of that verse.[35]

According to Ramah, scriptural departure from plain speech occurs "for one of two reasons. First, when language is incapable of explaining the idea to men except by way of parable and analogy, as in the use of terms for limbs of the body in regard to the Omnipresent, who is exalted above all this. And concerning this and things similar, the Sages have said: 'The Torah speaks in the language of men.'[36] And the second reason [is applicable] when that matter [discussed by Scripture] ought to be concealed from men like the [Messianic] End, told to Daniel."[37] This passage is, in context, purposely restrictive of nonliteral interpretation; yet it embraces a pillar of Maimonides' rationalistic exegesis: "The Torah speaks in the language of men."[38]

The sense in which this principle is Maimonidean requires clarification. The maxim itself is—as Ramah pointed out—something that "the [talmudic] sages have said."[39] It is the way in which Ramah uses it that is typically Maimonidean. In its talmudic context, "the Torah speaks in the language of men" means that scriptural Hebrew uses common speech patterns (like the doubling of verbs—infinitive followed by imperfect).[40] Ramah takes it to mean that Scripture makes figurative use of human language about God. This understanding was popularized by Maimonides and used by him to justify nonliteral interpretation of verses whose plain sense is anthropomorphic. And when Ramah and his friend Judah Alfakar as well[41] use it in precisely the same way, they speak in the language of the rationalists.

Again, there is nothing anomalous about this; for the Maimonidean twist given the talmudic maxim, "the Torah speaks in the language of men," has its source in the geonic-Andalusian tradition.[42] And the Spanish aristocrats of Ramah's circle—whatever their reservations about philosophical rationalism—were far from repudiating that tradition.

Like the scholars of northern France, R. Solomon of Montpellier seems to have rejected nonliteral interpretation of aggadah. Our major source of information on his views is the polemical letter of a bitter opponent, Abraham Maimonides.[43] R. Abraham's letter, which was sent from Cairo to rationalist circles in Provence in 1235,[44] gives a point-by-point response to now lost polemical writings of R. Solomon and his pupil, R. David b. Saul.

For Abraham Maimonides, the most important issue of the entire controversy was anthropomorphism—despite the denial by David b. Saul that the Provençal anti-rationalists had ever ascribed form or limbs to God.[45] R. Abraham accuses "these men—confused in their knowledge, corrupt in their faith, barren of understanding"—of gross inconsistency. They take literally the aggadic picture of God seated in heaven upon His Throne of Glory, surrounded by darkness and mist, and separated from his creatures by a curtain, and yet they claim to deny His corporeality; for their "impoverished minds" fail to grasp that anything located in a particular place is necessarily a body.[46]

Ramah's public commendation of R. Solomon as "a stock of faith, a fountain of wisdom and understanding"[47] could hardly contrast more sharply with Abraham Maimonides' expression of unmitigated contempt. But when it comes down to commenting on the Throne of Glory, Ramah is unmistakably Maimonidean: "[This does] not mean [that God] sits on a real throne. For He is not a body that He should have to sit on a throne. But rather any throne mentioned in connection with the Omnipresent, whether in Scripture or the words of the Sages, is nothing but an expression of sovereignty and kingship."[48] And so, argues Ramah, an aggadah that teaches that the "thrones" mentioned in Daniel 7:9 are for God and David[49] merely means that God's sovereignty and Davidic kingship are to be reestablished. Or alternatively, "it is possible to interpret that the throne [for God] referred to here indicates the Temple in which the *Shekinah* dwells, for which reason it is called the Throne of Glory."[50]

According to another aggadic interpretation the thrones of Daniel 7:9 are for the heavenly court; for "the Holy One blessed be He does nothing without consulting the heavenly household (*familia*)."[51] The latter, according to Ramah, is "the world of intellect (*'olam ha-madda'*) and it is called in Arabic by the philosophers (*hakme tushiyya*) *'ālam al-'uqūl* (the world of intellects)."[52] This explanation is probably borrowed from the *Guide for the Perplexed*.[53] Its adoption by Ramah indicates that his metaphysic was not dissimilar to that of the Arabic philosophers. Moreover, like Maimonides, Ramah associates the separate intelligences of the philosophers with the angels of biblical and talmudic literature—hardly the position of an antiphilosophical literalist.

If not metaphysics, then one might expect that at least eschatology would provide common ground between Ramah and his French allies. Ramah had single-handedly initiated the Resurrection Controversy because of his opposition to rationalistic reinterpretation of traditional eschatological terminology. In the controversy of the 1230s, the French anti-rationalists would seem to have been taking up Ramah's old cause;

for our sources indicate that their opposition to nonliteral interpretation centered particularly on aggadah dealing with eschatological reward and punishment.

But the French anti-rationalists went considerably further than Ramah. Ramah had insisted that 'olam ha-ba was to be experienced by reunited body and soul, whereas R. Solomon of Montpellier "staunchly maintained concerning the midrashim of our rabbis and their haggadot, that everything will come to pass in its plain sense—the future feast, the wine preserved and Leviathan, gehinnom and the palatial garden."[54] Likewise, our single surviving piece of northern French polemic brands readers of the Guide and Sefer ha-Madda' as

> heretics and deniers of the Sages and aggadot, and epiqorsim who dispute their masters. And how can they presume in their foolish hearts to make light of the reward of the Garden of Eden when countless halakot [sic] and aggadot [attest to it]. And should anyone, God forbid, reject this because of the words of R. Moses, he is like an epiqoros; for he rejects the words of the tannaim and amoraim. And likewise one who rejects other aggadot, the opening of the mouth of the ass [sic] and the feast on Leviathan which our rabbis interpreted literally.[55]

Ramah could hardly have agreed. For despite his insistence that body as well as soul will experience the reward of 'olam ha-ba, he is equally insistent on the purely spiritual nature of that reward. Aggadot to the contrary, he does not hesitate to interpret nonliterally. Thus, "the Garden of Eden, whenever mentioned in connection with 'olam ha-ba" is only a metaphor (mashal) for spiritual communion.[56] References to eating or drinking in 'olam ha-ba are to be taken figuratively. For example, "the wine preserved in its grapes from the six days of Creation" metaphorically describes the bliss of 'olam ha-ba: "And why is ['olam ha-ba] compared to wine? Because there is nothing that causes a man to rejoice in this world like wine ... That is why ['olam ha-ba] is compared to wine. For there is nothing that exceeds its joy. And what is the meaning of [its being] 'preserved in its grapes.'? To tell you that not a man in the world has grasped this joy. It is rather like wine preserved in its grapes, untouched."[57] This is just the sort of interpretation to which the French anti-rationalists objected so strenuously. By their standards, Ramah—no less than the Provençal rationalists—was deserving of condemnation.

The northern French letter treats tampering with the plain sense of both "the feast on Leviathan" and "the opening of the mouth of the ass" as sins of the same order, even referring to both as aggadot! The objection in the latter case is apparently to Maimonides' assertion that "the whole story of Balaam on the way and of the she-ass speaking . . . happened in a vision of prophecy (mar'eh ha-nebu'ah)."[58]

We do not know whether or not Ramah approved of Maimonides' interpretation of the Balaam story. His colleague Judah Alfakar took explicit exception to it (albeit for somewhat different reasons than the French);[59] and Ramah quite possibly concurred.[60] But he felt no compunctions about applying this same Maimonidean method in his aggadic exegesis. Thus, after explaining the talmudic account of how the Men of the Great Assembly slew the Evil Inclination for Idolatry and maimed its counterpart in charge of unchastity,[61] Ramah adds: "And, although I have explained all of these things according to their plain sense, it appears reasonable that they took place in a vision of prophecy (mar'eh ha-nebu'ah)."[62]

Ramah shares with Maimonides another exegetical device used when straightforward interpretation seems unreasonable. A talmudic scholar's response to a questioner is taken to be an "answer to a fool according to his folly" rather than that scholar's true opinion.[63] Ramah uses this principle to cover rabbinic response to a heretic;[64] but even when R. Judah the Prince seems to go along with his questioner's scientifically uninformed conception of the sun's daily movement, Ramah explains that "Rabbi gave him an answer in accordance with the understanding and supposition of the questioner."[65]

Similar concern with scientific correctness is evident in Ramah's comment on the following talmudic discussion:

R. Judah said in the name of Rab: "Primeval Adam [extended] from one end of the world to the other, as it is written: 'From the day in which God created man on the earth and from one end of the heaven to the other' (Deut. 4:32)." R. Elazar said: "Primeval Adam [extended] from the earth to the heaven, as it is written: 'From the day in which God created man on the earth and to the end of the heaven' (ibid.)." The verses contradict each other! [No, they do not.] Both indicate the same measure.[66]

Ramah's comment is as follows:

We find this matter quite baffling. For it is well-known that the earth is situated within the heavenly dome (kippah) like the center of a sphere. It follows that [the distance] from earth to heaven is equal to one half of the distance from one end of heaven to the other [the radius of a sphere equaling one half its diameter]. But according to this dictum, it seems to follow that the heavenly "sphere" is not as wide as it is long. Rather, it is long and narrow [that is, elliptical] enough for its width to equal half its length. And the earth is situated at the midpoint of its length. For it would then follow that the distance from earth to heaven would be equal to the distance from one end of heaven to the other. And the matter requires [further] deliberation. However, all of these statements [about the fantastic height of Adam] are hyperbolic, after the fashion of: "cities, great and fortified up to heaven" (Deut. 1:28), which means that they are exceedingly tall.[67] And this, it seems to us, is the way to interpret [our text]. And that's that.[68]

This remarkable comment illustrates the complexity of Ramah's attitude toward aggadah. Ramah declares his perplexity at the conflict between the aggadic text and "well-known" scientific data. He does not initially question the plausibility of an astronomically tall Adam. Instead, assuming a literal interpretation of the text, Ramah raises formal mathematical difficulties. He then contemplates drastic cosmographic revision on the basis of the aggadah, literally interpreted, and concludes that the problem requires further thought. Immediately reversing himself, Ramah then asserts that the matter is not deserving of further thought after all. The problematic statements are mere hyperbole; and the discussion is abruptly—almost impatiently—brought to a close. Reading this passage, one senses the tension that the question of literal versus nonliteral interpretation has injected into the interpretative process.

Reservations about rationalistic exegesis are evident here, not in Ramah's conclusion but in the apparent reluctance with which it is reached. A more rationalistic commentator would doubtless have been quicker to dismiss the literal sense of the aggadah; he would not likely have considered it a basis for fundamental scientific revision—even if only hypothetically.

Generally, Ramah's use of nonliteral aggadic exegesis is fairly restrained. His primary goal is to give the plain sense of the talmudic text (by no means an unchallenging task). A consistent exception is made when literal interpretation would endanger some fundamental theological principle such as God's incorporeality, perfection, omniscience, or omnipotence. In such cases, Ramah will invariably insist on a nonliteral interpretation.[69] But when no fundamental theological principle is at stake, he is sometimes content to give the plain sense of *aggadot* which most rationalists would find implausible, even fantastic.[70] This does not, in itself, imply that Ramah would have condemned allegorical interpretation of these *aggadot*. In fact, it is hard to see how he could have done so. For in Ramah's opinion, it is permissible to disagree outright with *aggadot* that do not reflect a broadly accepted tradition. There could, *a fortiori*, be no serious theological (as opposed to philological) objection to interpreting such *aggadot* nonliterally.[71] Ramah explicitly protests against nonliteral interpretation only in the case of 'olam ha-ba and tehiyyat ha-metim, whose plain sense he deems a broadly accepted tradition and hence authoritative. In this he is entirely consistent with the conservative wing of the geonic-Andalusian tradition.

The fact that Ramah and his Castilian colleagues were rooted in the geonic-Andalusian tradition left them vulnerable to charges of inconsistency on an important issue of the Maimonidean Controversy: the permissibility of philosophical study. The surviving northern French polemical letter bluntly condemns "any scholar who opposes the school of our masters who preceded us, all the geonim of Zarfat and Ashkenaz who never set their hearts to regard lying words, to leave the source of life—halakot and aggadot, and to occupy themselves with Greek wisdom (hokmah yevanit), the Sages having forbidden the teaching of one's son Greek wisdom."[72] To disciples of "the geonim of Zarfat and Ashkenaz" it seemed obvious that the talmudically banned Greek wisdom [hokmah yevanit] was philosophy.[73] But the geonim of Babylonia and Andalusia taught otherwise.

A geonic commentary very briefly states that "this 'Greek Wisdom' involved communication through hints."[74] Maimonides, after elaborating on this interpretation, concludes reassuringly: "And there is no doubt in my mind that this art has perished, and nothing whatsoever is left of it in the world today."[75] Judah Halevi's use of the term in his famous anti-Aristotelian line, "Be not deceived by Greek wisdom (hokmat yevanit) which has no fruit, but only flowers"[76] might suggest that he did apply the talmudic proscription to philosophy. But in fact, in twelfth-century Spain even the Aristotelian Abraham ibn Daud refers to science and philosophy as hokmah yevanit, and in an unmistakably laudatory context.[77]

An interpretation of the talmudic prohibition consistent with this usage is found in the Abot commentary of the late thirteenth-century Toledan R. Israel Israeli:

> "Study the Torah diligently" is juxtaposed to "Know what to answer the epiqoros," to teach us study procedure: that a man ought put first study of the Torah and the Talmud and its laws and to meditate therein and study meticulously until it sinks into his heart and he knows its principles and details, rules and regulations. And afterward, let him study the secular sciences in order to know the refutation of those who go astray, so that he may defeat them in their argumentation. That is why the Sages said: "Keep your sons from logic (higayon)"[78] and not "Keep yourselves." For the children have not quenched the thirst of their intellects with

Torah and Talmud . . . Likewise they said, "Cursed be he who teaches his son Greek wisdom" and did not say "Cursed be he who studies Greek wisdom," for the aforementioned reason.[79]

According to Ramah, the talmudically proscribed *hokmah yevanit* is astrology.[80] The exegetical considerations that led to this interpretation are not entirely clear; apparently Ramah felt that the plain sense of the term had to refer to at least some discipline that was part of the Greek intellectual tradition. His avoidance of the obvious interpretation of *hokmah yevanit* as Greek philosophy in favor of a more forced, restrictive interpretation indicates an unwillingness to put philosophy under blanket prohibition. And in this, Ramah is in accord with the geonic-Andalusian tradition.[81]

That the Castilian and French anti-rationalists were at variance on the issue of philosophical study did not go unnoticed. Kimhi, in his exchange with Judah Alfakar, makes the point bluntly: "And if I strive to ascend the Chariot [study metaphysics] upon the ladder which the master, the righteous teacher [Maimonides] has set up for us . . . there's nothing astonishing about that. For you too, along with other scholars, engage in the study of *hokmah* [wisdom] contrary to the words of the *Zarfatim* who have placed under the ban any who engage in the study of that kind of *hokmah*."[82] The statesmanlike Provençal *nasi* R. Meshullam b. Kalonymous makes the same point somewhat more subtly. His reconciliatory letter to Alfakar begins with a long chain of laudatory epithets climaxing in "the *nasi*, the sage, *the eminent philosopher*, R. Judah."[83]

Provençal rationalists went to some length in accentuating certain *Zarfati* practices generally frowned upon by the scholars of Spain. A Narbonnese circular to "our brethren the holy communities, sons of the exiles of Jerusalem who are in Sefarad" contains a furious denunciation of *Zarfati* superstition:

Praise to the God of our fathers, there is no breach, no ill repute, no shouting in our streets. There are none among us . . . whose heart turns away this day from the Lord our God to go and follow the abominations of the nations, to hearken to soothsayers and dreamers of false dreams, to lead boundlessly astray the people of God, with the vanities of [magical] names, appellations of angels and demons and to practice conjuration, and to write amulets, misleading fools . . . as we have heard concerning the great men of Israel among the *Zarfatim* and their scholars, their heads and men of understanding . . . They followed worthless paths and became themselves worthless. For they fancy themselves masters of the Name, like the true prophets of renown.[84] But they are fools and madmen full of delusions, their brains are polluted, as thorns thrust away, all of them. They dwell in abodes of darkness, have vain and foolish visions, immersed in stinking cave water . . . Woe for that shame, woe for that disgrace . . . Shall such men rule over the men of our land, shall they come to rebuke us in our abodes?[85]

Nahmanides, an admirer of Franco-German piety and scholarship, was at pains to defend some of these practices:

I am astonished for I have heard it reported with certainty that it is the practice of the pious men of Alamannia to occupy themselves with demons, and they conjure them, send them on missions, and use them in many ways. And I am of the opinion that it can be argued that works of demons must be distinguished from works of sorcery, as the Sages have said: "[when Pharaoh's magicians are described as performing] belatehem—this refers to works of demons, belahatehem—this refers to works of sorcery." And Rashi of blessed memory interpreted works of sorcery as those done through angels of destruction.[86] And it is these that the Torah forbade. But works of demons are permitted.[87]

Ramah was familiar with this line of reasoning, but rejected it: "Works of demons fall under the category of sorcery, and one who performs an act [using demons] is liable to [death by] stoning. And the distinction made between them [works of demons and words of sorcery] earlier [by the Talmud] is merely a matter of explaining the verses in which [the different forms] latehem and lahatehem appear. But both still come under the category of the sorcerer.[88] In effect, Ramah is declaring prominent representatives of the Franco-German tradition guilty of a stoning offense!

Ramah did not, like Maimonides, deny completely the existence of demons.[89] But his affinity to geonic-Andalusian—rather than Franco-German—sensibilities in matters demonological can be illustrated by his exegesis of the following talmudic passage: "One who dwelled in another's courtyard without the latter's knowledge is not bound to pay rent, for it is said: 'And the gate is smitten by she'iyyah [literally, destruction]' (Is. 24:12). Mar bar R. Ashi said: 'I have seen him and he was goring like an ox' (Baba Qamma, 21a)." According to Rashi, "A demon named She'iyyah destroys the gate of an uninhabited house . . . Alternatively: a house that is desolate (sha'uy) is destroyed by demons." In Ramah's view, however, "The reference is to the worm that causes the wood and beams of a house to rot. And [Mar bar R. Ashi] spoke hyperbolically—as if to say that he saw it cause as great a damage to a house as an ox goring the house's roof and walls." Ramah has abandoned the plain sense of the talmudic text, given by Rashi, in favor of a naturalistic interpretation, probably of geonic origin.[90]

To sum up, we have seen that on many of the important issues sep-
arating the Provençal rationalists and their French critics, Ramah—
loyal to the geonic-Andalusian tradition—was in accord with the
rationalist position. The "geonic-Andalusian tradition" is more than an
artificial construct; at the time of the controversy, there was an awareness of a coherent tradition of Babylonian, North African, and Spanish
scholars extending from Saadya to Maimonides. A sense of continuity
with this tradition served as a crucial element in the self-definition of
thirteenth-century Provençal rationalism. In their defense of Maimonides against northern French attack, the Provençal rationalists appealed
confidently and correctly to geonic-Andalusian precedent.[91]

Northern French polemic understandably takes as its authority "the
geonim of Zarfat and Ashkenaz"[92] rather than those of Babylonia and
Andalusia. Whether any coherent image of the latter tradition was
widespread among Franco-German scholars is difficult to say. But
Moses b. Hasdai, for one, is clear on the subject: the rationalist heresy
begins with Saadya Gaon; Ibn Ezra and Maimonides merely follow in
his wake; and the entire tradition is condemned as a whole.[93] The positions of Moses b. Hasdai and the Provençal rationalists are diametrically opposed, but they define the battle in the same way: to accept or
to reject the tradition of geonic-Andalusian rationalism. We may
therefore conjecture that the Lunel scholars, in expecting Ramah's support, had consciously or unconsciously syllogized roughly as follows:
"Maimonides represents the culmination of the geonic-Andalusian tradition. It is this tradition that we are now defending against blanket
condemnation. Ramah, despite isolated differences with Maimonides,
is firmly implanted in the geonic-Andalusian tradition. He is, therefore,
our natural ally."

The argument seems eminently reasonable. Why, then, did its conclusion prove wrong? Apparently, because the men in Ramah's circle
viewed the significance of the Maimonidean Controversy differently
from the Provençal rationalists. For the Castilian anti-rationalists, the
issue at stake was not whether to repudiate geonic-Andalusian rationalism in favor of Franco-German talmudic culture; it was rather the radicalization of the Spanish tradition itself. Provençal rationalists and
Castilian anti-rationalists could define the same controversy differently
because the two groups perceived the geonic-Andalusian tradition and
Maimonides' relationship to it in different ways.

The Provençal rationalists seem to view geonic-Andalusian rationalism as a relatively unified tradition—as indeed it is, when defined
against the background of prephilosophical French culture. Maimonides' works were seen as the crowning achievement and quintessential
statement of that tradition. Those who viewed the geonic-Andalusian
tradition from within were not so apt to see it as a static, undifferen-

tiated whole; they were more conscious of internal complexity and development. And this holds true for rationalists as well as anti-rationalists.

Spanish rationalists do sometimes speak of the geonic-Andalusian tradition as a whole. Thus, Abraham Maimonides (who can, for our purposes, be considered a representative of Spanish rationalism) speaks of an undifferentiated tradition extending from Saadya Gaon to Abraham ibn Ezra.[94] But Abraham Maimonides was polemicizing against French anti-rationalism, and invocation of a unified geonic-Andalusian tradition was natural in that context. In a nonpolemical context, there is frank recognition of important elements of discontinuity. Ibn Ezra, for example, makes this acknowledgement.[95] And Maimonides, in somewhat unexpectedly decisive fashion, separates his philosophical school from that of the *geonim* and their followers.[96]

In some of these shifts, the anti-rationalists found cause for alarm. During the Resurrection Controversy, when the Provençal Aaron b. Meshullam claimed geonic support for Maimonides' position, Ramah correctly pointed out that Maimonides had, in fact, broken with geonic tradition.[97] Such breaks are not made explicit in the samples of Castilian anti-rationalist polemic that survive from the 1230s. But they must have been much in mind; for they determine the issues that dominated Castilian criticism of Maimonidean rationalism. The root change is a tendency—especially with the ascendancy of Aristotelianism in the twelfth century—toward a more stringent naturalism. Most of the concerns of Castilian anti-rationalism stem from this new naturalism and its attendant radicalization of the religious stance of Spanish rationalism.

Maimonides himself had defined the ultimate issue between Aristotle and the Bible with utmost clarity. Discussing the conflict between the biblical doctrine of creation and the Aristotelian conception of an eternal universe, Maimonides points out that the underlying issue is really God's free will. Biblical God stands above nature and can freely create, change, and control as He wills. The God of Aristotle, first cause though He be, is absolutely constrained by the natural order. He cannot, as Maimonides graphically puts it, even alter the wing of a flea.[98]

Maimonides rejected the Aristotelian view; but Castilian critics of the *Guide* remain uneasy. They fear that Maimonides has not been unambiguous, decisive, sweeping enough in maintaining direct divine initiative in the workings of the world; too much is conceded to nature. And when the Castilian anti-rationalists turn to certain anonymous contemporaries, uneasiness gives way to certainty that there has been a partial or even complete capitulation to Aristotelian naturalism.

We have seen how Ramah called attention to the role of philosophical naturalism in the rationalistic conception of 'olam ha-ba. In a few dry sentences of his postscript to the Resurrection Controversy, Ramah uncovered the far-reaching consequences of an eschatology enclosed entirely within the confines of natural law.[99] At the same time, Ramah clarified his original assumptions in initiating the controversy. He had assumed that Maimonides denied the *possibility* of permanent bodily resurrection.[100] Maimonides' *Treatise on Resurrection* softened his opposition with its assertion that no miracle is impossible, but that to accept the conception of a permanently resurrected body without bodily functions would be to postulate unworthily an everlasting redundancy in God's activity.[101] Ramah now disagrees without condemnation.[102] Thus the problem of naturalism was, at least from Ramah's point of view, central to the Resurrection Controversy.

Ramah studied Maimonides' works carefully. Several passages in *Perate-Sanhedrin* draw upon key Maimonidean formulations.[103] These passages are not only a measure of Maimonides' impact on Ramah; they point even more finely to some of Ramah's reservations about Maimonidean rationalism. For Ramah does not borrow verbatim; he adapts—and with discrimination. One such variation on a theme by Maimonides is of interest with regard to the question of Aristotelian naturalism.

A talmudic discussion of the Messianic redemption contains the following: "What is [meant by], 'For the day of vengeance is in My heart' (Isaiah 63.4)? Said R. Yohanan: [It means] 'To My heart I have revealed it; to My limbs I have not revealed it.' "[104] Ramah argues for a figurative interpretation of this aggadah:

> God forbid [to entertain the idea] that He has heart and limbs; for He is not a body. For a body is finite. And any finite thing has finite power. And our God (blessed be His name and exalted be His kingdom for ever and eternity) since His power is infinite—for He maintains (*nose*) the entire universe with His power while His power remains undiminished and unchanged; and even more: for He has brought all existents into existence *ex nihilo* from which it follows that His power is infinite—He is certainly infinite. And since He is infinite, it follows that he is not a body. And wherever you find—whether in the Torah or the Prophets or the Writings or in the words of our Sages of blessed memory—[things to the contrary], they are not to be taken literally; they are rather [said] by way of metaphor. And the Torah speaks in the language of men.[105]

This argument for God's incorporeality and for its attendant exegetical corollary is—in logic, language, and structure—heavily indebted to Maimonides. It is adapted from the first chapter of *Sefer ha-Madda'*,[106] a section of that work unpopular with Maimonides' French critics.

Ramah thought highly enough of Maimonides' argument to borrow it. But his alteration of the segment arguing the infinitude of God's power is significant:

Maimonides	*Ramah*
And our God (blessed be His name) since His power is infinite and never ending—For the Sphere rotates always—His power is not the power of a body.	And our God (blessed be His name and exalted be His kingdom for ever and eternity) since His power is infinite—for He maintains (*nose*) the entire universe with His power while His power remains undiminished and unchanged; and even more: for He has brought all existents into existence *ex nihilo* from which it follows that His power is infinite—He is certainly infinite. And since He is infinite, it follows that he is not a body.

Ramah has changed Maimonides' first argument and added a second. Maimonides, in Aristotelian fashion, argues from God's activity as a first mover imparting eternal motion to the heavens. Ramah refers instead to God's "maintaining the entire universe [*kol ha-'olam kullo*]"—as if to protest that He is not just an unmoved mover but rather the One who directly maintains the world and all it contains. Why did Ramah insert an additional argument from creation *ex nihilo* and stress that it is of even greater force than the first? Probably because, as Maimonides indicates in the *Guide*, his argument here was based on a hypothetical acceptance of the eternity of the world.[107] And so Ramah's adaptation adds that accepting creation *ex nihilo* makes the argument even stronger.[108] In short, Ramah likes Maimonides' argument for God's incorporeality but is sensitive to its Aristotelian overtones; and with these he is unhappy.

Just how central the question of Aristotelian naturalism was to the Castilian anti-rationalists can be seen from Judah Alfakar's brief but incisive critique of the *Guide*.[109] Maimonides' penchant for exegetically minimizing the miraculous comes in for particularly acute criticism. There is no middle ground, insists Alfakar; either you concede God's power to abrogate the laws of nature or deny it. But trying to keep biblical miracles to a minimum by forced exegesis makes no sense in either case. Are three flying camels less likely than one? asks Alfakar, making his point with mordant wit.[110] To put Alfakar's criticism in a nutshell: biblical teaching and Greek naturalism are irrevocably opposed and ir-

reconcilable. Maimonides muddies clear waters in attempting to strad-
dle the issue:

> His [Maimonides'] intention was [to explain the Bible such] that
> the laws of nature not be abrogated, so that the Torah might be at
> one with Greek philosophy. And he imagined the former and the
> latter to be twin gazelles. But [instead] there is mourning and lam-
> entation; for the earth cannot bear them dwelling together as sis-
> ters; for not like unto the Egyptian women are the Hebrew women!
> This Torah declares: "Not so—my son is the live one and your son
> the dead!" And her rival vexes her sorely.[111]

For the Castilian anti-rationalists, nonliteral exegesis becomes an
issue of concern when it goes beyond geonic guidelines and serves as a
tool for imposing philosophical naturalism on the classical texts.
Ramah had already indicated as much in connection with the Resurrection Controversy.[112] Alfakar's letter pursues the same line of argument
more explicitly and broadly. Interestingly, Alfakar is unhappy about
the implications of Maimonidean exegesis for bodily resurrection—the
Treatise on Resurrection, apparently notwithstanding.[113] But resurrection
is mentioned only in passing as part of a fundamental critique of the
Guide's exegetical paring down of the miraculous.

At the outset, Alfakar attempts to drive a wedge between legitimate
nonliteral interpretation and exegesis of a more radical sort. Maimonides, in a famous passage of the *Guide,* writes that had he been faced
with compelling Aristotelian proof of the eternity of the world he could
have interpreted the creation story figuratively, as easily as he had biblical anthropomorphism.[114] The analogy annoys Alfakar: "It is clear
that the question of eternity is in no way comparable to corporeality!"
God's incorporeality is attested by both Scripture and rabbinic tradition. And so concerning biblical anthropomorphism "our rabbis of
blessed memory have said: 'The Torah speaks in the language of
men.' "[115] In short, Alfakar dissociates the kind of nonliteral exegesis
universally accepted within the geonic-Andalusian tradition from that
practiced by its newer, more naturalistic wing.

A similar stance is implicit in the attitude of the Castilian anti-rationalists to philosophical study. The notion that a well-rounded education
should include science and philosophy, that a well-educated Jew
should be able to defend his faith with philosophical weapons—this
had become commonplace in the geonic-Andalusian tradition. Ramah
and Alfakar were themselves representative of this educational ideal.
They rejected not the permissibility, but the primacy of philosophical
study—its claim to be the royal road to salvation.[116] And here too,

Ramah sees a form of naturalism at the root of the rationalistic view; for the attainment of immortality by the intellect—actualized through philosophical study—is (according to the philosophers) a natural process. Unfortunately, Aristotelian nature fails to provide for the reward of nonphilosophical good: "The upshot [of the philosophical conception of immortality] is that there is no lasting benefit to Torah and good deeds since the matter [of immortality] is determined by Nature."[117]

The philosopher's soteriology has curricular consequences. As the path to perfection and salvation, philosophy lays claim to the lion's share of study time. Traditional talmudic study is the big loser; thus Alfakar's complaint to Kimhi that the latter "sets aside the discussions of Abbaye and Raba attempting [instead] to ascend the *Merkabah* [metaphysics]."[118] There is probably a disparaging allusion here to a famous passage in *Sefer ha-Madda'* in which Maimonides, after having identified metaphysics with *ma'aseh merkabah*, quotes the Talmud on the latter's superiority to the discussions of Abbaye and Raba.[119]

Kimhi denies the charge that he neglects talmudic study. His policy is that of King Solomon: "It is good that you should take hold of this, and from that withhold not your hand (Eccles. 7:18)."[120] And there is no reason to disbelieve him.[121] Alfakar may have been projecting on Kimhi an attitude that he held to be implicit in the rationalist position and that was already common among Spanish rationalists.[122]

In the same letter to Kimhi, Alfakar refers to the opponents of Solomon of Montpellier as "violators of religion."[123] Kimhi is indignant. With eloquence and passion he eulogizes the learning, piety, and good deeds of Provençal Jewry.[124] Here again, Alfakar may be projecting on Provence his "ideal type" of the rationalist drawn from Spanish realities. The Castilian anti-rationalists were aware that the philosopher's contemplative ideal bears the seeds of antinomianism.[125] And whatever the situation in Provence, antinomianism *was* a problem in Spain.

At about the time of the Maimonidean Controversy, Nahmanides was embroiled in communal conflict with the aristocratic *nesi'im* of Barcelona. The latter were, we recall, staunch Maimunists. Nahmanides paints quite a picture of his opponents: ". . . men suspected of sexual immorality . . . men who do not pray for their lives, nor recite the benedictions over their food; nor are they strict about their bread and wine. And in private, they do not keep the Sabbath; for they are Ishmaelites.[126] But there are, of course, many reasons for violation of religious law that have nothing to do with philosophical rationalism.[127] And Nahmanides makes no connection between his opponents' religious laxity and their rationalistic sympathies.

Religious laxity and rationalism *are* directly linked by Ramah's brother, Joseph b. Todros.

> "Most of the supporters of this book [the *Guide*] in our regions . . .
> fall into two groups. The first group is that of the hypocrites who
> make a sham of the Torah and freely indulge in secret trans-
> gression, whose Torah consists of bowing their heads like a reed;
> they assume the mantle of righteousness, but it clothes them not.
> The second group is that of the rich pleasure-seekers who remove
> the age-old boundaries; they are the ones who go astray and lead
> [others] astray . . . who have grown fat and sleek, and kicked, who
> thrust the poor off the road, who abandon the paths of righteous-
> ness, neglecting the Torah out of wealth.[128]

In short, most Spanish Maimunists are either hypocritical intellectuals or hedonistic aristocrats. Both groups are accused of consistent reli- gious transgression; and this is somehow connected with their rational- istic sympathies, although Joseph does not say exactly how. The impli- cation would seem to be that rationalistic antinomianism serves as a convenient justification for the religious transgressions of these groups. Of course, allowance must be made for hyperbole in R. Joseph's report; polemicists are wont to overstate the opposition's faults.[129]

Ramah too, with polemical license, sweepingly characterizes the ra- tionalists as antinomians. But Ramah's "ideal type" of the rationalist provides an interesting corrective to R. Joseph's "ulterior motive" ex- planation; for Ramah stresses the philosophical, even spiritual, bases of these antinomians,

> . . . makers of breaches who follow after their own counsels to lop
> off with axes the branches of commandments, statutes and righ-
> teous laws, to pervert upright paths, to falsify the [divine] decree
> and to give distasteful reason[s for the commandments][130] to break
> the yoke of the commandments, to sever the bonds by saying:
> "The Creator has no desire for shekels with agio,[131] nor is there
> jealousy before Him that he should exact [punishment for] offense
> [against Him]. Remote is the Exalted One, there is no accountabil-
> ity.[132] For He desires only that each man in his heart apprehend
> knowledge of his Creator and the wisdom of His Chariot [meta-
> physics]. For what pleasure [can God possibly take] in the body—
> whether it be pure or impure, whether it hunger or thirst?"[133] They
> lead their spirits into error, pervert their paths, make crooked their
> ways . . . in making [philosophical] knowledge the [supreme] end,
> to practice ungodliness, to utter error against the Lord, to empty
> the soul which craves *mizvot* and Torah, setting its heart aboil like a
> pot, to deprive of drink [the soul] thirsty for His word, to bring
> death to souls that ought not die.[134]

Ramah assigns "distasteful reasons [for the commandments]" a role in the ideology of antinomianism. But this does not mean that Ramah opposed the idea that commandments have reasons. An enigmatic aggadah characterizing the Torah as *"debarim shel tohu* [vain things] upon which the world is founded"[135] elicits the following clarification in *Perate-Sanhedrin:* "Vain things—that is, things whose reasons are not manifest like the prohibition of mixed species, mixed linen and wool and the like which seem to people to be vain things which are without substance. It is these which are called statutes (*huqqot*) as it is written: 'You shall keep my statutes etc.' (Lev. 19:19). And the world is founded upon them . . . for they are based on great principles (*'iqqarin*), great as the mightiest mountains."[136] But explanatory principles that subordinate the Law to an ultimate contemplative goal could justify bypassing the means in favor of the end; and it is probably such explanations that Ramah finds distasteful. Ramah attributes these explanations to anonymous antinomians. He makes no explicit mention of Maimonides' famous theory of the Law in part 3 of the *Guide.*[137] Joseph b. Todros does; and it is probably no coincidence that he dubs Maimonides' explanations distasteful with the same clever pun used by his brother.[138]

To recapitulate, the Provençal rationalists misjudged Ramah's circle because the two groups defined the problem of Maimonidean rationalism differently. French anti-rationalism represents a reaction of Franco-German talmudic culture to the challenge of the geonic-Andalusian tradition. Much of that tradition was acceptable, even sacred, to the Castilian anti-rationalists. They were concerned with the increased influence of uncompromised Aristotelianism in Spain and its possible spread to Provence. The issues of primary concern to them—naturalism, salvation by philosophy, antinomianism—are hardly mentioned, perhaps not even grasped, in the French arena of the Maimonidean Controversy. The men of Ramah's circle were not merely aiding the cause of their French allies with rhetorical and dialectical weapons more sophisticated than the latter possessed; they were, in important respects, fighting a different battle.[139]

Though their polemical writings express solidarity with the French anti-rationalists, Ramah and his colleagues must have been aware that their own opposition to Maimonidean rationalism was of a more complex and selective sort. An obscure "in-house" exchange between Joseph b. Todros and Judah Alfakar may preserve written expression of this recognition.[140] Joseph's letter has not survived, perhaps because it was written in Arabic. Alfakar begins his response by indulging an Andalusian inclination for enlivening polemic with extraneous linguistic criticism:[141] he takes Joseph to task for "speaking like an Arab in the desert (*midbar*)."[142] Joseph, for his part, may have intended by writing in Arabic to limit the circulation of his letter; for it apparently criticized Alfakar for having been too lavish in his praise of Solomon of Montpellier and too harsh in his blame of the Provençal rationalists. Alfakar concedes both points. R. Solomon, it appears, was not one of Alfakar's heroes:

> I praised Solomon so extravagantly not because of his greatness but rather on account of his mighty deeds. For he has done battle for Israel against the *Guide*, and raked it over the coals, its head with its legs and entrails; and the altar-fire set it aflame. I have praised him more than he deserves and continue to overlook his faults in order that Israel not stray after it [the *Guide*] nor attend to all its words; for it is time to strengthen the hands of the faithful and time to act for the Lord.[143]

Nor, concedes Alfakar, had the Provençal rationalists been deserving of his denunciations. He had hoped to shock them into realization of their errors, but now regrets "having spoken proudly against rulers and nobles, men wise and renowned." They are not to blame; for "the nature of the *Guide* is concealed from their eyes."[144] But why should "the nature of the *Guide*" be concealed from men renowned for their wisdom? Alfakar is apparently excusing the Provençal rationalists on grounds of insufficient philosophical sophistication![145]

Kimhi's earlier letter provides unexpected elucidation of Alfakar's thesis. Pointing out that Alfakar and his friends are students of philosophy, Kimhi adds: "I had indeed craved your fellowship to ask you in person about some of my [philosophical] problems which I felt ought not to be put in writing. For ever since our brother, the great scholar, R. Samuel ibn Tibbon of blessed memory was gathered to his fathers, I have found no one with whom to discuss these matters."[146] In all of Provence, bastion of support for Maimonidean rationalism, Kimhi can find no adequate philosophical companionship! His intellectual isolation indicates an as yet incomplete assimilation of philosophical learning on the part of native Provençal scholars.[147] There is, then, a kind of internal unity to both the Provençal and Spanish arenas of the Maimonidean Controversy. Within each, rationalism and its opposing anti-rationalism stand at corresponding stages of maturity.[148]

This is not to suggest that the Maimonidean Controversy breaks down intellectually into two separate and distinct debates taking place within airtight compartments. French and Castilian anti-rationalism, for example, had different origins and concerns; but this does not mean that Ramah and his circle were impervious to French influence or that their support for the French anti-rationalists was nothing more than a tactical maneuver. The talmudic learning and piety of the French were probably not without impact on the Castilian anti-rationalists—especially so in light of the latter's rejection of Aristotelian soteriology and reassertion of the centrality of "Torah and good deeds." Thus the undeniably deep differences between these groups should not obscure the obvious—that enough consciousness of common ground did exist for Ramah and his colleagues to take the side of the French anti-rationalists.

A common denominator of all who joined the anti-rationalist camp in the Maimonidean Controversy was an at least partially critical stance toward Maimonides. For it was in the nature of that controversy that impersonal issues—theological, exegetical, educational—were inextricably bound up with Maimonides—his stature, teaching, and authority. And just as there were different perceptions of the issues at stake in the controversy, so there were different images of Maimonides himself. Let us look for a moment at the opposition to Maimonides through thirteenth-century Castilian eyes. Two young Toledan contemporaries have left us brief reactions to the Maimonidean Controversy. Both were defenders of Maimonides and of similar intellectual-spiritual complexion, yet they characterize Maimonides' opponents quite differently. The first is Ramah's pupil Judah ibn Matka, author of the scientific and philosophical encyclopedia *Midrash Hokmah*; the second is the philosopher-kabbalist Isaac ibn Latif.

Ibn Matka illustrates nicely the concerns of a sophisticated Castilian anti-rationalist. Though he took the trouble to master and twice summarize the Aristotelian corpus,[149] Ibn Matka takes the "alien woman" of Proverbs 2:16 "who speaks so smoothly" to be none other than "heretical wisdom which takes on the appearance of truth and seduces one, like some of the words of Aristotle, on the eternity of the world." Aristotle himself is not to be condemned: without prophetic tradition, he apprehended God's existence, unity, and incorporeality. But he erred in affirming the eternity of the world and has led his Jewish followers astray. "May the Holy One, blessed be He, bring us back in perfect repentence unto His Presence."[150] Refuting the Aristotelian proof of eternity, Ibn Matka adds that "this will be accounted an act of righteousness on our part. And whoever provides additional refutation, may he receive a blessing."

More basically, Ibn Matka challenges the Aristotelian methodology whereby one reasons from the empirical to the supraempirical. And so, "why should we abandon our holy and perfect Torah to follow after vain things that profit not. We ought, therefore, to strive, with all our might for the sake of our faith and our Torah."[151] Ibn Matka vigorously rejects identification of the Torah's "Divine Wisdom" (*hokmah elohit*) with Aristotelian metaphysics. The highest knowledge provided by the latter "is axiomatic [even] to our children." The true Divine Wisdom is accessible not through philosophical reasoning but only through an unbroken tradition (*qabbalah*) that goes back to Revelation.[152]

If Aristotelianism is so dangerous, unproductive, and far from true Divine Wisdom, why, one wonders, did Ibn Matka labor so assiduously to propagate its knowledge? "Only," according to Ibn Matka, "in order to make known the extent of the benefit [to be gained] from the [scientific and philosophical] works of the nations, and so that the Israelite not be innocent of them lest they [the nations] grow haughty toward him with their sciences. And this work will teach him how to refute the heretic (*epiqoros*) from his [own] science and how to return one who has gone astray after their works, to our holy Torah."[153] Moreover, *Midrash Hokmah* provided its readers with "hints about our [Israel's] Divine Wisdom. And the man of understanding will grasp [them]. And if he be worthy, he will distinguish [between our Divine Wisdom and Aristotelian metaphysics]."[154]

Though this evaluation of Aristotelian philosophy and its study sounds considerably more conservative than that of Maimonides, Ibn Matka strongly rejected suspicions about the *Guide* entertained by certain contemporaries:

> I acknowledge that the . . . book of the Teacher of Righteousness [Maimonides' *Guide*] planted in my heart a burning desire to study the works of the philosophers whereby I achieved the little that I have. My true opinion is that the author's intent . . . was merely to cause those who erred after the words of Aristotle to repent and to hold fast once again to our holy Torah, and that one ought not suspect the lamp of the exile of Ariel [Jerusalem] of the things that he has been suspected by some people of this generation. Those who err in their study of his treatise . . . resemble the eyes of a bat that gazes at the sun.[155]

These people were not French anti-rationalists. The latter were not suspicious of Maimonides; they were alarmed by explicit teachings of the *Guide* and *Sefer ha-Madda'*. Ibn Matka is probably referring to fellow Castilian anti-rationalists. Their view of the *Guide* was fraught with tension and uncertainty.

The second Toledan, the philosopher-kabbalist Isaac ibn Latif, is in many ways similar to Ibn Matka. To quote the succinct characterization of R. Isaac b. Sheshet: "[Ibn Latif] was apparently quite accomplished in philosophy and was, nevertheless, a traditionalist and a man of piety (*toriyyi ve-hasid*)."[156] He too was a defender of Maimonides. But unlike Ibn Matka, Ibn Latif refers to critics who attacked *Sefer ha-Madda'*, and he regards these men with a full measure of condescension. Reared, as they were, on corporealism and ignorance, "they were unable to apprehend intelligibles and spiritual matters too exalted for their minds." And so, when they came upon matters beyond their grasp at the beginning of *Mishneh Torah* "and in other distinguished works," they slandered their master. Because they sinned only out of ignorance, Ibn Latif refrains from mentioning their names,[157] but we have no difficulty in recognizing them as anti-rationalists of the French school.

Northern French polemic seems to have adopted an attitude toward Maimonides that was almost diametrically opposed to that of the Provençal rationalists. For the latter, Maimonides was a figure of heroic proportions, zenith of the geonic-Andalusian tradition and symbolic personification of a new cultural ideal. Northern French polemic responded with an equally sweeping condemnation of both the *Guide* and *Sefer ha-Madda'* as inimical to the Franco-German tradition. Nor did the northern French mince words about Maimonides himself, as can be seen by Nahmanides' pungent rebuke:

> Even whores paint one another—scholars how much more so! . . . you have uttered arrogance, words seemingly said out of jealousy and hatred; it is forbidden even to hear them—certainly to write and declare them; for you have written and declared concerning that holy one [Maimonides], peerless in all the exile of Zarfat and Sefarad . . . erudite in all species of sciences . . . opening your mouths without right, multiplying words heard far and wide when you said about about that *gaon* [Maimonides]: "We had a greater man than he who became a Sadducee!"[158]

Though not far from the northern French position on substantive issues, Solomon of Montpellier and his circle recognize—whether out of principle or prudence—an obligation to honor Maimonides. R. Solomon shifts the brunt of condemnation to Samuel ibn Tibbon, "the translator who has revealed all that the master [Maimonides] concealed."[159] Concealment of odious opinions must surely seem a somewhat damning defense! But, in any case, R. Solomon rejects as slanderous the charge that he has "reviled the armies of the living God and spoken against the great master who has increased and spread Torah in Israel, R. Moses son of the rabbi, the *dayyan* R. Maimon of blessed memory."[160]

This denial was important in winning, or at least keeping, Spanish friends. Nahmanides attached particular importance to this point: "In apologizing that you did not put forth your hand against the anointed of the Lord [Maimonides] you have done well, as befits you . . . the honorable men of our city, our scholars and elders have all read [your letter] . . . praised it, found it like honey in their mouths. I have also shown it to the common people and read it to them to explain your case to them, to justify you in their eyes."[161] In Spain, even anti-rationalists would tolerate no dishonoring of Maimonides; (nor would the "common people"—who can appreciate a hero better than abstract issues).

But the Spanish anti-rationalists would not accept a heroic image of Maimonides without reservation. Ramah's brother, Joseph b. Todros, is an interesting case in point. His letter begins with a recitation of Maimonides' glories, echoing even Aaron b. Meshullam's contention that "none has arisen like him since the days of Rabina and R. Ashi."[162] But he also sounds a different note:

> Even if he [Solomon of Montpellier] openly rejected his [Maimonides'] words, what has come over them [the Provençal rationalists] that they judge him a rebellious elder for disagreeing with the *Guide?* Do they consider every word of that obscure book a tradition handed down from Moses at Sinai . . . standing fast for ever and ever . . . and that the gates of refutation of his books have, from the first, been locked in the face of all men, that one may not question him in the manner of honest and upright scholars?[163]

Generous, though somewhat more restrained than Joseph, Judah Alfakar plainly denounced the heroic image: "Why have you [rationalists] violated the word of God and made the *Guide* into a new *Torah?* . . . And you thought to elevate R. Moses of blessed memory above the prophets!"[164] In their attitude toward Maimonides, Alfakar and Joseph b. Todros were following along lines set by Ramah during the Resurrection Controversy: honor—yes; infallibility—no.[165]

In protesting the canonization of the *Guide*, Alfakar and Joseph b. Todros pointedly neglect to mention *Sefer ha-Madda'*. The omission is significant; for the French critics of Maimonides, whom the Castilian anti-rationalists publicly supported, had criticized *Sefer ha-Madda'* as well as the *Guide*. Apparently, the Castilian anti-rationalists did not wish to be identified with the French attacks on *Sefer ha-Madda'*.

The attitude of Spanish anti-rationalists to *Sefer ha-Madda'* is particularly instructive. These men were quite capable of taking the full measure of that work's rationalism; yet their overall view was favorable. They do not, like the French anti-rationalists, object to *Sefer ha-Madda'* as a unit. To the contrary, Nahmanides and Joseph b. Todros express admiration for *Sefer ha-Madda'*.[166] This admiration illustrates once again (this time in integrated fashion) the rootedness of the Spanish anti-rationalists in the geonic-Andalusian tradition. For *Sefer ha-Madda'* is—among other things—an eloquent statement of the fundamental religious ideas and values of that tradition. Castilian statements in support of French anti-rationalism simply ignore the latter's attacks on *Sefer ha-Madda'* and address themselves instead to the *Guide*.

Why should admirers of *Sefer ha-Madda'* dislike the *Guide?* For one thing, the tendency toward naturalistic explanation is more pronounced, explicit, and encompassing in the *Guide* than it is in *Sefer ha-Madda'*. But the unhappiness of the Castilian anti-rationalists with the *Guide* was probably also related to the way in which it was used by some contemporaries. Judah Alfakar indicates that the *Guide* serves as a peg upon which unnamed rationalists hang unspecified radical views.[167] And there is, in fact, a school of both medieval and modern commentators who attribute to the *Guide* an esoteric teaching more radically Aristotelian than its exoteric defense of traditional religion. Consider, for example, the *Guide's* position on Creation. Maimonides, we recall, states that had he found Aristotle's proofs convincing, he would have had no trouble explaining the beginning of Genesis in terms of the eternity of the world.[168] According to the fourteenth-century commentator Joseph ibn Kaspi, what Maimonides says in the subjunctive, he really means in the indicative.[169] Could the existence of such an interpretation a century earlier help explain Alfakar's particular annoyance at this passage?

The way in which the Castilian anti-rationalists themselves understood and evaluated the *Guide* cannot be delineated with any precision. We know the issues of concern to them and the general ways in which these issues relate to Maimonidean rationalism. But the Castilian anti-rationalists will not say explicitly just what objectionable doctrines they impute to the *Guide*. Apparently, they were not quite sure.

Ibn Matka, we recall, says that "one ought not suspect Maimonides of the things that he has been suspected by some people of this generation." Reflecting somewhat less certitude, Alfakar remarks that "we are obligated to judge [Maimonides] in the scale of merit."[170] Benefit of the doubt becomes necessary only when doubt exists. And this doubt may explain something of the obscurity with which Castilian anti-rationalists speak of the *Guide*.

Ramah's brother, Joseph b. Todros, describes his first reading of the *Guide* as an unsettling experience: "Had I not shut my eyes, covered my face with fear, sanctified myself sufficiently, knowing my unworthiness, and turned my face away—then my feet would almost have stumbled, my steps well nigh slipped."[171] Ramah's two surviving statements on the *Guide* are contradictory. In his letter to Nahmanides, written during the 1230s, Ramah's attitude is akin to that of his brother. But in his poetic eulogy on the death of Maimonides, Ramah had given high and un-

qualified praise to the *Guide*.[172] The more than a quarter-century sep-
arating these conflicting appraisals is not quite as helpful as might
seem; for in his letter to Nahmanides, Ramah is describing his critical
conclusion to a study undertaken "when this book [the *Guide*] reached
me."[173]

Brody, who first published Ramah's eulogy, noticed this contradiction and suggested the following chronological solution: Ramah received the *Guide* shortly before Maimonides' death. An incomplete
reading impressed him, whence the glowing praise in his eulogy. But
further study soon changed his opinion to that expressed in his letter to
Nahmanides.[174]

Without denying that Ramah's mistrust of the *Guide* may have increased in the years following Maimonides' death, one suspects that
there is a further explanation for his conflicting appraisals. When eulo-
gizing "the great master" it was both natural and appropriate for
Ramah to give expression to his most positive sentiments. In espousing
the anti-rationalist cause, Ramah expresses his deep reservations; yet
even here he shows painful ambivalence.

Following is the difficult but suggestive passage on the *Guide* from
Ramah's letter to Nahmanides:

> And as for me, when this book [the *Guide*] reached me, I made
> bold to traverse its sections, moving back and forth through its
> various gates[175] in order to search out and taste its flavor upon my
> palate, so that I might know whether to partake of its bread.[176] And
> when I looked, behold, its [the *Guide's*] shoot strengthens the roots
> of religion but lops off its branches,[177] repairs the breaches of its
> foundations but breaks down its fences. The exaltation of God is in
> its throat, but both death and life are upon its tongue; once it turns
> to the left, another time to the right; it accepts with the left hand
> and rejects with the right. And I realized that there was perverse-
> ness in its midst; none who have contact with it will remain unsul-
> lied. So I removed my way far from it. But I have not allowed my
> mouth to sin against the great master who lightens my darkness,
> who has sown the light of his *Mishneh Torah* over the very edges of
> oblivion, planting therein trees of knowledge and wisdom. For
> who knows, perhaps the author of that book [the *Guide*], who has
> sealed it, was of a different spirit?[178]

A litany of conflicts and contradictions is the rhetorical device by
which Ramah characterizes the *Guide*. Though making allusive use of
phrases from Proverbs classically associated with heresy,[179] he remains
inexplicit. That Ramah feels impelled to suspect a man whom he so ad-
mires appears to be a source of deep pain. And his last word on the

subject suggests that the *Guide*—obscure book that it is—is perhaps not guilty of heterodox teaching, after all.[180]

What precisely was it that troubled Ramah about the *Guide?* What were his doubts and suspicions? Ramah does not tell us; for he will "not allow [his] mouth to sin against the great master who lightens [his] darkness." The historian's curiosity remains unsatisfied; but he can hardly begrudge Ramah his silence.

VI

ANTI-RATIONALISM
AND MYSTICISM

RAMAH'S MATURE YEARS saw two developments that shaped subsequent Hispano-Jewish controversy over rationalism. The first was the consolidation of Spanish rationalism under the banner of Maimonides. Of this development, Ramah took regretful notice. But an equally momentous development goes unmentioned in his surviving writings—the arrival and impact of kabbalah.[1] Soon after reaching Spain from Provence at the turn of the twelfth century, kabbalah's longstanding tradition of esotericism began to crumble.[2] Kabbalah spread with remarkable rapidity and gained important adherents among Spain's Jewish leadership. Such extraordinary impact suggests an extraordinary receptivity.[3]

The period in which kabbalah came upon the Spanish scene was one of disequilibrium and spiritual crisis. Ramah defined some of its central problems: the correct interpretation of classical texts; the relationship of the natural and divine economies; the quest for spirituality and its relationship to halakah and eschatology; the search for the secrets of the Torah and the universe. Maimonidean rationalism represented a distinctive and forceful response to these questions, but one that increasingly came to be viewed as dangerous and destructive by important elements of Spanish Jewry's intellectual and communal leadership. Meanwhile the first generation of Spanish kabbalists had begun to show that kabbalah could offer a different response to this same set of questions. Many members of the Hispano-Jewish elite found that response not only more satisfying spiritually, but also more in consonance with their conservative impulse. The perception of kabbalah as a native rival of rationalism that could claim true authority and check rationalistic corrosion and corruption led naturally to a link between kabbalah and anti-rationalism. A partial alliance is already evident during the Maimonidean Controversy.[4]

Ramah's anti-rationalism, strong Provençal connections, and friendship with Nahmanides naturally raise the question of his relationship to kabbalah. A generation after Ramah's death, a tradition linking him with kabbalah is reported by his nephew, the kabbalist Todros b. Joseph Abulafia:

> I have heard it said of my uncle, R. Meir Halevi of blessed memory, that he used to issue many warnings not to gaze at the moon, just as our rabbis of blessed memory warned not to gaze at the rainbow (*Hagigah*, 16a). And happy is he and happy his portion *for he was privileged to receive the perfect Torah and internal hidden wisdom.* Woe unto the generation from which his glory was taken! And woe unto me—for the only Torah that I was privileged to study with him was the chapter "He who gathers sheep . . ." (*Baba Qamma*, chap. 6) when I was about ten years old. Blessed be the Omnipresent who granted that I see the beauty of his face in his old age. And he laid his two hands upon me and blessed me with the threefold benediction (Num. 6:24-26). [It is] that very [benediction] which has stood me in stead even unto old age and gray hair.[5]

Though unmistakably authentic in conveying his youthful impressions of a venerable uncle, R. Todros' testimony on Ramah's "internal hidden wisdom" must be treated cautiously. As a boy, R. Todros studied a little Talmud or Mishnah with Ramah—not kabbalah. Todros never quotes Ramah in his kabbalistic works. His information on Ramah's kabbalah seems to be secondhand. The report that Ramah based a normative decision (prohibiting gazing at the moon) on presumably kabbalistic considerations and propagated it through repeated warnings inspires further skepticism.[6] Moreover, other important figures—even Maimonides—were claimed by legend for kabbalah.[7] R. Todros' testimony must therefore be examined against the evidence of Ramah's writings.[8]

I would venture to say that there is only one comment in Ramah's surviving writings that probably reflects kabbalistic influence. It deals with the talmudic aggadah that God made a secret tunnel so that a repentant Manasseh could be smuggled up unnoticed by the Attribute of Justice. Ramah, we recall, refused even to quote Rashi's literal interpretation "because it contains unfitting statements concerning Heaven." Instead he explained the passage as a figurative way of saying that God graciously accepted Manasseh's repentance though it ought not, in strict justice, to have been accepted.[9] But, Ramah adds, "there is another explanation (*pitron*) of the matter. [Namely] that this attribute (*middah*) which was designated to accept Manasseh in repentance is a profound one and is 'hidden from the eyes of all living.' And it is unknown to the Attribute of Justice, like someone who tunnels [under a house], working secretly so that the householder does not know where he entered from."[10] The notion that one divine attribute is more profound and hidden than another seems neither philosophical nor midrashic in inspiration. It may well be kabbalistic in origin. For example, Binah, the *sefirah* associated with repentance, could easily be considered more profound and hidden than Justice.[11] Description of this attribute as "hidden from the eyes of all living" (Job 28:21) may reflect an awareness of early kabbalistic exegesis of Job 28.[12] Ramah, attempting in good geonic-Andalusian fashion to interpret aggadic anthropomorphism figuratively, may have mentioned an explanation suggested by kabbalah. If this is correct, then Ramah was in contact with kabbalists and acquainted with their ideas.[13]

But despite this probable adaptation, Ramah almost certainly did not accept the central kabbalistic doctrine of the *sefirot*—at least not in its usual sense.[14] Although he nowhere discusses this question, there is a basic element in the doctrine of the *sefirot* that Ramah can be shown to deny. Kabbalists identified the biblical Kabod and the rabbinic Shekinah with the last of the *sefirot*, Malkut.[15] So fundamental is this identification that the usual geonic-Andalusian interpretation of Shekinah and Kabod as a luminous "creature, distinct from the glorious Name, blessed be He" elicits an exoteric "Heaven forbid" from Nahmanides.[16] But Ramah's colleague, Judah Alfakar, emphatically identified this interpretation with the position of classical Judaism.[17] And it appears certain that Ramah too stood, quite characteristically, within the geonic-Andalusian tradition on Shekinah and Kabod.[18] Although he may have made ad hoc use of a kabbalistic notion in order to remove aggadic anthropomorphism, his own doctrine of God's unity and attributes remained essentially Andalusian.[19]

There are other passages of Ramah's aggadic exegesis that would seem very strange coming from the pen of a kabbalist. "No kabbalist was ever embarrassed . . . by an old aggadah; in particular those aggadahs which were anathema to 'enlightened' Jews were enthusiastically hailed by the kabbalists as symbols of their own interpretation of the universe."[20] Ramah, on the other hand, not only fails to expound or even allude to the secret sense of such *aggadot;* he can even confess the "doubts and perplexity" aroused by a difficult aggadah as part of his "obligation to the truth."[21] The particular aggadic notion that occasioned this confession is that of the "heavenly Jerusalem." Among kabbalists it is associated with the last of the *sefirot*, Malkut.[22] If this interpretation was known to Ramah, it did nothing to alleviate his perplexity.

There are sometimes suggestive links between classical aggadah and medieval kabbalistic ideas. These provide a further test of Ramah's commitment to kabbalah. If we find Ramah not just ignoring such a link but straining to sever it, exegetically, the hypothesis that he was a kabbalist is further damaged. Even the strictest esotericism cannot make sense of a kabbalist unnecessarily blowing up bridges between kabbalah and the classical tradition. Consider, for example, the following talmudic passage: "Whoever occupies himself with the Torah for its own sake causes peace to reign in the heavenly *familia* and the *familia* [that is, servants] here below."[23] This passage is suggestive of the mystical activism so characteristic of kabbalah[24] and was, in fact, seized upon by kabbalists.[25] Following, however, is Ramah's comment on this passage: "[He] causes peace to reign . . . in the heavenly *familia*, for their pleasure (*nahat ruah*) is done in that they are not obliged to punish him."[26] The point of this explanation is to *avoid* the notion, fundamental to kabbalah, that human action can serve as an efficient cause of cosmic harmony.

A similar tendency is evident in Ramah's exegetical neutralization of the mystical possibilities in *Abot* 3:14: "Beloved are Israel for to them was given the precious instrument through which the world was created. [Still] greater love [is theirs in that] it was made known to them that to them was given the precious instrument through which the world was created, as it is written: 'For I have given you good doctrine (*lekah tob*); do not forsake my Torah' (Prov. 4:2)." This aggadic view of the preexistent Torah as the instrument of Creation serves as a springboard for the kabbalistic view of the Torah as "the concentrated power of God himself."[27] Ramah exerts considerable exegetical effort in pointing the passage in the opposite direction:

> The precious instrument through which the world was created is the good, as it is written: "And God saw all that He had made and behold it was very good" (Gen. 1:31). For God brought all that exists into existence only because he saw that there is good in its existence. And this [good] consists of worship and love of the Omnipresent, as it is written: "Everything called by my name, for my glory have I created it, formed it and made it" (Isa. 43:7). This is the final purpose for which the world was created. And it is well known that the principles and particulars of the Torah, from beginning to end, come only to command worship of the Omnipresent. Thus the Torah brings about worship of the Omnipresent and worship of the Omnipresent brings about the creation of the world. Therefore the Torah is called "knowledge of the good" (*leqah tob*)—that is to say [knowledge of] the thing for which the world was created, the very [good] concerning which it is written in the account of the creation: "And God saw that it was good"

(Gen. 1:12). And because that good was the cause of the creation of the world it follows that that good was, in the creation of the world, like an instrument in the hands of the Creator.[28]

For Ramah, there is no real instrument of Creation. The Creator "says and it's done, all without toil or act, without instrument."[29] His monotheistic razor would allow nothing to come between divine will and deed. The "instrument" of Creation refers figuratively to its purpose, the good—worship and love of God. Painstakingly stripped of any cosmic significance and interpreted on a purely moral plane, the passage's mystical potential is defused and implicitly denied.[30]

These comments probably date from the first decade of the thirteenth century.[31] An about-face in subsequent years appears unlikely in light of Ramah's introduction to *Masoret Seyag la-Torah*, composed in 1227.[32] Only occasionally, reports Ramah, could his "intellect succeed in finding a correct *explanation*" for *plene* and defective spellings. The phenomenon, he thinks, is currently unexplainable: "For who can find a reason for every *plene* and defective [spelling] except those who follow in the footsteps of the ancient *midrashot* which are far from us on account of our sins."[33] Conspicuously absent is the explanation prominently advanced by contemporary Spanish kabbalists, that there is a mystical reading of the Torah which makes accuracy of defective and *plene* spellings meaningful and crucial.[34] Even talmudic sources that point in this direction are ignored.[35]

For Ramah, in 1227, the unsolved problem of Masoretic fine points is just part of a more general ignorance of the secrets of the Torah. "Who among us is greater than David . . . and many secrets of the Torah were far from him, as he said: 'Open my eyes so that I may see what is far from me in your Torah' (Ps. 119:18). How much more so we, whose lives are cut off in the pit of Exile; and we have tasted naught but the bread of idleness; and the wisdom of our wise men has perished and the discernment of our discerning men has been hidden—until a spirit of knowledge and fear of the Lord shall be poured upon us from on high."[36] There's no shame, Ramah implies, in admitting ignorance of the Torah's secrets: it occurred even among the best of men in the best of times; little chance then of these secrets being revealed in Ramah's own dark days—the very birth hour of Spanish kabbalah!

Ramah's frankly confessed ignorance of secret wisdom is consistent with the temper and style of his anti-rationalism. Based in a geonic-Andalusian tradition of conservatism, Ramah viewed rationalism as a danger to *qabbalah peshutah* (broadly accepted tradition).[37] For kabbalistic anti-rationalists it was also a usurper, claiming for itself what rightfully belongs to the esoteric *qabbalah*, the "secrets of the Torah." No kabbalist would have followed Maimonides in using classical Merkabah terminology to describe philosophy.[38] Ramah and Judah Alfakar do—rhetorically, at least;[39] and for Ramah's brother, Joseph b. Todros, the identification seems substantive.[40] Ramah criticized rationalism not for arrogating title to the Torah's secrets but for seeking after ultimate secrets in the first place.[41]

Ramah's anti-rationalism thus differs from that of kabbalists like Nahmanides. Occasionally, we have seen, his aggadic exegesis can even read like rationalistic antikabbalism.[42] In Chapter 5 we saw how Ramah's differences with French anti-rationalism stem from his rootedness in the geonic-Andalusian tradition. The same is true with regard to his distance from kabbalah: Ramah's apparent innocence of mysticism and his uncompromisingly antimythic religious sensibility are characteristic of his hero, Saadya, and the entire geonic-Andalusian tradition.

The differences between Spanish and French anti-rationalism were primarily a product of geocultural division. In part, the split over kabbalah within Spanish anti-rationalism was also geocultural. Kabbalah gained influential adherents in Catalonia somewhat earlier than in Castile.[43] In the controversy of the 1230s, kabbalistic anti-rationalism seems to have been restricted to Catalonia. This lag reflects both the proximity of Catalonia to kabbalah's Provençal roots and the tenacity of Andalusian cultural patterns among the Castilian aristocracy.

But within a generation after Ramah's death, the diffusion of kabbalah in Spain seems to have been fairly uniform. And yet nonkabbalistic anti-rationalism remained important.[44] Ramah's stance thus represents more than a vestige of Andalusia; it points also to a lasting internal division within Spanish anti-rationalism.

When we place Ramah next to a "typical" rationalist and a "typical" kabbalist, Ramah's position in the resulting triad seems one of cautiously conservative minimalism: he shares much of the kabbalist's criticism of rationalism and apparently also much of the rationalist's criticism of kabbalah. Moreover, fundamental tendencies common to both rationalism and kabbalah remain alien to Ramah. Often, Spanish rationalism and kabbalah provide opposing yet parallel responses to the same set of problems.[45] The "hidden love" that unite them—despite "open rebuke"[46]—emerges boldly when both are juxtaposed to Ramah. This convergence serves, at the same time, to emphasize the particular character of Ramah's anti-rationalism and the extent to which it represents a denial of powerful historical impulses.

Ramah's conservatism is evident in his approach to aggadic exegesis. Ramah shared with his Spanish contemporaries a perception of the plain sense of classical texts as, at times, problematic. His approach to these problems was closer, in important respects, to rationalism than to kabbalah. Drawing on standard geonic-Andalusian methods, he may rationalize some *aggadot* a bit, deny the authority of others, regard some as dreams and others as "responses to a fool."[47] But his exegetical energies are still most heavily invested in a search for the plain sense of the text. He *never* views aggadah as communicating profound secrets to an elite.[48] In this respect, his approach contrasts with both Maimonidean rationalism and kabbalah. Kabbalistic interpretation of aggadah was a preoccupation of Spanish kabbalah from its start.[49] A parallel program for finding philosophical teachings in aggadah, though actually executed only in a few instances, is fully articulated in Maimonides' writings.[50] Ramah, on the other hand, as a nonkabbalistic anti-rationalist, could not find the secrets of the Torah in aggadah for the simple reason that he did not claim to know them.[51]

Maimonides' version of the secrets of the Torah is closely related to the laws of nature—much too closely, Ramah thought. The problem of nature—its boundaries and its relationship to religious phenomena—is crucial to the controversy over rationalism.[52] Here kabbalah and rationalism might seem diametrically opposed. Thus Nahmanides appears hostile to the very idea of nature: "A man has no portion in the Torah of Moses our Teacher unless he believes that all the things that happen to us are miracles—none of them are [determined by] nature."[53] In fact, the matter is a bit more complex. Nahmanides not only has a conception of nature, he assigns it a significant role in his religious system.[54]

It is instructive to compare Nahmanides to Ramah on the issue of eschatological naturalism. Ramah saw rigorous naturalism as the fundamental problem with Maimonidean eschatology;[55] but Nahmanides accepted the view that immortality is a natural phenomenon.[56] The following formulation seems almost Maimonidean: "[King] Solomon wished to establish [in Ecclesiastes] that a man ought not say that the world is passing [and] without permanence and hence there is no purpose in the Creation . . . no merit or guilt. For this reason [Solomon] mentioned that its genera are permanent and its Creator created it [that is, Creation] for a great permanence. For Wisdom inheres in its genera. And should a man gain wisdom of them, his wisdom will be everlasting. And this is immortality of the soul through Wisdom."[57]

Nahmanides stresses that, although immortality is natural, Providence remains miraculous.[58] But on this point a later kabbalist, Meir ibn Gabbai, takes him to task for fundamental inconsistency:

> In [Nahmanides'] opinion, the prosperity and success promised in the Torah do not follow [directly] upon the [performance of] *mizvot* nor are they rendered necessary by them at all. Thus there is no [causal] relationship between the performance of *mizvot* and, [for example] . . . the falling of rain when the land is parched . . . The

fact that all this happens after [the performance of] *mizvot* [Nahmanides] rather views as occurring like a miracle—the *mizvot* not being their cause at all. But from his hints concerning the secrets of the Torah, in accordance with his tradition [*qabbalah*]—as interpreted by his students who received from him . . .—the opposite appears to be the case, and is, in fact, the truth. Namely, that the upper worlds are blessed through the arousal of those below—by their worship—whence blessing flows to causal agents. For one who understands the Truth, this cannot be said to occur in the manner of a miracle. It is rather that the nature of worship makes it necessary.[59]

Ibn Gabbai goes on to suggest that Nahmanides' denial of natural providence is merely an exoteric stance, whereas his true and contrary opinion is expressed in his kabbalistic teachings.[60]

Though himself an arch-representative of kabbalistic anti-rationalism, Ibn Gabbai's remarks suggest an unintended parallel between the kabbalistic and rationalistic secrets of the Torah. Although the kabbalist's "nature" is quite different from its rationalistic counterpart, both view the entire cosmos—the spiritual realm included—as bound up in a causal network that operates with lawlike necessity. Indeed, Ibn Gabbai sees the greater range of kabbalah's causality as a mark of its theoretical superiority to Maimonidean rationalism.[61] Ramah rejected Maimonides' eschatological naturalism in favor of free divine judgment. He also avoided, exegetically, the kind of causal nexus between lower and upper worlds fundamental to kabbalah. As a nonkabbalistic anti-rationalist, he tends to separate between the natural and spiritual realms, leaving the latter to divine will and judgment. Ramah did not have a comprehensive science of the divine; nor did he seem to want one.

For both rationalist and kabbalist the "divine science" plays a central and structuring role in the pursuit of spirituality. It is, in fact, possible to view rationalism and kabbalah as parallel programs for the preservation of spirituality in halakic Judaism. Both assign primacy to ethical-theological disciplines over legal dialectic. And both stress "duties of the heart" while attempting to infuse "the duties of the limbs" with spiritual significance.[62]

Ramah pointed out, in connection with the Resurrection Controversy, that rationalistic spirituality could translate theologically into a sharp body-soul dualism and a denial of physical resurrection.[63] Kabbalists seem much more conservative on this score.[64] Nahmanides' classic statement of eschatology in his *Sha'ar ha-Gemul* attempts a complex combination of mystical spirituality and anti-rationalistic traditionalism.[65] But there may be an early kabbalistic parallel to the radical

spirituality of Sheshet Benveniste that predates kabbalah's consciousness of anti-rationalistic mission. In an epistle to Burgos, R. Azriel of
Gerona describes the ascent of the soul as follows:

> When the soul leaves this world, namely the world of bodies . . . it
> goes to the world of souls . . . and from the world of souls, it as-
> cends to the world of spirits . . . and from the world of spirits, the
> souls ascend to the world of life . . . And whoever is not worthy of
> long life in the world of life and deserves to receive measure for
> measure in the world of bodies comes back through resurrection
> (tehiyyat ha-metim). That is why it says "and many of those who
> sleep in the dust of the earth shall awake" (Dan. 12:12) and it does
> not say "and all." And whoever is worthy of long life in the world
> of life has no interruption [in his incorporeal existence] for ever
> and all eternity.[66]

This negative interpretation of tehiyyat ha-metim is in a way even more
radical than the interpretation of Sheshet Benveniste. Sheshet took tehiyyat ha-metim as a metaphor for immortality of the soul.[67] R. Azriel
took it literally (that is, physically), but as a punishment—apparently
identified with gilgul (transmigration)![68] These two interpretations may
seem far apart; but both serve the same function—to preserve a purely
spiritual state from descent into the corporeal.[69] Kabbalistic spirituality
could thus pull in the same direction as its rationalistic counterpart.

Ramah understood the relationship of rationalism to spirituality. He
even attributed rationalistic antinomianism to excessive spirituality
rather than self-serving hedonism.[70] But Ramah's own refusal to sur-
render traditional ground to spirituality does not mean that it held no
attraction for him—to the contrary. Ramah may insist, on the basis of
tradition, that 'olam ha-ba is to be experienced by the reunited body and
soul; but he, no less than Maimonides, stresses the purely spiritual nature of its reward. He is as insistent as any rationalist that the aggadic
feasts of 'olam ha-ba are metaphors for spiritual perception.[71] Moreover,
Ramah rejected the notion of material reward for Torah in this world as
well as the next. He is thus at one with Maimonides in denying the legitimacy of professionalized scholarship as an unacceptable compromise with the demands of spirituality.[72]

The very fragmentary remains of Ramah's commentary to Abot indicate that he borrowed the framework and basic principles of his ethics
from Maimonides: the sphere of inner moral qualities (de'ot) as a universe of discourse distinct from the norms of action;[73] the rule of the
mean as one of its governing principles;[74] "let all your deeds be for the
sake of Heaven" as another overarching principle;[75] the superiority of
virtue that stems from an internal state to mere self-control;[76] the pursuit of disinterested service of God motivated by love.[77] Ramah thus

shared Maimonides' stress on inner character and purity of motivation. But his borrowing is selective, as in the following variation on a Maimonidean interpretation:

> This form (*zelem*) [of God, in which man is created] does not refer to the form of the body either in the Torah or in our *mishnah* (*Abot*, 3:14) . . . but to the form of the intellect through which a man apprehends truths. And concerning this it was said: "For in the form of God made He man" (Gen. 9:6). And why all this [stress on man being made in God's form]? To tell you how much a man ought to thank his Creator for the kindness He has shown him in causing him to have this perfect [form of] existence . . . And so that he will pursue correct opinions (*ha-de'ot ha-nekonot*) in order to preserve the form of intellect graciously granted him by the Omnipresent, that it be pure and free of blemish. And Solomon already said in his wisdom: "Fear God and keep his commandments" (Eccles. 12:13).[78]

Along with Maimonides' interpretation of Genesis 1:27 has come some of his intellectualistic spirituality.[79] But absent in Ramah's formulation is any hint of a salvational role for knowledge or even its association with philosophy. And in "the end of the matter," Ramah, as if recoiling from the implication that all but reason might be "vanity," reasserts the more integrative image of "the whole of man" at the end of Ecclesiastes—"fear God and keep his commandments."[80] As a nonkabbalistic anti-rationalist, his spirituality was focused on the cultivation of exoteric religious experience. While drawing inspiration from Maimonidean spirituality, he sought to moderate it and to disengage it from soteriology and the quest for cosmic wisdom.[81]

Ramah would doubtless have liked a reliable source of theological wisdom. When Aaron b. Meshullam rebuked him for not "searching out and investigating the matter [of *'olam ha-ba*] from an elder and master, 'a man of understanding (*maskil*) who seeks after God,'" he responded: "Would that I knew where to find him!"[82] This is not, however, the fervent wish of a potential believer. Ramah reminds Aaron that (according to Ps. 14:2-3) the Almighty himself could not find a single "man of understanding who seeks after God." Aaron's allusion to "wonderful secrets that are covered and concealed from many wise men but revealed to the pure-hearted *maskilim*" evokes annoyed sarcasm: "My brother, keep what you've got to yourself; what's mine is mine and what's yours is yours; let them be yours alone and not for strangers with you; and let the thunder stop and the hail and rain cease pouring earthward."[83]

This desire "to seek after great things," Ramah thought, was part of the allure of philosophical speculation. In counseling self-denial, he al-

ludes to the famous advice of Ben Sira: "... you've no concern with
hidden things."[84] Nahmanides, in the introduction to his *Commentary on
the Torah*, can quote the same advice to would-be kabbalists.[85] But
Nahmanides is warning the noninitiate against independent speculation on kabbalistic hints that he himself has nevertheless placed in his
commentary. Implicit is an invitation to share these secrets by seeking
out a qualified master.[86] Ramah's formulation uses the first person plu-
ral: "We must interpret ... in accordance with what we have received
from our fathers and teachers and the tradition spread throughout Israel ... and not ... seek after hidden things, that belong to the Lord our
God and are none of our concern, to know their what and their wherefore."[87]

There is a striking parallel to this passage in one of Ramah's poems.
Ramah links the search for hidden wisdom to the primeval temptation
of the Tree of Knowledge. The following warning is addressed to an
obviously paradigmatic Adam:

Cast behind your back the search for profundities
Busy yourself not with what is too great for you
Incline your ear to the King's commands
Bind them upon your heart always.[88]

Both Maimonidean rationalism and kabbalah represent a different
religious sensibility. Their parallel tendencies—the pursuit of new
depths in classical texts, the quest for an all-embracing "natural" order,
and the search for spirituality—all converged in an educational-con-
templative ideal that set knowledge of "divine science" as its highest
goal. That knowledge was a supreme religious value, the deepest
meaning of the Torah, a key to the cosmic plan, the truest form of
spirituality, and a "natural" source of salvation. This complex of ideas
was foreign, perhaps distasteful, to Ramah. In an age of widespread
conversion to both Maimonidean rationalism and kabbalah, he remained rooted in geonic-Andalusian conservatism.

Ramah's denial of so powerful a historical impulse may seem an inherently unstable posture. And we can never really disprove the possibility that, in his last years, Ramah became a kabbalist. But even if—as I
believe likely—he did not, Ramah was more than a fossil left behind by
the flow of intellectual history. For his urbane traditionalism remained
an alternative to both rationalism and kabbalah. Figures like Judah Alfakar, Abba Mari of Lunel, Nissim Gerondi, Isaac b. Sheshet Perfet,
Hasdai Crescas, Isaac Arama, and Isaac Abarbanel illustrate its continuing significance. Even less than rationalism or kabbalah is this traditionalism a pure, uniform, or static type; but its representatives fit a
rough common profile: broad learning, conservative sensibility, exo-

teric spirituality, a tendency to disengage religion from nature, cautiously selective use of the esoteric sciences, and reluctance to enthrone theoretical knowledge or wholeheartedly embrace a contemplative ideal. These nonkabbalistic anti-rationalists were not timid, colorless, or narrow. Their determination to deny themselves the greatest of medieval passions is not without a touch of the heroic.[89]

NOTES

I. Islam to Christendom

1. For the twelfth century as a turning point in Jewish history, see H. H. Ben-Sasson, "Jewish Reflections on Nationhood in the Twelfth Century" (Heb.), in *Peraqim*, II, ed. E. S. Rosenthal (Jerusalem, 1974), pp. 145–218. There was an important though temporary eastward shift in the center of gravity of Jewish life in the sixteenth century.

2. On these developments see Yitzhak Baer, *A History of the Jews in Christian Spain*, trans. L. Schoffman (Philadelphia, 1961), I, 46–96. For a history of the Christian Reconquest and Muslim resistance, see D. Lomax, *The Reconquest of Spain* (London, 1978), pp. 49–156. For a general synthesis of Spanish history during the Reconquista, see A. MacKay, *Spain in the Middle Ages* (London, 1977), pp. 1–117.

3. On Toledo, see E. Ashtor, *Qorot ha-Yehudim be-Sefarad ha-Muslamit* (Jerusalem, 1966), II, 325–334.

4. See Baer, *History*, I, 59–65.

5. At mid-century, Judah Halevi and Joseph ibn Megash had just died, Abraham ibn Ezra and Abraham ibn Daud had reached maturity, and Maimonides was a teenage prodigy. There would seem then to be no lack of internal momentum in Hispano-Jewish culture.

6. See Abraham Halkin, "Le-Toledot ha-Shemad Bimay ha-al-Muwahhidun," *Joshua Starr Memorial Volume* (New York, 1953), pp. 101–110; D. Corcos, "Le-Ofi Yahasam shel Shelite ha-al-Muwahhidun Lihudim," *Zion* 32 (1967): 135–60.

7. *Sefer ha-Qabbalah*, trans. and ed. G. Cohen (Philadelphia, 1967), pp. 37–38, 96–99.

8. Ibid., p. 87; for the source of this expression see *Yebamot*, 62b; cf. Cohen's note to *Sefer ha-Qabbalah*, p. 87.

9. For a description of Ibn Daud's world, see Cohen, *Sefer ha-Qabbalah*, pp. xvi–xxv.

10. Ibid., p. 99. Of course, Ibn Daud's perceptions do not do complete justice to the complexities of historical reality. First, Jewish history in pre-Almohade Christian Spain was not quite so insignificant. A poem by Judah Halevi gives a more balanced perception: *galut zion asher be-sefarad be-'arab mefuzzar ube-edom meforad* (*Dīwān*, ed. H. Brody, III [Berlin, 1910], p. 172). Second, not everyone moved from Muslim to Christian Spain. Some, like Maimonides' fam-

ily and Joseph ibn Aqnin, stayed within the Islamic world. Others remained behind in Andalusia; see, e.g., Baer, *History*, I, 113–114. Still others, like Judah ibn Tibbon, Joseph Kimhi, and Solomon ibn Parhon, moved to southern France or Italy.

11. See Cohen, *Sefer ha-Qabbalah*, pp. xxvi–xxviii, 88, 97–99.

12. Judah Alharizi, *Tahkemoni*, ed. Y. Toporofsky (Tel Aviv, 1952), p. 345.

13. *Ha-Shirah ha-'Ibrit be-Sefarad ube-Provence*, ed. Hayyim Schirmann (Jerusalem, 1961), I, 487, l. 31; see Baer, *History*, I, 67–77.

14. Alharizi, *Tahkemoni*, p. 345.

15. See Cohen, *Sefer ha-Qabbalah*, pp. xxvi–xxvii.

16. Cf. too the contemporary impressions of E. Ashtor, *Qorot ha-Yehudim be-Sefarad ha-Muslamit* (Jerusalem, 1966), I, 211. Poetic identification of Toledo with Jerusalem implies no abandonment of Messianic hopes on Alharizi's part. Judah Halevi, after all, did the same with a pretty girl! See Schirmann, *Ha-Shirah ha-'Ibrit*, I, 434, l. 6, playing on Psalm 137:5. In fact, pilgrimage to Palestine was among the reasons Alharizi left Spain for the East; and he describes his journey in a style indebted to Halevi; see Schirmann, ibid., II, 99. For Alharizi's concern "that the nations and princes may be shown her beauty" (Esther 1:11), cf. Isadore Twersky, "Aspects of the Social and Cultural History of Provençal Jewry," *Journal of World History* 11 (1968): 190, 204–205. Note that Alharizi is concerned with the political and aesthetic as well as the intellectual image of the Jews. Alharizi's use of Esther 1:11 may have been suggested by Maimonides' letter to R. Jonathan ha-Kohen of Lunel; see *Teshubot ha-Rambam*, ed. J. Blau, III (Jerusalem, 1961), p. 57.

Alharizi also describes Sefarad as "the garden of God" (*Tahkemoni*, p. 3); see Ezek. 31:8–9. This reflects the Arabic image of Andalusia as Paradise; see T. Glick, *Islamic and Christian Spain in the Early Middle Ages* (Princeton, 1979), pp. 53–54. But Alharizi has significantly applied this image to all of Spain. Contrast the harsh landscape perceptions of Moses ibn Ezra in Christian Spain a century earlier; see Baer, *History*, I, 59–64; D. Pagis, *Shirat ha-Hol ve-Torat ha-Shir le-Mosheh ibn Ezra* (Jerusalem, 1970), p. 258. Ibn Ezra's wild and bleak image of Christian Spain is part of its perception as antithetical to the civilized gardens of Andalusia.

17. Alharizi, *Tahkemoni*, p. 346.

18. See Alharizi, *Tahkemoni*, pp. 348–349 and pp. 388–389; Shmuel Stern, "Rabbi Yehudah Alharizi be-Shebaho shel ha-Rambam," in *Hagut 'Ibrit be-Eropa*, ed. Menahem Zohari and Arie Tartkover (Tel Aviv, 1969), pp. 91–103; Isadore Twersky, "The Beginnings of Mishneh Torah Criticism," in *Biblical and Other Studies*, ed. Alexander Altmann (Cambridge, 1963), p. 167.

19. *Sanhedrin*, 97a and Ramah's commentary in *Hiddushe ha-Ramah 'al Maseket Sanhedrin* (New York, 1953), p. 168a (hereafter cited as *HRS*). I have checked most citations against the first edition (Salonika, 1798).

20. See, e.g., on R. Jonah Gerondi, Baer, *History*, I, 250–257; note that R. Jonah Gerondi was considered Ramah's successor in Toledo; see Menahem b. Zerah, *Zedah la-Derek* (Warsaw, 1880), p. 6.

Scattered legal sources further attest to Ramah's social and religious concerns. On Ramah's departure from a talmudic ruling on the grounds that "nowadays . . . insolence and licentiousness abound," see R. Joseph Karo, *Bet Yosef, Eben ha-'Ezer*, beginning of no. 17 (p. 30b); see too Ramah's formulation preserved by an anonymous Spanish commentator in Hebrew University MS. 4° 14, p. 141b: "If you say [that nowadays a woman who says to her husband, 'you have divorced me,' is believed] you won't have a single woman remaining with her husband." On Ramah's reaction to base, violent men who arrogate for themselves the title *nasi* (born quite legitimately by himself), see in B. Septimus, "Ma'abaq 'al Shilton Zibburi be-Barcelona be-Tequfat ha-Pulmus 'al Sifre ha-Rambam," *Tarbiz* 42 (1973): 396, n. 45. On powerful individuals who flout communal authority, see Ramah's responsum in *Or Zaddiqim* (hereafter cited as *OZ*) (Warsaw, 1902), no. 258, p. 298. On the problem of judicial and sexual misconduct among scholars and religious leaders, see Chapter 4, n. 87. The possibility that Ramah may have taken some action to bring about reforms is suggested by the report of Jonah ibn Bahlul, below, n. 77.

In comparing Alharizi to Ramah it should also be remembered that Alharizi had the benefit of instructive comparison. His *Tahkemoni* was written during his journey to the East; see Schirmann, *Ha-Shirah ha-'Ibrit*, II, 99–101. Confronted with the rapidly deteriorating situation of the Jewish communities still under Islamic rule, Alharizi's pessimism was spent on the very real decline around him.

21. Isaac Israeli, *Yesod 'Olam* (Berlin, 1848), 4:18, p. 35.

22. See Menahem b. Zerah, *Zedah la-Derek*, p. 6; Abraham b. Solomon Ardutiel, *Sefer ha-Qabbalah*, in *Medieval Jewish Chronicles*, ed. A. Neubauer (Oxford, 1887), I, 103; Abraham Zacuto, *Sefer Yuhasin*, ed. H. Filipowski, 2d ed., with an introduction by A. H. Freimann (Frankfurt, 1925), p. 220a; below, n. 48.

23. See L. Zunz, *Zur Geschichte und Literatur* (Berlin, 1845), p. 432; F. Cantera, "La judería de Burgos," *Sefarad* 12 (1952): 62; Institute of Microfilmed Hebrew Manuscripts in the Jewish National and University Library, no. 18467 (from Paris MS, 82); the name Meir for Todros' father can also be derived from Ramah's poetry; see Hayyim Brody, ed., "Shirim u-Miktabim mi-Rabbi Meir Halevi Abulafia," *Yedi'ot ha-Makon le-Heqer ha-Shirah ha-'Ibrit* 2 (1936): 4. Brody's excellent edition of Ramah's surviving poetry is preceded by a brief but very useful biographical-genealogical introduction.

24. On this name see M. Steinschneider, "An Introduction to the Arabic Literature of the Jews," *Jewish Quarterly Review* 11 (1899): 488.

25. See Brody, "Shirim," p. 5; Chapter 2, n. 27.

26. Brody, "Shirim," p. 5. R. Zerahyah was murdered, possibly in Toledo, in 1215. Ramah's beautiful letter of condolence to his cousin R. Todros reveals little about the circumstances of his death. R. Zerahyah is eulogized as "the most glorious of the princes of Israel . . . a faithful shepherd who reigned over the holy people, a counselor and teacher, who sought the good of his people and placed a spirit of peace upon them, who rescued those condemned to die and even offered his life as ransom for them to save their lives from death." Ramah concludes with the prayer that R. Zerahyah's blood be avenged and exhorts his cousins to take courage "lest the hands of your enemies be strengthened"; see Brody, "Shirim," pp. 83–85; Y. Baer, *Toledot ya-Yehudim be-Sefarad ha-Nozrit* (Tel Aviv, 1965), p. 482, n. 36. I wonder whether the old manuscript of

Mishneh Torah that R. Menahem de Lonzano reports had belonged to "R. Zerahyah ha-Levi" did not belong to this uncle of Ramah. This assumption would solve a difficult chronological problem; see Y. Ta-Shema, "Zemanim u-Meqomot be-Hayyav shel R. Zerahyah," *Bar-Ilan Annual* 12 (1974): 134; S. Z. Havlin's introduction to the facsimile of *Mishneh Torah of Maimonides, Moses ben Shealtiel Edition* (Jerusalem, 1975), pp. 7, 15. Cf. also N. ha-Kohen, *Ozar ha-Gedolim*, III (Haifa, 1968), p. 209.

27. See Chapter 2, n. 17; Brody, "Shirim," p. 8, confuses Ramah's uncle and brother, both named Joseph.

28. In his letter to Ramah *Kitāb al-Rasā'il*, ed. Yehiel Brill (Paris, 1871), p. 33; on this work, see Chapter 3. I have checked citations from the printed edition against Cambridge MS Add. 1178, which is often superior to the manuscripts available to Brill.

29. Edited by S. Z. H. Halberstam in *Jeschurun*, ed. J. Kobak, VIII (1872–1875), 41.

30. See, e.g., Ibn Daud, *Sefer ha-Qabbalah*, pp. 87–88, on the Ibn Megash family; this would explain the allusion to Genesis 48:22, a reference to Joseph (ibn Megash).

31. See Schirmann, *Ha-Shirah ha-'Ibrit*, II, 67–69, 87. For more information on these poets see E. Fleischer, " 'En Mishpat," *Qiryat Sefer* 48 (1973): 329–339. Fleischer points out that the identification of the "Abraham" to whom Ibn Shabbetai dedicated his poem as Abraham Alfakar is Steinschneider's suggestion and remains conjectural. In light of the importance of Ramah's mother it is interesting that *Women's Aid* is dedicated to the wife of R. Todros. Such a dedication is unique in this period. The text implies that she will understand the poem. Moreover, the heroine of the poem is modeled after her; see D. Pagis, *Hiddush u-Masoret be-Shirat ha-Hol ha-'Ibrit* (Jerusalem, 1976), p. 220; Fleischer, "En Mishpat," p. 336; A. H. Habermann, *Shalosh Maqamot 'al ha-Nashim* (Jerusalem, 1971), pp. 32, 43–44.

32. See Baer, *History*, I. 95.

33. Judah ibn Shabbetai, *Milhemet ha-Hokmah veha-'Osher*, ed. A. M. Habermann (Jerusalem, 1952). There is a chronological problem here: *Milhemet ha-Hokmah veha-'Osher* is standardly dated 1214, but Ramah's father died in 1213; see below, n. 36. Judith Dishon, "On the Identification of Todros Halevi," *Journal of Jewish Studies* 24 (1973): 84–87, proposes the existence of a second Todros Halevi to whom Ibn Shabbetai dedicated his poem. Note, however, that the date, which appears twice in mock legal documents in this work, is designed to be read as a word (תִּתְקְעִ׳ד) which fits the rhyme scheme and may therefore be, chronologically, imprecise. The discrepancy does not seem to be sufficient grounds for postulating a second contemporary R. Todros who is a Levite and so similar to Ramah's father. I have therefore taken Ibn Shabbetai's patron, R. Todros Halevi, to be Ramah's father. But the identification remains uncertain.

34. But it would be imprudent to take Messianic language *too* seriously in light of the permissibility of extravagant hyperbole in medieval Hebrew poems of praise; see, e.g., Pagis, *Shirat ha-Hol*, pp. 154–155. Cf., however, Cohen, *Sefer ha-Qabbalah*, pp. 275–276.

35. See Solomon Grayzel, *The Church and the Jews in the Thirteenth Century* (New York, 1966), pp. 112–113.

36. Brody, "Shirim," p. 46.

37. Ibid., p. 49 in the introductory remark (to poem no. 24) by the anonymous editor of Ramah's *dīwān*. This editor's all too brief introductory notes describe the occasions on which Ramah's poems were composed; these notes are valuable in reconstructing Ramah's biography.

38. *Ozar ha-Geonim, Ketubot,* ed. B. M. Lewin (Jerusalem, 1929), I, p. 163.

39. Brody, "Shirim," p. 47.

40. Ibid., p. 51.

41. Kobak, *Jeschurun*, VIII, 41; see Baer, *History*, I. 95.

42. Cf. Brody, "Shirim," p. 2, who estimates a birth date of 1170. Ramah died in 1244. But by the turn of the century he was already a recognized scholar and confident enough to launch a major intercommunal challenge to the authority of Maimonides; see Chapter 3. I have, therefore, moved the date back a bit, to 1165. Ramah composed commentaries to most of the tractates of *Nashim* and *Neziqin*; see below, n. 152. The commentaries on *Sanhedrin, Horayot,* and *Abot* were composed in the first years of the thirteenth century; see below, n. 156; Chapter 3, n. 109. It is quite possible that Ramah commented on the tractates roughly in order. This would imply substantial literary activity before the end of the twelfth century and suggest that the estimated birthdate of 1165 is, if anything, not early enough.

43. See Baer, *History*, I, 192.

44. See Abraham b. Nathan Ha-Yarhi, *Sefer ha-Manhig,* ed. Y. Raphael (Jerusalem, 1978), II, pp. 686, 729, 727.

45. Ibid., pp. 677, 683; see too G. Sed-Rajna, "Toledo or Burgos," *Journal of Jewish Art* 2 (1975): 6–21.

45. Baer, *History*, I, 92, and *Die Juden im christlichen Spanien* (Berlin, 1936), II, 19–21; Brody, "Shirim," pp. 5, 8–9.

47. See Brody, "Shirim," p. 12; cf. ibid., p. 59.

48. See Kobak, *Jeschurun*, VIII, 45. Baer locates Todros, Meir, and Joseph Abulafia in Toledo; see his *History*, I, 91, 95, 108–109, 398, 400. But the cumulative evidence that Todros lived in Burgos, that Meir originated there, and that Joseph remained there is quite strong; see above, nn. 21 and 22; on Joseph see Frank Talmage, "David Kimhi and the Rationalist Tradition," *Hebrew Union College Annual* 39 (1968): 177; Joseph refers to his father's role in suppressing Karaism "in our region," which argues for a location of both north of Toledo; see above, n. 41. Ramah communicates with his father and brother in writing, which would have been unnecessary had they been together in Toledo; see below, n. 53. The incident surrounding R. Todros' successor (see below, n. 54) seems extremely unlikely in Toledo, where Ramah's position was quite strong. The support for the Provençal rationalist *herem* which Joseph describes in his city seems unlikely for Toledo; see Chapter 4, n. 67. Note too that Joseph communicates in writing with Judah Alfakar of Toledo; see Chapter 5, n. 140.

49. See Ramah's responsum to the scholars of Burgos, quoted by Menahem Ha-Meiri, *Qiryat Sefer,* ed. M. Hershler (Jerusalem, 1956), pp. 46–48.

50. Brody, "Shirim," pp. 36–37; Schirmann, *Ha-Shirah ha-'Ibrit*, II,

272–273. On the device of having the deceased speak and its source in Halevi's poetry, see A. Mirsky, " 'Erke ha-Shirah ha-'Ibrit be-Sefarad," *The Sephardi Heritage*, ed. R. D. Barnett I (London, 1971), 212. For closing references to resurrection in Spanish elegies, see e.g., Ibn Gabirol in Schirmann, *Ha-Shirah ha-'Ibrit*, I, 201, and the references in Pagis, *Shirat ha-Hol*, p. 219. On this poem of Ramah see I. Levin, *'Al Mavet* (Tel-Aviv, 1973), pp. 222–225.

51. Jacob b. Asher, *Tur, Yoreh De'ah*, no. 240; see G. Blidstein, *Honor Thy Father and Mother* (New York, 1975), pp. 40–41. Contrary to the claim of Graetz, there is no evidence that Ramah's relationship to his father was anything but exemplary; see H. Graetz, *Dibre Yeme Yisrael*, trans. and ed. S. P. Rabinowitz, V (Warsaw, 1897), 38, and the critical notes of A. Harkavy to that volume, p. 10.

52. Joseph ibn Sahl in *Mibhar ha-Shirah ha-Ibrit*, ed. H. Brody and M. Wiener (Leipzig, 1922), p. 152; see *Sanhedrin*, 105b.

53. *OZ*, pp. 185–186, no. 294.

54. Brody, "Shirim," p. 49. On Isaac Benveniste, see Chapter 2.

55. Ibid., the words of Ramah's medieval editor.

56. Ibid., p. 52.

57. See Chapter 4.

58. For the Jews in Toledo in the eleventh and first half of the twelfth centuries, see Ashtor, *Sefarad ha-Muslamit*, I, 211ff. and II, 137–143, 325–334; Baer, *History*, I, 49–52, 60, 66–69; Joseph ibn Megash, *She'elot, u-Teshubot* (Jerusalem, 1959), pp. 34ff.; Y. Ta-Shema and H. Ben-Shammai, "Shemonah Teshubot Hadashot le-Rabbenu Yosef ibn Megash," *Kobez 'al Yad* (new series), 8 (1975): 167–185. For a general survey of Toledo in the years following its reconquest that attempts to examine the transition from a Muslim to a Christian society, see R. Pastor de Togneri, *Del Islam al Cristianismo* (Barcelona, 1975), pp. 87–128.

59. Zacuto, *Sefer Yuhasin*, p. 221b.

60. See Baer, *History*, I, 418–419.

61. Alharizi, *Tahkemoni*, p. 346; see B. Z. Dinur, *Yisrael ba-Golah*, vol. II, bk. II (Jerusalem, 1966), 179, n. 93.

62. Alharizi, *Tahkemoni*, pp. 345–346.

63. See Ha-Yarhi, *Sefer ha-Manhig*, I, 153; F. Cantera Burgos, *Sinagogas españolas* (Madrid, 1955), pp. 42–45, 56–64; Cantera Burgos, "La Sinagoga," in *Simposio Toledo judaico* (Toledo, 1973), I, 22–23; Ashtor, *Sefarad ha-Muslamit*, II, 268–269, 412–413. The standard for "peerless beauty" in this period is still Arabic; see too Sed-Rajna, n. 45 above.

64. *Yad Ramah, Baba Batra* (Warsaw, 1887), 1:87 (hereafter cited as *YRB*).

65. Baer, *History*, I, 79.

66. See ibid., pp. 47–49, 79–80, 89. Baer's *History* seems to me to contain a properly balanced presentation of the development of Jewish-Christian relations in medieval Spain. The conception of *convivencia* developed by A. Castro, *The Spaniards* (Berkeley, 1971), pp. 509–585 and passim, may be useful in underscoring the Arabic and Jewish impact on medieval Hispanic culture and the unique relationship between Spanish kings and Jewish courtiers; but it tends to

suggest a static and exaggerated picture of Jewish security and power. T. Glick in his sensible critique of the theories of Castro and Sánchez-Albornoz (*Islamic and Christian Spain*, pp. 6–15, 165–166, 290–299, 314–316, and passim) rightly emphasizes that cultural diffusion and ethnic conflict are not mutually exclusive.

The beginning of the thirteenth century marks a hardening of the Church's position toward the Jews that found expression in the decisions of the Fourth Lateran Council in 1215. The Hispano-Jewish aristocracy understood the implications of these developments. Little more than a year after his correspondence with Ramah, "the great *nasi*, the prince of princes, R. Isaac Benveniste" was leading an ultimately futile attempt by the Aragonese and Provençal communities to head off the anti-Jewish measures anticipated at the forthcoming IV Lateran; see Solomon ibn Verga, *Shebet Yehudah*, ed. A. Shohet (Jerusalem, 1947), p. 147; Grayzel, *The Church and the Jews*, pp. 63–65. Benveniste was able to win for Aragonese Jewry a postponement of the council's decree that all Jews be distinguished by wearing a distinctive badge. Likewise, the men around Ramah were still sufficiently powerful to win grudging temporary exemption. Honorious III in acceding to a royal request on this matter writes: "The Jews in the Kingdom of Castile are so seriously wrought up over . . . the matter of wearing a sign that some of them choose rather to flee to the Moors than to be burdened with such a sign. Others conspire because of this and make secret agreements. As a result, the King, whose income in large measure derives from these very Jews, can hardly raise his expenses and serious misfortune may befall his kingdom" (Grayzel, *The Church and the Jews*, pp. 150–151). The real possibility of Castilian Jews fleeing to the Almohades, at this point, seems nil; see below, n. 89. The Pope's claim probably reflects the arguments put forward by the Castilian court in order to justify its request for a postponement.

67. Brody, "Shirim," p. 28. Cf. for this theme in the elegy for a political leader in Schirmann, *Ha-Shirah ha-'Ibrit*, I, 199–200, and the even closer parallel in Judah Halevi, *Dīwān*, ed. H. Brody, II (Berlin, 1909), p. 81.

68. This is the interesting and plausible interpretation suggested by Cohen, *Sefer ha-Qabbalah*, pp. 293–302.

69. See S. D. Goitein, "Ha-Parashah ha-Aharonah be-Hayye Yehudah Halevi le-Or Kitbe ha-Genizah," *Tarbiz* 24 (1955): 32; B. Dinur, ed., *Yisrael ba-Golah*, vol. II, bk. III (Tel Aviv, 1968), p. 409 and n. 37. For Halevi's rejection of "enslavement to kings," see Schirmann, *Ha-Shirah ha-'Ibrit*, I, 498.

70. See Baer, *History*, I, 92; thus Ibn Shoshan and Alfakar controlled communal taxation; see Chapter 2, nn. 71–72; for a "noble *wazir*," unknown from other sources, see Brody, "Shirim," pp. 59–61.

71. See Brody, "Shirim," pp. 4–10; see further Baer's review of A. González Palencia, *Los mozárabes de Toledo en los siglos XII y XIII* (Madrid, 1926–1930), in *Tarbiz* 5 (1934): 228ff.

72. See Ramah's succinct comment on *Abot*, 1:10, quoted by Samuel de Uceda, *Midrash Shemuel* (Jerusalem, 1960), p. 13b; for the circumstances under which, Ramah felt, "lordship" and seeking royal authority were justifiable, see

HRS, 164b s.v. *tanna;* see also *HRS*, 177a, for the interesting distinction between authority gained through power and through spiritual stature; note too the justification of inherited authority. On advising kings, see *YRB*, 1:36, 12b.

73. See Baer, *History*, I, 81ff.

74. See Brill, *Kitāb*, p. 34 and Brill's note. D. J. Silver, *Maimonidean Criticism and the Maimonidean Controversy* (Leiden, 1965), pp. 145–146, n. 6, mistakes a poem written for a less wealthy friend for a description of Ramah's own condition; see Brody, "Shirim," p. 36, no. 13.

75. See *OZ*, pp. 145–146, no. 248.

76. Brody, "Shirim," p. 83. J. Schirmann, "The Function of the Hebrew Poet in Medieval Spain," *Jewish Social Studies* 16 (1954): 239, claims that Ramah earned his living as a talmudic teacher. This would have been both unnecessary and against Ramah's principles.

77. This sentence follows directly the quotation below, n. 146. Ibn Bahlul is apparently using *bigde ha-serad* in a sense similar to Nahmanides, *Commentary on the Torah*, Exod. 31:10. The preponderance of Ramah's halakic writings would seem to have been devoted to legal topics; see below, n. 152. This may reflect his perception of current need. A good picture of the kind of fundamental guidance Ramah provided in the very important area of communal government is given by S. Albeck, "Yesodot Mishtar ha-Qehillot be-Sefarad 'ad ha-Ramah," *Zion* 25 (1960): 85–121.

78. See *YRB*, 1:77, pp. 25–31.

79. *OZ*, p. 194, no. 303.

80. See, e.g., H. H. Ben-Sasson, *Peraqim be-Toledot ha-Yehudim Beme ha-Benayim* (Tel Aviv, 1969), p. 90.

81. *Baba Batra*, 8a.

82. See his *Commentary on Baba Batra*, ed. M. Shapiro (Bene-Beraq, 1973), p. 6d (to 8a); see too *Hiddushe ha-Ramban* to *Baba Batra*, 8a.

83. *YRB*, 1:87; see too 1:85; cf. Abraham Ha-Yarhi, *Sefer ha-Manhig*, I, 19. The notion that discriminatory taxation ensures continued Jewish existence is not entirely absent under Islam; see, e.g., S. Baron, "Economic History," *Encyclopaedia Judaica* (Jerusalem, 1972), XVI, 1279. But the notion that taxes constitute a direct purchase of the king's protection seems possible only in the new Christian environment. For Ramah's limitation of the legality of royal taxation, see S. Shilo, *Dina de-Malkuta Dina* (Jerusalem, 1974), pp. 203–204.

84. See Baer, *History*, I, 85–86.

85. See ibid., p. 397.

86. *Rosh, Baba Batra*, 1:29.

87. See Baer, *History*, I, 396–397, n. 31.

88. On the struggle with the Almohades and the Christian victory, see Lomax, *The Reconquest of Spain*, pp. 118–159.

89. See Maimonides, *Iggeret Teman*, ed. A. Halkin (New York, 1952), p. 94; Bahya b. Asher, *Perush 'al ha-Torah*, ed. C. Chavel (Jerusalem, 1974), III, 439–440.

90. See Baer, *History*, I, 89, 397, n. 31.

91. See G. Cohen, "Esau as a Symbol," in *Jewish Medieval and Renaissance Studies*, ed. A. Altmann (Cambridge, 1967), p. 48.

92. Brody, "Shirim," p. 70, l. 93. The phrase also occurs in a beautiful hymn of Ramah's own composition that he used to sing on the eve of the Sabbath (ibid., pp. 74–75). It is structured around classical rabbinic motifs linking the Sabbath with Redemption. A final twist gives a symbolic meaning to "Sabbath" itself:

> Turn away, O day of my toil (*yom 'abodati*) / harness your chariot
> Take your weapons and get out / get out O bloody man!

The Hebrew *yom 'abodati* is "my work-day" in obvious juxtaposition to the literal Sabbath; but it is also "the day of my slavery" which precedes the Messianic Sabbath. The first meaning connects with the preceding lines of praise to the literal Sabbath. The second meaning forces itself on the reader when he attempts to continue. "Take your weapons and go out" are words addressed, in Gen. 27:3, to Esau. The "bloody man" (*ish ha-damim*) whose exit coincides with the entrance of the Messianic Sabbath is thus Edom (Christendom). The hymn ends with a prayer for the revelation of God's kingship that links the Sabbath of Redemption and the original Sabbath of the Creation story:

> Look with favor, we beseech you, O God / and restore the Day of Kingship.
> As when in ancient times you alone / completed all Creation.
> May You grant Your Glory / a royal throne
> A seat formed of Your Splendor / upon which You might sit enthroned forevermore.

A Sabbath hymn by Judah Halevi may have suggested this concluding prayer for a renewal of the primeval Kingship; see Judah Halevi, *Dīwān*, ed. H. Brody, IV (Berlin, 1930), p. 4. But Halevi's Messianic Sabbath is initiated by the defeat of Islam as well as Christendom. In Ramah's hymn, the new political-religious order is evident.

For a case of Messianic expectation on the part of a Toledo resident at about the time of Ramah's arrival, see the appendix to Halkin's edition of Maimonides' *Iggeret Teman*, pp. 108–111. Ramah thought Messianic speculations and predictions an exercise in futility and an invitation to disillusionment. Following his literal exposition of a strange Messianic aggadah, Ramah adds: "This is the simple meaning of these words. But as to these matters, we don't know how they will occur until the time that they come about" (*HRS*, 170b). Ramah has paraphrased Maimonides, *Mishneh Torah, Melakim*, 12:2, substituting "we don't know" for Maimonides' "no one will know." For Maimonides (ibid.) denied that "the Sages have any tradition concerning these matters"; cf. Ibn Ezra to Daniel 11:31. But Ramah (probably with Maimonides' claim in mind) insists that "it is impossible that the date of the Messianic Redemption (*qez mashiah*) was not transmitted to the Sages; but the reason that they did not make it explicit is because of 'announce His salvation from day to day' (Ps. 96:2)" (*HRS*, 169a). Elsewhere (*HRS*, 160b) Ramah explains that if Daniel had revealed how far off the End really is, "many of the wicked of Israel in those days and *nowadays too* would have become apostates." Apparently, then, Ramah did not feel the Messianic Age to be imminent.

93. Brody, "Shirim," p. 71. For "the bread of falsehood" as the host, see also Simon b. Zemah Duran in Schirmann, *Ha-Shirah ha-'Ibrit*, II, 590; cf. *Zohar*, III, 192a. The pressure of Christian polemic is evident in Ramah's explanation that the Mishnaic charge, "know what to answer the *epiqoros*" (*Abot* 2:4), "refers also to those who accept the Written Law but distort its meaning as the disciples of Jesus of Nazareth have done. For the very verse in which the Father of all Prophets . . . enjoined belief in God's unity, they have taken as grounds for their heresy of polytheism" (quoted in *Perush R. Yizhaq b. R. Shlomoh 'al Maseket Abot*, ed M. Kasher and Y. Blochrowitz [Jerusalem, 1965], p. 75). For the probable source of Ramah's ironic allusion to the Trinitarian exegesis of Deut. 6:4, see J. Finkel, ed., "Maimonides' Treatise on Resurrection," *Proceedings of the American Academy for Jewish Research*, IX (1939), p. 1 (Heb. sec.); cf. J. N. Hillgarth, *The Spanish Kingdoms*, I (Oxford, 1976), p. 212. See too *HRS*, 172a, s.v. *pisqa*, on the prohibition to read *sifre minim*. Ramah's language is based on Alfasi, *Sanhedrin*, 19b; but Ramah seems to take *sifre minim* as Christian books, whereas for Alfasi it means scriptural interpretation not based on the Oral Torah.

94. Samuel ibn Tibbon, *Ma'amar Yiqqavu ha-Mayim* (Pressburg, 1837), p. 175.

95. For the term, see E. R. Curtius, *European Literature and the Latin Middle Ages* (Princeton, 1953), p. 541, and A. Deyermond, *A Literary History of Spain: The Middle Ages* (London, 1971), pp. 55–58. For science and philosophy, see, e.g., the strong statement of G. Fraile, *Historia de la filosofía española* (Madrid, 1971), I, 148–149.

96. S. Halberstam, ed., "Milhemet ha-Dat," in Kobak, *Jeschurun*, VIII (1872–75), 117. The word " 'eber" is missing there, making the text incomprehensible.

97. See the edition of this letter by S. Abramson in *Sefer Hayyim Schirmann* (Jerusalem, 1970), p. 404. Once it is realized that Nahmanides was borrowing the formulation of Halevi's letter, the emendation indicated in the previous note becomes obvious.

98. Cf. too Nahmanides' *Commentary on the Torah*, Num. 26:13.

99. By the time Ramah arrived in Toledo, only a few poor Muslims remained in the city; but there was a very significant Mozarabic community which perpetuated Arabic influence; see, e.g., the Arabic documents in González Palencia, *Los mozárabes de Toledo* and Baer's review in *Tarbiz* 5 (1934): 228 ff. For the continuity of Arabic among the Jews of Toledo into the fourteenth century, see, e.g., Asher b. Yehiel, *Responsa* (New York, 1954), 55:9; G. Vajda, *Recherches sur la philosophie et la kabbale* (Paris, 1962), pp. 117–120; M. Steinschneider, *Die hebraeischen Uebersetzungen des Mittelalters* (Berlin, 1893), II, 913.

A brief comment in *HRS*, 114b gives some sense of Ramah's knowledge of the Islamic religion. Ramah was clearly aware of some of the practices at the Meccan cult; but his knowledge was no longer of the same quality as that of Andalusian figures like Maimonides or Judah Halevi. Ramah's erroneous assumption (ibid.) that the lapidation rite is done backwards through the thighs probably stems from a Hispano-Jewish polemical tradition. There is a full treatment of these questions in B. Septimus, "Petrus Alfonsi on the Cult at Mecca," *Speculum* 56 (1981): 517–533. A source overlooked in that study is quoted by G. Vajda, "Joseph Ben Shalom Ashkenazi," *Archives d'histoire doctrinale et littéraire du moyen age* 23 (1956): 134–136.

100. See e.g., Chapter 3, on *Kitāb al-Rasā'il.*

101. See, e.g., *HRS,* 128a, 143a; *YRB,* 5:136, 138, 139.

102. See, e.g., Halevi in S. M. Stern, *Hispano-Arabic Strophic Poetry* (Oxford, 1974),pp. 133–134. On Jewish use of Romance in eleventh century Muslim Spain, see Ibn Gabirol quoted by Schirmann, *Ha-Shirah ha-'Ibrit,* I, 25.

103. See Brody, "Shirim," p. 23 and Brody's note. See also Schirmann, *Ha-Shirah ha-'Ibrit,* II, 272, 274. On the Arabic poet-king, Al-Mu'tamid of Seville (1040–1095), whom Ramah translates, see E. Ashtor, *Qorot ha-Yehudim be-Sefarad ha-Muslamit* (Jerusalem, 1966), II, 288 ff. Preference for things Arabic was not restricted to the literary and intellectual spheres, as can be seen from the naughty poem written by a member of the Abulafia family in the second half of the thirteenth century in Schirmann, *Ha-Shirah ha-'Ibrit,* II, 434–435.

104. See Ya'aqob ben El'azar, *Kitāb al-Kāmil,* ed. N. Allony (Jerusalem, 1977).

105. See especially the linguistic and exegetical material in Brill, *Kitāb,* pp. 97–102; on this material see Chapter 3, n. 72. Ramah consciously attempts to interpret rabbinic exegesis as being consistent with the plain meaning of the biblical text; see, e.g., Ramah quoted by Jacob ibn Habib, *'En Ya'aqob* (Jerusalem, 1961), V, 90; *HRS,* 143b s.v. *amar,* 169b s.v. *amar Rab,* 175a s.v. *va-yehi,* 185a s.v. *itmar;* Ramah quoted in *Perush R. Yizhaq b. R. Shlomo'al Maseket Abot,* pp. 171–172; see too *YRB,* 1:2, 1:5, 8:80; see also Ramah's *Masoret Seyag la-Torah* (Florence, 1750), introduction, especially the reference to the methods of the lexicographers.

106. Quoted by Yeruham b. Meshullam, *Toledot Adam ve-Havah* (Tel Aviv, 1960), I, 16, cited by Joseph Karo, *Bedeq ha-Bayit* to *Bet Yosef, Yoreh Deah,* no. 246. Note, however, that רמ'יה in our texts of R. Yeruham often refers to R. Meir of Rothenberg rather than to Ramah. It is, therefore, not certain that this quotation belongs to the latter.

107. See Chapter 2.

108. See Schirmann, *Ha-Shirah ha-'Ibrit,* II, 97–103, 689–690.

109. See ibid., pp. 207–210, 690–691.

110. See ibid., pp. 67–70, 689.

111. See Ramah's little poetic boast in Brody, "Shirim," p. 16, l. 29. Concerning the quality of Ramah's poetry, Brody was quite enthusiastic; see "Shirim," pp. 2–3. Schirmann is more reserved in his judgment; see *Ha-Shirah ha-'Ibrit,* II, 271–272.

112. See, e.g., Schirmann, *Ha-Shirah ha-'Ibrit,* I, 24–29; Pagis, *Hiddush u-Masoret,* pp. 56–58.

113. On Alharizi, see, e.g., Pagis, *Hiddush u-Masoret,* p. 203.

114. Ibid., p. 221. The centrality of competition with Arabic in the work of Jacob b. El'azar has been underscored by Allony, *Kitāb al-Kāmil,* pp. 6–10.

115. Pagis, *Hiddush u-Masoret,* p. 184.

116. See Brody, "Shirim," p. 3.

117. See Schirmann, "The Function of the Hebrew Poet in Medieval Spain," *Jewish Social Studies* 16 (1954): 235-252.

118. Brody, "Shirim," pp. 11-12. A poem in praise of Ibn Shoshan upon his recovery from illness was published by I. Davidson (*Ginze Schechter*, III [1928], 290-291), who suggested Alharizi as a possible author (ibid., p. 282). Brody ("Shirim," p. 8) suggests Ramah.

119. See Baer, *History*, I, 95, 390-391; cf. too the letter of Abraham ibn Hasdai to Joseph's son Judah Alfakar in *Qobez Teshubot ha-Rambam ve-Iggerotav*, ed. A. Lichtenberg (Leipzig, 1859), III, 7b.

120. Brody, "Shirim," pp. 96-99.

121. Ibid., pp. 12-13. Ramah was of the opinion that the rejoicing of a wedding day has status as a biblical commandment; see *Rosh, Ketubot*, 1:5.

122. On Alfakar, see Graetz, *Dibre Yeme Yisrael*, IV, 244-245; Brody, "Shirim," pp. 6-7; A. S. Yahuda, *'Eber ve-'Arab* (New York, 1946), pp. 106-110.

123. Brody, "Shirim," p. 41; cf. ibid., p. 25, ll. 125-126.

124. Ibid., p. 41.

125. See B. Klar, *Mehqarim ve-Iyyunim* (Tel Aviv, 1954), pp. 353-354, n. 115; cf. Brill, *Kitāb*, p. 97 (Brill's emendation is unnecessary).

126. Brody, "Shirim," p. 41.

127. The seventeenth-century North African historian of Spain, al-Maq-qarī, quoted by Yahuda, *'Eber ve-'Arab*, p. 106.

128. See Dinur, *Yisrael ba-Golah*, vol. II, bk. VI, p. 200, no. 21; Stein-schneider, *Die hebraeischen Uebersetzungen*, I, 132-133.

129. Brody, "Shirim," pp. 41-42.

130. See Chapter 4.

131. See Julius Guttmann, *Philosophies of Judaism* (London, 1964), p. 134; see also Chapter 4.

132. See Guttmann, *Philosophies of Judaism*, pp. 143-152.

133. See Chapter 3, n. 122.

134. See the testimony of Ramah in his letter to Nahmanides, in Lichten-berg, *Qobez*, III, 6d.

135. See S. Pines, *Scholasticism after Thomas Aquinas and the Teachings of Hasdai Crescas* (Jerusalem, 1967), pp. 98-101. Note too Pines's suggestion that Ibn Daud's *Zikron Dibre Romi* was designed to inform the Jewish community— now living under Christian rule—about the historical tradition of their new environment.

136. On the translation movement, see M. Steinschneider, *Die europäischen Übersetzungen aus dem Arabischen* (reprint ed.: Graz, 1956); C. H. Haskins, *The Renaissance of the Twelfth Century* (Cambridge, 1927), pp. 278-302; R. Walzer, "Arabic Transmission of Greek Thought to Medieval Europe," *Bulletin of the John Rylands Library* 29 (1945-46): 160-183; D. Lindberg, "The Transmission of Greek and Arabic Learning to the West," in *Science in the Middle Ages*, ed. D. Lindberg (Chicago, 1978), pp. 52-90.

137. See Lindberg, "Transmission of Greek and Arabic Learning," pp. 67-70.

138. See Steinschneider, *Die hebraeischen Uebersetzungen*, I, 1.

139. See Baer, *History*, I, 59-64, 90-91.

140. See Chapter 2 on Abraham Ha-Yarhi.

141. Brody, "Shirim," pp. 79–82; on the affinity of this poem to a similar one, by Moses ibn Ezra, see Brody's notes. Brody also points out borrowings from Bahya ibn Paquda's *Hobot ha-Lebabot*. For the influence of Judah Halevi see, e.g., Chapter 4, n. 17. For more on Ramah's familiarity with and use of philosophical terminology and reasoning, his attitude toward philosophical study, and his relationship to Maimonidean philosophy, see Chapter 5.

142. See Ramah's appreciation of Saadya in Brill, *Kitāb*, p. 57; for a full discussion of Ramah's relationship to rationalism, see Chapters 3, 4, and 5 passim.

143. See Steinschneider, *Die hebraeischen Uebersetzungen*, I, 1–4. Anyone acquainted with the vast literature in the fields of philosophy and kabbalah produced by the Jews of Christian Spain will find very strange the assumption of A. Castro (*The Spaniards*, pp. 537–540, 547–548) that their learning was essentially "practical," oriented toward the attainment of power, and without the "theoretical meditation" present in northern European culture.

144. *Midrash Hokmah*, Cambridge MS Dd. 9.65, p. 61b. I am unable to locate the passage in the Jerusalem Talmud to which Ibn Matka refers. There are, however, numerous medieval citations of "Yerushalmi" that are not in our texts of the Palestinian Talmud. Often "Yerushalmi" is a misnomer for later sources, sometimes nonextant; see, e.g., L. Ginzberg, *Geonica* (New York, 1909), I, 85; Twersky, *Rabad*, pp. 242–243; S. Abramson, *Rab Nissim Gaon* (Jerusalem, 1965), pp. 199, 205–206, 208, 210–211, 419.

145. Cf. too the chronicles of David of Estella and Isaac Lattes in Neubauer, *Medieval Jewish Chronicles*, II, 232, 236. Description of Ramah as a Toledan in no way contradicts the reports of his origin in Burgos; see, e.g., I. Twersky, *Rabad of Posquieres* (Cambridge, 1962), p. 4, n. 14.

146. Oxford MS, Opp. Add. 4°1 19, fol. 3b; quoted by N. Wieder, "Sifro ha-Nisraf shel Yehudah ibn Shabbetai," *Mezudah*, 2 (1944): 124. For the correct identification of this "R. Meir" as Ramah, see N. ha-Kohen, *Ozar ha-Gedolim*, IV (Haifa, 1968), 172–173.

147. *Zedah la-Derek*, p. 6.

148. See Alharizi, *Tahkemoni*, pp. 348–349; Stern, "Rabbi Yehudah Alharizi," p. 102.

149. *Hobot ha-Lebabot*, ed. and trans. J. Kafih (Jerusalem, 1973), p. 24. See too Ibn Daud quoted by H. Wolfson, *Studies in the History of Philosophy and Religion*, I (Cambridge, 1973), pp. 543–545. For later examples, see Twersky, "Provençal Jewry," pp. 194–195. Bahya was more committed to talmudic study than Alharizi; nor would he have approved the way Alharizi spent the time he saved by not studying talmudic minutiae; see *Hobot ha-Lebabot* 5:5, pp. 253–254 and especially p. 274, where the evil inclination teams up with the ideal of *adab* to urge neglect of both talmudic and philosophical study; see further B. Safran, "Bahya ibn Paquda's Attitude toward the Courtier Class," in *Studies in Medieval Jewish History and Literature*, ed. I. Twersky (Cambridge, 1979), pp. 154–196.

150. See *Masoret Seyag la-Torah*, introduction.

151. See Chapter 5.

152. I. Ta-Shema, "Yezirato ha-Sifrutit shel R. Meir Halevi Abulafia," *Qiryat Sefer* 43 (1968): 569–576. Ta-Shema's bibliographical essays are an important contribution to the study of Ramah's career as a halakist; see below, n. 162; Chapter 2, n. 89.

153. The *Sanhedrin* commentary is missing the tenth chapter.

154. Brody, "Shirim," p. 83.

155. On scarcity of books, see Twersky, *Rabad*, p. 198 and the references. Alternatively, Ramah was interested in a northern manuscript for comparative purposes.

156. Hayyim Yosef David Azulai, *Shem ha-Gedolim* (Livorno, 1838), I, 52b. Like other lost commentaries of Ramah, numerous fragments of these works are quoted in the writings of later Sefardic authors; see I. Ta-Shema, "R. Meir Abulafia," *Qiryat Sefer* 43 (1968): 574–576.

157. See Ta-Shema, "R. Meir Abulafia," pp. 570–571.

158. Extracts from his *Qiryat Sefer* in Neubauer, *Medieval Jewish Chronicles*, II, 236; perhaps based on Menahem Ha-Meiri, introduction to *Bet-ha-Behirah, Abot*, ed. B. Z. Prague (Jerusalem, 1964), p. 54.

159. See I. Joel, *Reshimat Kitbe ha-Yad ha-'Ibriyim ha-Nimzaim be-Bet ha-Sefarim ha-Le'umi* (Jerusalem, 1934), no. 88.

160. Isaac b. Sheshet, *She'elot u-Teshubot* (Jerusalem, 1968), no. 318.

161. See *YRB*, 3:248, and *Tosafot, Shabbat*, 80a s.v. *abal* (quoting *Riba*).

162. See I. Ta-Shema, "R. Meir Abulafia," *Qiryat Sefer* 44 (1969): 429–435. An important but very poorly preserved index to some of Ramah's responsa (in Montefiore MS 86) requires careful study, to which I hope to return.

163. See ibid.

164. See ibid.

165. *YRB*, 8:136, p. 318.

166. Later commentators often take note of the novelty of Ramah's theories; see the two examples cited by Ta-Shema, "R. Meir Abulafia," *Qiryat Sefer* 43 (1968): 573. Ramah himself sometimes underscores the originality of his views; see, e.g., *OZ*, p. 169, no. 279 and the interesting citation from Ramah in *Tur, Hoshen Mishpat*, no. 97; note the use in both cases of the term *meleket shamayim*; cf. *YRB*, 3:233; see on this term I. Twersky, *Introduction to the Code of Maimonides* (New Haven, 1980), pp. 170–175. For an interesting example of Ramah's originality, see *YRB*, 1:3. Ramah is addressing himself to a question raised by the Tosafists; his answer anticipates by six centuries that of Aryeh Leb ha-Kohen, *Qezot ha-Hoshen* (Jerusalem, 1955), 157:3. For a simple but striking example of Ramah's aggadic exegesis, see the explanation of *'atir sil'in* (*Baba Batra*, 145b) quoted (from *Perate Horayot*) by Jacob ibn Habib, *'En Ya'aqob*, V, 91 (cf. *YRB*, 9:65, where the passage is quoted without explanation). Cf. too *'En Ya'aqob*, V, 91, where Ramah rejects Hai Gaon and Rashi for a clear, simple interpretation of his own. Cf. too Chapter 6, n. 5.

167. See Ibn Daud, *Sefer ha-Qabbalah*, p. 88. Ibn Daud is our only source on their activity.

168. Alharizi, *Tahkemoni*, p. 346.

169. See Abraham Ha-Yarhi, *Sefer ha-Manhig*, II, 677.

170. Alharizi, *Tahkemoni*, p. 346.

171. See Brody, "Shirim," p. 4.

172. Ibid., pp. 53–54. For Ramah's positive attitude toward medicine and the maintenance of health (through bathing), see *HRS*, 37a; note the implicit rejection of Rashi to *Sanhedrin* 17b, s.v. *rofe*.

173. Bezalel Ashkenazi, *Shittah Mequbbezet, Baba Mezia* (New York, 1953), p. 438 (to 108a).

174. See, e.g., Schirmann, *Ha-Shirah ha-'Ibrit*, I, 358.

175. See, e.g., Ashtor, *Ha-Yehudim be-Sefarad ha-Muslamit*, II, 247.

176. See also S. Abramson, *Be-Leshon Qodemin* (Jerusalem, 1965), pp. 56–57.

177. See above, n. 169.

178. Brody, "Shirim," p. 15; cf. too ibid., p. 83.

179. See, e.g., *HRS*, 55a, 131a; *YRB*, 3:102, 3:103, 3:248, 4:54, 6:87, 8:190; *Magid Mishneh, Malveh ve-Loveh*, 15:1; cf. too H. Y. D. Azulai, *Sha'ar Yosef* (Jerusalem, 1970), p. 22b.

180. See, e.g., *HRS*, 133b; cf. B. Dinur, ed., *Yisrael ba-Golah*, vol. I, bk, III (Tel Aviv, 1961), pp. 116–117.

181. *Kitāb al-Rasā'il*, pp. 79–80. On the Nagid's library, see Ibn Daud, *Sefer ha-Qabbalah*, pp. 74–75.

182. Ibn Daud, *Sefer ha-Qabbalah*, p. 76.

183. Ibid., p. 80.

184. Ibid., pp. 86–87.

185. See ibid., p. 87.

186. Ibid., p. 81; Joseph ha-Nagid's wife also found refuge in Lucena; see ibid., p. 77.

187. Ibid., pp. 87–88.

188. On talmudic studies in Muslim Spain, see M. Margalioth, *Hilkot ha-Nagid* (Jerusalem, 1962), pp. 1–67; see too I. Ta-Shema, "Yezirato ha-Sifrutit shel R. Yosef Halevi ibn Megash," *Qiryat Sefer* 46 (1970–71): 136–146, 541–553; ibid., 47 (1971–72): 318–322.

189. Brody, "Shirim," p. 83, taking "פ ר'" as *perush*—i.e., *perush Rashi*.

II. New Northern Connections

1. See Chapter 1, n. 8.

2. *Bet ha-Behira 'al Maseket Abot*, p. 55.

3. See Moritz Steinschneider, *Die Geschichtsliteratur der Juden* (Frankfurt, 1905), p. 56.

4. See, e.g., E. E. Urbach, *Ba'ale ha-Tosafot* (Jerusalem, 1955), pp. 15–217; B. Z. Benedict, "Le-Toledotav shel Merkaz ha-Torah be-Provence," *Tarbiz* 22 (1951): 85–109; Twersky, *Rabad*, and "Provençal Jewry," pp. 185–207.

5. See Ibn Daud, *Sefer ha-Qabbalah*, pp. 88–90 and Cohen's note, pp. 142–143. Ha-Meiri's judgment is to be preferred to that of Graetz, *Dibre Yeme Yisrael*, IV,. 327, who takes Ibn Daud's description as an accurate evaluation of mid-twelfth century Jewish culture.

6. See Steinschneider, *Die hebraeischen Uebersetzungen*, I, 1–3.

7. Ibn Matka, *Midrash Hokmah*, Parma MS 421, p. 110a.

8. David Kimhi, *Ha-Perush ha-Shalem'al Tehillim*, ed. A. Darom (Jerusalem, 1967), p. 247 (to 108:1).

9. The Toledo response, written for Ibn Shoshan by Abraham Ha-Yarhi (*Sefer ha-Manhig*, ed. Raphael, II, 723–736), is addressed "to the rabbis, great scholars, princes and nobles in all the region (hebel) of Aragon, from the assembly of the congregation of Israel which is in Toledo."

10. See Chapter 4.

11. See H. Michael, *Or ha-Hayyim* (Jerusalem, 1965), p. 524, no. 1098.

12. See, e.g., the introduction of R. Joseph b. Isaac ibn al-Fawwāl, the translator of Maimonides' *Perush ha-Mishnayot*, *Mo'ed* (published in the Vilna ed. of *Shabbat*).

13. See Twersky, "Provençal Jewry," p. 202, n. 61a; Benedict, "Merkaz ha-Torah be-Provence," pp. 98–103.

14. On R. Zerahyah's relationship to the Provençal tradition of halakah, see B. Z. Benedict, "R. Mosheh b. Yosef mi-Narbonne," *Tarbriz* 19 (1948): 19–34; for Zerahyah's return to Gerona, see Menahem He-Meiri, *Magen Abot* (Jerusalem, 1958), pp. 28–29. For Zerahyah's biography, see I. Ta-Shema, "Zemanim u-Meqomot be-Hayyav shel Rabbenu Zerahyah," *Bar Ilan Annual* 12 (1974): 118–136.

15. Twersky, *Rabad*, p. 35.

16. See the communal letters of these communities published by A. Neubauer in *Israelitische Letterbode*, IV (1878–1879), 162–168; cf. Baer, *History*, I, 94–95, and B. Septimus, "Piety and Power in Thirteenth-Century Catalonia" in *Studies in Medieval Jewish History and Literature*, ed. I. Twersky (Cambridge, 1979), pp. 197–230.

17. Brody, "Shirim," pp. 61–63, 88–90.

18. Alharizi, *Tahkemoni*, p. 346.

19. Brody, "Shirim," pp. 38–39, 48–49; see also p. 9.

20. On Nahmanides' teachers, see C. Chavel, *R. Mosheh b. Nahman* (Jerusalem, 1967), pp. 38–46; on R. Jonah Gerondi, see ibid., pp. 54–55; Urbach, *Ba'ale ha-Tosafot*, pp. 395–396; Chapter 4; on R. Samuel ha-Sardi, see Chavel, *R. Mosheh b. Nahman*, p. 51; cf. too R. Solomon of Montpellier's letter to R. Samuel, in Kobak, *Jeschurun*, VIII, 99.

21. See the sources cited by I. Ta-Shema, "R. Meir Abulafia," *Qiryat Sefer* 44 (1969): 431 and n. 9.

22. See, e.g., Salo Baron, *A Social and Religious History of the Jews*, VII (New York, 1958), 48, 238–239; see too Dinur, *Yisrael ba-Golah*, vol. II, bk, VI, pp. 175–176 (quoting Judah ibn Tibbon's introduction to his translation of *Sefer ha-Riqmah*). Graetz, *Dibre Yeme Yisrael*, IV, 92, maintains that by "Zarfat," Ibn Chiquitillia means, here, Catalonia; H. Gross, *Gallia Judaica* (Paris, 1897), p. 538, thinks this unlikely, and that the reference is to southern France. The Ibn Tibbon text supports this. If so, the statement of Benedict, "Merkaz ha-Torah be-Provence," p. 90, that there is no record of cultural relations between Spain and Provence prior to the time of Ibn Megash, must be revised.

23. See Steinschneider, *Die hebraeischen Uebersetzungen*, II, 912.

24. See Judah Halevi, *Dīwān*, ed. H. Brody, I (Berlin, 1894), 219–225; see also Halevi's poetic invitation to dinner to "the French (*Zarfati*) rabbi,"

ibid., p. 38; Dinur, *Yisrael ba-Golah*, vol. II, bk. III (Jerusalem, 1968), pp. 57, 325–326, n. 40.

25. Halevi, *Dīwān*, I, 217–218; Dinur, *Yisrael ba-Golah*, vol. II., bk. III, p. 32, n. 18.

26. See Twersky, "Provençal Jewry," pp. 195–202; Benedict, "Merkaz ha-Torah be-Provence," pp. 99–106.

27. Brody, "Shirim," pp. 44–46, 86–88. See Ramah's beautiful letter of mourning, apparently for his brother Samuel, inserted in a responsum to Tudela, published in *OZ*, p. 156 (the letter should be the beginning of no. 160, rather than the end of no. 159); that Samuel died before his brother proves correct Brody's contention ("Shirim," p. 10) that he is not to be identified with the Samuel Halevi Abulafia who served as a translator at the court of Alfonso X.

28. See *OZ*, p. 181, no. 292. On Ramah's questioner, R. Joseph b. Gershom, see Ha-Meiri, *Bet ha-Behirah 'al Abot*, introduction, p. 56.

29. This emerges from the letter of Aaron b. Meshullam of Lunel to Ramah; see, e.g., Brill, *Kitāb*, pp. 28, 39; see also Chapter 3.

30. See Ramah's responsum in Menahem Ha-Meiri's *Qiryat Sefer*, p. 46.

31. See Ibn Tibbon's introduction to his translation of Aristotle's *Meteora* in Dinur, *Yisrael ba-Golah*, vol. II, bk. VI, p. 200, n. 21; Steinschneider, *Die hebraeischen Uebersetzungen*, I, 132–133.

32. Dinur, *Yisrael ba-Golah*, vol. II, bk. VI, p. 200; Steinschneider, *Die hebraeischen Uebersetzungen*, I, 132–133. Joseph requested Hebrew translations of Aristotle from Ibn Tibbon. Fifty years earlier the idea of a Toledo Jew with philosophical interests, unable to read philosophical Arabic, applying to a Provençal friend for translation, would have been absurd.

33. Brody, "Shirim," pp. 16–21; Ramah's praise is profuse but highly general. Rabbi Naftali Hakohen identified him with a colleague of Rabad; see his *Ozar ha-Gedolim* (Haifa, n.d.), II, 39; see *The Itinerary of Benjamin of Tudela*, ed. Adler (London, 1907), p. 4, n. 31 (Heb. sec.); R. Abraham ben David, *Teshubot u-Pesaqim*, ed. J. Kafih (Jerusalem, 1964), no. 63. But in neither of these sources is Abraham b. Moses associated with Carcassonne. On the tendency to praise in universal terms, see Pagis, *Hiddush u-Masoret*, pp. 21, 146–147.

34. Thus when Ramah writes to Aaron b. Meshullam of Lunel following the conventions of Spanish epistolary style and with accompanying poetry, the latter responds in kind; see the letters in *Kitāb al-Rasā'il*; note too that Ramah's poem of friendship to Abraham b. Mosheh was in response to the latter's poem, adopting its rhyme and meter; cf. Pagis, *Shirat ha-Hol*, pp. 126–30. Among the roles played by Judah ibn Tibbon's famous "will" may have been the spreading of Spanish values and conceptions of correct style in Provence; see I. Abrahams, ed., *Hebrew Ethical Wills* (Philadelphia, 1948), I, 51ff.

35. See E. Fleischer, *Shirat ha-Qodesh ha-'Ibrit beme ha-Benayim* (Jerusalem, 1975), pp. 12–13.

36. See Gershom Scholem, *Ursprung und Anfänge der Kabbala* (Berlin, 1962), pp. 324ff.

37. See ibid., pp. 349–350.

38. See ibid., pp. 199–200, 347.

39. The question of Ramah's relationship to kabbalah is fully discussed in Chapter. 6.

40. See Benedict, "Merkaz ha-Torah be-Provence," pp. 98–106; Twersky, "Provençal Jewry," pp. 191–194.

41. See, e.g., Twersky, Rabad, pp. 232–236; S. Friedman, The Commentary of R. Jonathan Ha-Kohen of Lunel on the Mishnah and Alfasi Tractate Bava Kamma (New York, 1969), introduction, pp. 27ff.

42. For example, R. Aha Gaon in Perate Baba Mezia, quoted by Meir b. Simon, Sefer ha-Me'orot, end of "Hilkot Mezuzah"; Simon Qayyara in YRB, 3:102; R. Sherira in HRS, 7a, 36b; R. Hai in YRB, 3:102, 3:224 and HRS, 24a, 35a, 60b, 68b.

43. For example, R. Hananel in YRB, 3:103, 4:40 and HRS, 3b, 24a, 45a, 58b, 72a, 93a, 99a, 128a.

44. For example, Alfasi in YRB, 3:102, 3:103, 3:252; HRS, 7b, 70a; Joseph ibn Megash in YRB, 3:102, 3:103: HRS, 21b, 43a, 43b.

45. Yizhaq b Abba Mari, 'Ittur Soferim, quoted in HRS, 8a; this is the only reference to a Provençal work that I can locate in Ramah's commentaries. Note that Ha-Yarhi was a relative and student of R. Yizhaq b. Abba Mari and uses his 'Ittur in Sefer ha-Manhig; see Raphael's introduction to Sefer ha-Manhig, I, 17.

46. Rashi is quoted on almost every other page of HRS; Rashbam, in YRB, 3:103, 3:234; R. Tam, in HRS, 15b.

47. R. Isaac b. Asher (Riba) in HRS, 21a.

48. For the influence of Saadya, see Ozar ha-Geonim, Megillah, ed. B. M. Lewin (Jerusalem, 1933), I, 52, n. 12; for R. Nissim Gaon, see Ta-Shema, "R. Meir Abulafia," Qiryat Sefer 43 (1968): 573, n. 18; for the influence of an early Spanish responsum, see Ta-Shema, "R. Meir Abulafia," p. 572; for further examples of Ramah's borrowing, see S. Abramson, R. Nissim Gaon, 230–231. Ramah's Baba Batra commentary makes abundant use of the earlier commentary of Ibn Megash; see, e.g., YRB, 8:40, 8:60, 1:46, 1:82, 1:103, 1:192. For examples of Franco-German influence, see, e.g., YRB, 9:168; Tosafot, Baba Batra, 159a s.v. ve-lemru and Shittah Mequbbezet, ad loc. See too HRS, 121a s.v. amar; Ramah is clearly aware of the dispute between Rashbam and R. Tam (see Tosafot and Rosh, ad loc.) and emphatically rejects the view of the latter. For further examples of Franco-German influence, see below, n. 50.

49. See, e.g., YRB, 8:33 s.v. beram; Ramah is reasserting the view of "the rabbis of Spain" against that of R. Tam; see the commentary of Nahmanides here (Baba Batra, 114a). See too YRB, 3:10 and the comments of Magid Mishneh, Shekenim, 11:4.

50. For a striking example, see Nahmanides, Milhamot Hashem, Baba Batra, 82b, defending Alfasi from the stricture of Zerahyah Halevi. Nahmanides asserts that Alfasi's view is that of "the early geonim . . . and the later geonim and all the rabbis of Spain." But Ramah has already adopted the Provençal view; see YRB, 10:149. Note that Ha-Yarhi's teacher, the great Tosafist Isaac of Dampierre, had also rejected Alfasi's view; see Hagahot Maymoniyot, Malveh ve-Loveh, 11:3. See too YRB,1:149 (to 12a) and the commentary of Nahmanides, ad loc. For another example, see YRB, 4:45; Tosafot, Baba Batra, 66a–b s.v. Miklal and Kesef Mishneh, Miqva'ot, 4:2. See also YRB, 9:98, Milhamot, Baba Batra, 70a, and Magid Mishneh, Zekiyya u-Mattanah, 9:8.

51. See Chapter 4.

52. Brody, "Shirim," p. 82; translated in S. Baron, *A Social and Religious History of the Jews*, VII (New York, 1958), 164. The poem is not even conclusive evidence that Ramah traveled at all; see Todros Abulafia in Schirmann, *Ha-Shirah ha-'Ibrit*, II, 419. Todros' poem is required reading for anyone attempting to reconstruct history on the basis of Spanish Hebrew poetry.

53. See the court document in Ha-Yarhi's *Sefer ha-Manhig*, II, 677; for biographical and bibliographical information on Ha-Yarhi, see M. Higger, "Yarhi's Commentary on Kallah Rabbati," *Jewish Quarterly Review* 24 (1934): 331–339; Twersky, *Rabad*, pp. 240–244; Raphael's introduction to *Sefer ha-Manhig*, I, 11–86.

54. See Alharizi, *Tahkemoni*, p. 403; Ha-Yarhi, *Sefer ha-Manhig*, I, 11.

55. According to Higger, "Yarhi's Commentary," p. 331, he was born in Avignon rather than Lunel. Cf., however, Raphael's introduction to *Sefer ha-Manhig*, I, 11.

56. See Twersky, *Rabad*, p. 241.

57. See below, nn. 71 and 72.

58. See Twersky, *Rabad*, pp. 242–243.

59. See below, nn. 71 and 72.

60. See Raphael's introduction to *Sefer ha-Manhig*, I, 14.

61. See Chapter 1, n. 44.

62. See Raphael's introduction to *Sefer ha-Manhig*, I, 15.

63. See Brill, *Kitāb*, p. 107; Raphael's introduction to *Sefer ha-Manhig*, I, 15, on Ha-Yarhi's return from France in 1211.

64. Ha-Yarhi, *Sefer ha-Manhig*, I, 9–10.

65. See Twersky, *Rabad*, pp. 241–242; Raphael's introduction to *Sefer ha-Manhig*, I, 20–73.

66. Ha-Yarhi, *Sefer ha-Manhig*, II, 763.

67. See ibid., pp. 729, 731; note Ha-Yarhi's reference to "one of our beloved friends among the scholars of Toledo."

68. Ibid., 723–736; see too pp. 616–617.

69. Ibid., pp. 729–731.

70. See especially ibid., pp. 20, 27. But Ha-Yarhi can also say with confidence that Toledo custom is consistent with that of "Provence and Burgundy, Ile-de-France (*Zarfat*) and Champagne, Lotharingia and Alamannia." For a later Provençal parallel to this emotional defense of local custom under outside attack, see Menahem ha-Meiri's *Magen Abot*.

71. Brody, "Shirim," p. 36.

72. Ibid., pp. 23–25. Ramah's view of the "social function" of the poet thus somewhat unconventionally includes helping scholars in financial difficulty. On another poetic request for tax relief, see Y. Baer, "Todros ben Yehudah ha-Levi u-Zemano," *Zion* 2 (1937): 30, n. 31. The latter's request is for himself.

73. *Perush Maseket Kallah Rabbati*, ed. B. Toledano (Tiberias, 1906); another fragment was published by M. Higger, "Yarhi's Commentary on Kallah Rabbati," *Jewish Quarterly Review* 24 (1934): 331–348; Twersky, *Rabad*, p. 244.

74. Alfasi, *Berakot*, 21b.

75. *Perush Kallah Rabbati*, ed. Toledano, p. 20.

76. See Chapter 1; Schirmann, *Ha-Shirah ha-'Ibrit*, II, 67–69, 87; A. M. Habermann, *Shalosh Maqamot al ha-Nashim* (Jerusalem, 1971); note that Alharizi too engaged in this sport; see *Tahkemoni*, chap. 6.

77. *Perush Kallah Rabbati*, ed. Toledano, p. 21.

78. Ibid., p. 19. For a recognition of the "social function" of this type of poetry and its implications for the equitable distribution of communal tax burdens incurred in the recitation of such poetry, see Ramah's interesting responsum, *OZ*, pp. 136–137, no. 241.

79. Cf. too *HRS*, 173b. Note, however, the erotic prologue to Ramah's wedding poem in honor of Abraham Alfakar (Brody, "Shirim," pp. 12–13). Technically it might have met Ha-Yarhi's standards because it is a wedding poem. But one doubts that Ramah's expertise in this area was developed solely by composing wedding poems. In fact, this prologue is a completely independent component—the complaint of a rejected lover. Transition to the main theme comes when the poet (Ramah) tells his stunningly beautiful rejectors that Alfakar's friendship makes them dispensable. This sort of introduction, common in poems of praise, almost never occurs in wedding poems; see Pagis, *Hiddush u-Masoret*, p. 158.

80. Quoted by Jacob b. Asher, *Tur Orah Hayyim*, no. 68.

81. Ha-Yarhi, *Sefer ha-Manhig*, I, 93–94.

82. Ha-Meiri, *Magen Abot*, pp. 28–29; on the history of this custom, see Y. Ta-Shema, "El Melek Ne'eman—Gilgulo shel Minhag," *Tarbiz* 39 (1969): 184ff.

83. Quoted by Jacob b. Asher, *Tur Orah Hayyim*, no. 61.

84. See Ha-Yarhi, *Sefer ha-Manhig*, I, 66; cf. *Hiddushe ha-Ramban* (Jerusalem, 1938), I, 1.

85. Meir b. Simon, *Sefer ha-Me'orot, Berakot*, 11a.

86. According to Urbach (*Ba'ale ha-Tosafot*, p. 201, Ha-Yarhi served as the link between the scholars of his native Lunel and the school of R. Isaac of Dampierre. But the source for this statement is not clear.

87. On midrash and kabbalah in *Sefer ha-Manhig*, see Twersky, *Rabad*, pp. 242–243; see *Sefer ha-Manhig*, I, 153 for what may be a kabbalistic interpretation of a liturgical custom of Ibn Shoshan's synagogue.

88. See Chapter 3.

89. On the nature and influence of this work, see I. Ta-Shema, "Yezirato shel R. Meir Abulafia," *Qiryat Sefer* 45 (1970): 119–126; M. Breuer, *Keter Aram Zobah veha-Nusah ha-Mequbbal shel ha-Miqra* (Jerusalem, 1976), pp. 12–17, 88–94 and passim. The brief sketch given here is heavily dependent on Breuer's interpretation of Ramah's Masoretic enterprise. The date 1227 is preserved in a colophon; see J. Llamas, "Las manuscritos hebreos de la real biblioteca de San Lorenzo de el Escorial," *Sefarad* 1 (1941): 16. For an illustration of Ramah's increasing interest in the problems of Masorah, cf. his treatment of Deut. 11:18 in *HRS*, 6b s.v. *u-mi* to that preserved from *Masoret Seyag la-Torah* by Yedidyah Norzi, *Minhat Shai* (Vienna, 1814), to Deut. 11:18. For sensitivity to Masoretic problems in Ramah's talmudic commentaries, see *HRS*, 176a s.v. *pisqa*; *YRB*, 1:106. On the last source, see the note of R. Matityahu Strashun to *Baba Batra*, 9a.

90. See, e.g., Maimonides, *Mishneh Torah, Sefer Torah,* 7:11.

91. *Qiddushin,* 30a.

92. *Masoret Seyag la-Torah* (Florence, 1754), introduction.

93. "Therefore I, Moses son of Maimon the Sefardi, girded my loins . . ."

94. *Masoret Seyag la-Torah,* introduction. Cf. the "three scrolls" account in *Sifre on Deut.,* sec. 356 and parallels. Ramah's procedure of following the majority is already suggested in Judah Halevi's *Kuzari,* 3:26–27; cf. too *YRB,* 6:77; see also S. Assaf, *Meqorot u-Mehqarim be-Toledot Yisrael* (Jerusalem, 1946), pp. 183–184.

95. See Breuer, *Keter Aram Zobah,* pp. 12–17, 88–94.

96. See ibid., p. 13 and passim.

97. See *Masoret Seyag la-Torah,* introduction.

98. See Ha-Meiri, *Qiryat Sefer,* pp. 45–49.

99. Ibid., pp. 48–49; cf. N. Kohen, *Ozar ha-Gedolim,* VI, 127.

100. See, e.g., the sources in Dinur, *Yisrael ba-Golah,* vol. II, bk. I, 322 and bk. II, 40–41. *Erez ha-Ma'arab* could refer specifically to Muslim Spain; see, e.g., Schirmann, *Ha-Shirah ha-'Ibrit,* I, 386, l. 25 and 462, l. 4. Note too its extension by Nahmanides to the Toledo region; see Chapter 1, n. 96.

101. See the letter published by A. S. Halkin as an appendix to his edition of Maimonides' *Iggeret Teman* (New York, 1952), p. 109.

102. See I. Ta-Shema, "R. Meir Abulafia," *Qiryat Sefer* 44 (1969): 434.

103. *She'elot u-Teshubot R. Yosef Megash* (Jerusalem, 1959), p. 17, no. 101.

104. The attribution to Ramah is based on the questioner's address to *nesi nesi'e ha-levi*—a usual title for Ramah. However, it was also used in address to other prominent Levites; see, e.g., the address to Judah Halevi quoted in Dinur, *Yisrael ba-Golah,* vol. II, bk. III, 56, no. 21.

105. See Ha-Meiri, *Qiryat Sefer,* pp. 46–48.

106. Breuer, *Keter Aram Zobah,* pp. 26–27.

107. Brody, "Shirim," p. 42.

108. Ibid., p. 43.

109. Ibid.

110. Ibid., p. 44.

111. See *Sefarad* 1 (1941): 16; *Sefarad* 2 (1942): 277. On this colophon and the manuscripts of *Masoret Seyag la-Torah,* see also M. Benayahu, "Iggeret ha-Sofer R. Abraham Hassan," *Sefunot* 11 (1971–1977): 195–199. Ramah's colophon, after recording the date (5 Elul, 4987) and place ("the city of Toledo") of his work's completion, adds the cryptic letters ל׳יא ה׳יא ח׳ית ב׳ית א׳׳ב. Mr. Jordan Penkower informs me that these are the first letters of the words of Ps. 46:6 ("God is in her midst, she shall not be moved, God will help her at the dawn of day"). Ramah's reference is thus to "the city of Toledo." But in its biblical context Ps. 56:6 refers to "the city of God, the holiest habitation of the Most High." We thus have a striking parallel to Alharizi's poetic linkage of Toledo and Jerusalem; see Chapter 1, n. 16. However, in Ramah's reference, "the dawn of day" is probably the time of Redemption (see Kimhi to Ps. 56:6), when Toledo Judaico will be helped by God and restored to the true Jerusalem.

III. The Resurrection Controversy

1. *YRB*, 1:184, p. 80; *Mishneh Torah* (hereafter cited as MT), *Sefer Torah*, 9:9. An authoritative study of *Mishneh Torah* is I. Twersky, *Introduction to the Code of Maimonides* (New Haven, 1980).

2. See I. Twersky, "The Beginnings of Mishneh Torah Criticism," in *Biblical and Other Studies*, ed. A. Altmann (Cambridge, 1963), pp. 161–183.

3. See Ramah's responsum to Burgos quoted by Menahem ha-Meiri, in *Qiryat Sefer*, ed. M. Hershler (Jerusalem, 1956), p. 46.

4. Lichtenberg, *Qobez*, II, 44b. It is possible, however, to construe Maimonides' phrase "you and the cities around you" as referring more broadly to the communities of Christian Europe. There was, in any case, at least some contact between Spanish Jews and Maimonides; see ibid., p. 27a. Alharizi was able to send a poem of praise to Maimonides "from Spain"; see *Tahkemoni*, p. 389. See also S. D. Goitein, *A Mediterranean Society*, I (Berkeley, 1967), 57.

5. See below, n. 33; on the correspondence between Maimonides and the Lunel scholars, see *Teshubot ha-Rambam*, ed. A. H. Freimann and J. Blau, 3 vols. (Jerusalem, 1958–1961), III, 42–44, 49–57; S. M. Stern, "Halifat ha-Miktabim ben ha-Rambam ve-Hakme Provence," *Zion* 16 (1951): 18–29; Maimonides' replies were written 1198/1199; see Stern, "Halifat Miktabim," p. 24.

6. See Ramah's responsum, cited by Joseph Karo, *Kesef Mishneh, Lulab*, 7:7. Maimonides' reversal is confirmed by his son; see ibid. Ramah says that his Provençal friend saw Maimonides' responsum, written toward the end of his life, in which he reverses himself. R. Asher b. Yehiel adds the significant information that Maimonides' reversal was in response to the questioning of the Lunel scholars; see *Rosh, Sukkah*, 3:14; *Kesef Mishneh*, Lulab, 7:7; the question (whether it is permissible to use more than two *'arabot*) does not appear in the extant exchange between the Lunel scholars and Maimonides, but it does fit their pattern; for this issue too was the subject of one of Rabad's *hassagot*; see below, n. 41; *Hassagot, Lulab*, 7:7. Note that Ramah was in possession of the first set of Maimonides' answers to the Lunel scholars before Maimonides' death, but found out about this responsum orally, after Maimonides' death; this would imply that there was a second, hitherto unknown, halakic exchange between Maimonides and the scholars of Lunel! On the halakic issue in question and the history of Maimonides' views on the subject, see the additional sources in S. Lieberman, *Tosefta Ki-Fshutah*, IV (New York, 1962), 863.

7. See further below, Chapter 4.

8. See Twersky, "Provencal Jewry," pp. 191–194.

9. See Chapter 1, n. 148.

10. See Chapter 4, nn. 91 and 93.

11. See Chapter 4, n. 89.

12. See I. Twersky, "Non-Halakic Aspects of Mishneh Torah," in *Jewish Medieval and Renaissance Studies*, ed. A. Altmann (Cambridge, 1967), pp. 95–118; Twersky, *Introduction to the Code of Maimonides*, pp. 356–514.

13. *MT, Teshubah*, chap. 8; see Joseph Karo, *Kesef Mishneh, Teshubah*, 8:2 and 8:8. Maimonides explicitly links *'olam ha-ba* with the notion of immortality

propounded by "the philosophers"; see *Mishnah 'im Perush R. Mosheh b. Maimon*, trans. and ed. J. Kafih, 7 vols. (Jerusalem, 1963–1968), IV, 205. Modern scholars are divided on the question of whether Maimonides' identification of *'olam ha-ba* and immortality of the soul has any valid support in the classical rabbinic sources; see, e.g., C. Albeck, ed., *Mishnah Neziqin* (Jerusalem, 1959), p. 454; E. Urbach, *Hazal: Pirqe Emunot ve-De'ot* (Jerusalem, 1969), p. 587.

14. M. Higger, ed., "Yarhi's Commentary on Kallah Rabbati," *Jewish Quarterly Review* 24 (1934): 342.

15. See, e.g., *Ha-Nibhar be-Emunot ube-De'ot*, trans. and ed. J. Kafih (Jerusalem, 1970), chaps. 6:5–7, 7, 9:4–5.

16. This is already pointed out by Nahmanides; see his *Torat ha-Adam* in *Kitbe ha-Ramban*, ed. C. Chavel (Jerusalem, 1964), II, 311; see, e.g., the definition of *'olam ha-ba* in Ibn Gabirol's "Keter Malkut," in Schirmann, *Ha-Shirah ha-'Ibrit*, I, 273, ll. 257–262.

17. Julius Guttmann, *Philosophies of Judaism* (London, 1964), p. 73. D. J. Silver, *Maimonidean Criticism and the Maimonidean Controversy* (Leiden, 1965), p. 115, incorrectly claims that the talmudic teacher Raba (quoted in *Baba Batra*, 16a) took Job 7:9 as biblical denial of resurrection; Raba merely says that Job denied resurrection.

18. Brill, *Kitāb*, p. 13; cf. the similar language in Ramah's letter to Nahmanides, in Lichtenberg, *Qobez*, III, 7a. There is no denial of resurrection in *Mishneh Torah*; the reasoning seems to be that a purely spiritual interpretation of *'olam ha-ba*—defined in classical rabbinic literature as the postresurrection period—is tantamount to denial of bodily resurrection. It was objected that *Mishneh Torah* itself declares the denier of resurrection (*tehiyyat ha-metim*) a heretic; see Aaron b. Meshullam, *Kitāb*, pp. 35–36. (Aaron refers to "several places in *Sefer ha-Madda'* "; I can locate only *Teshubah*, 3:6.) But the term *tehiyyat ha-metim* is itself susceptible to figurative interpretation; see below, n. 65; cf. too *Mishnah 'im Perush R. Mosheh b. Maimon*, IV, 206–207, where an assertion of the centrality of *tehiyyat ha-metim* is followed by quotation of a talmudic dictum using "death" and "life" figuratively and an assertion of the inevitability of death and decomposition. Note that Maimonides seems to take the "judgment day" of *Rosh ha-Shanah*, 16b–17a, not as a postresurrection judgment (see Rashi, ad loc.), but as the day of death; see *MT, Teshubah*, 3:5–6. For a similar reinterpretation, see the striking poem of Moses ibn Ezra in Schirmann, *Ha-Shirah ha-'Ibrit*, I, 406–407. An early discussion of conflicting views on physical resurrection by David al-Muqammis is quoted by R. Judah b. Barzilai of Barcelona, *Perush Sefer Yezirah*, ed. S. Halberstam (Berlin, 1885), pp. 153–154. For a reading of Maimonides as denying physical resurrection, see S. D. Luzzatto, *Mehqere ha-Yahadut* (Warsaw, 1913), pp. 166ff.; see further Chapter 5, n. 113.

19. Brill, *Kitāb*, p. 13. For explicit opposition to the philosophical view of death, see Nahmanides in *Kitbe ha-Ramban*, ed. C. Chavel (Jerusalem, 1964), II, 14. Maimonidean eschatology as a source of disillusionment and despair is a frequent theme in the polemical poetry of Meshullam da Piera; see, e.g., H. Brody, "Shire Meshullam b. Shelomoh da Piera," *Yedi'ot ha-Makon le-Heqer ha-Shirah ha-'Ibrit*, 4 (1938); 16–17.

20. Brill, *Kitāb*, p. 15.

21. Ibid.

22. Ibid. On the date of Ramah's first letter to Lunel, see N. Brüll, "Die Polemik für und gegen Maimuni im dreizehnten Jahrhunderte," *Jahrbücher für judische Geschichte und Literatur* 4 (1879): 4–5; cf. Chapter 4, n. 54.

23. See Benedict, "Merkaz ha-Torah be-Provence," *Tarbiz* 22 (1951): 100.

24. See below, n. 57.

25. Brill, *Kitāb*, p. 15, corrected by Cambridge MS Add. 1178, p. 2d.

26. See the critical glosses of Rabad on *MT, Teshubah*, 8:2, 4, and 8. Note that Ramah's friend Ha-Yarhi was a student of Rabad; see Twersky, *Rabad*, pp. 240–244.

27. Brill, *Kitāb*, p. 15.

28. Ibid.; alluding to the interpretation of Prov. 21:30 in *'Erubin*, 63a.

29. The first instance of a theme frequently sounded regarding problematic views of Maimonides; see Twersky, "Non-Halakic Aspects of Mishneh Torah," p. 110.

30. Brill, *Kitāb*, p. 15.

31. Ibid., p. 16.

32. Ibid., pp. 16–25.

33. Ibid., pp. 19–25.

34. See below, n. 110.

35. See Twersky, "Mishneh Torah Criticism," pp. 178–179.

36. Brill, *Kitāb*, p. 16. The statement of Baer (*History*, I, 101–102) that Ramah sought to enlist support "for his plan to place the writings of Maimonides under the ban" is without foundation.

37. See Brill, *Kitāb*, pp. 1–2, 25–40; on Aaron b. Meshullam, see H. Gross, *Gallia Judaica* (Paris, 1897), p. 280; Twersky, *Rabad*, pp. 251–253. The suggestion of Brill (*Kitāb*, p. 52) and Brody ("Shirim," p. 64) that Ramah was Aaron's student is highly unlikely. Ramah's medieval editor identifies a poem as having been written to Aaron b. Meshullam in connection with their controversy over the *Guide* ("Shirim," p. 64). This is probably a slip; the poem occurs in *Kitāb*, p. 105, in connection with the Resurrection Controversy.

38. See S. Friedman, ed., *The Commentary of R. Jonathan Ha-Kohen of Lunel on the Mishnah and Alfasi Tractate Bava Kamma* (New York, 1969), introduction, p. 41.

39. Twersky, *Rabad*, pp. 247–250; Friedman (*Commentary of R. Jonathan Ha-Kohen*, pp. 41–43) is, however, skeptical on this score.

40. Twersky, *Rabad*, pp. 125–197.

41. See A. H. Freimann in *Teshubot ha-Rambam*, ed. Freimann and Blau, III, 43.

42. See n. 26 above.

43. Though Aaron had corresponded with Rabad; see Twersky, *Rabad*, pp. 251–252.

44. See Brill, *Kitāb*, pp. 25–40.

45. Ibid., pp. 40–49.

46. See ibid., pp. 36–38 and Ramah's rebuttal, pp. 53–58.

47. Ibid., p. 2.

48. Ibid., pp. 103–104.

49. Ibid., p. 39.

50. See Chapter 1, n. 17.

51. See also Brill, *Kitāb*, pp. 13–16; note, e.g., the pun on *Mishneh Torah* (ibid., p. 13).

52. See the examples cited by Twersky, *Rabad*, pp. 191–193.

53. See above, n. 28.

54. Brill, *Kitāb*, p. 30; for Ramah's reply see ibid., pp. 99–100, 102–103.

55. See, e.g., Chapters 4 and 5 on the controversy of the 1230s. In the controversy over rationalism in Spain and Provence at the beginning of the fourteenth century, the anti-rationalists exclude Maimonides and his works completely from their criticism; see, e.g., J. Sarachek, *Faith and Reason: The Conflict over the Rationalism of Maimonides* (New York, 1935), pp. 167, 196. There were, of course, always exceptions such as Shem Tob b. Shem Tob; see, e.g., E. Gottlieb, *Mehqarim be-Sifrut ha-Kabbalah* (Tel Aviv, 1976), pp. 347–356.

56. See, e.g., Brill, *Kitāb*, pp. 103–104.

57. See ibid., pp. 26, 28, 30 and especially pp. 39–40.

58. Brody, "Shirim," p. 63; for the expression *"yehid ha-dor,"* cf. Samuel ha-Nagid, *Dīwān*, ed. Dov Yarden (Jerusalem, 1966), p. 212; Mosheh ibn al-Taqanah in Schirmann, *Ha-Shirah ha-'Ibrit*, 1:290.

59. Most of the sources on Sheshet Benveniste were collected by Graetz, *Dibre Yeme Yisrael*, IV, 408–409; Steinschneider took exception to Graetz's claim that all these sources refer to the same man; see *Hebraeische Bibliographie* 13 (1873): 106–110; on the basis of archival material, Baer removed Steinschneider's objections and showed that Graetz was correct; see *Die Juden im christlichen Spanien*, I, 34–35; A. Marx, "Texts by and about Maimonides," *Jewish Quarterly Review* 25 (1935): 408, reaffirms Steinschneider's view; Brody ("Shirim," p. 10) adds that it is unlikely that a man whom Ramah's poetry shows to have been a friend could have written a harsh polemic against him. In fact, their identity can be proved: the polemic against Ramah is signed by Sheshet b. Isaac b. Joseph of Saragossa (Marx, "Texts," p. 428); an author of precisely this name corresponded with the *nesi'im* of Narbonne mentioning the death of his only son about 1195; see D. Kaufmann, "Lettres de Scheschet b. Isaac de Saragosse aux Princes de Narbonne," *Revue des études juives* (1899): 224–225; the name of Sheshet's son was apparently Samuel; see Kaufmann, "Lettres," p. 220; thus Ramah's poem on the death of "R. Samuel b. Sheshet, the Saragossa *nasi"* ("Shirim," p. 61) is clearly for the son of his future opponent. Baer's thesis would seem to be correct. It is possible, however, that there was a second, less famous Spanish *nasi* Sheshet whose son(s) did survive him; see, e.g., Baer, *History*, I, 398, n. 43; D. Baneth, "R. Yehudah Alharizi ve-Shalshelet ha-Targumim shel Ma'amar Tehiyyat ha-Metim," *Tarbiz* 11 (1939): 269. On an interesting medical success of R. Sheshet, see V. Aptowitzer, *Mabo le-Sefer Rabiah* (Jerusalem, 1932), p. 421.

60. Alharizi (*Tahkemoni*, p. 346) refers to Sheshet as "the pillar of the world and the foundation of all saints." This sounds like something more than idle praise for a former patron.

61. Marx, "Texts," pp. 406–428.

62. Ibid., pp. 414–415.

63. See Kaufmann, "Lettres," pp. 62–75, 217–225. Kaufmann even suggests that R. Sheshet was a native of Narbonne; Baer thinks this incorrect; see *Die Juden im christlichen Spanien,* I, 35.

64. Marx, "Texts," pp. 414–417.

65. Ibid., pp. 417–426.

66. Ibid., p. 425.

67. Ibid., pp. 425–426; see Chapter 4, n. 89.

68. Zacuto mistakes Sheshet's family name for his father's name; this misled Steinschneider, cited above, n. 59.

69. *Sefer Yuhasin,* ed Filipowski, p. 229b. R. Joseph's second son, Isaac, was Ramah's son-in-law. Alharizi's poetic picture of Maimonides greeting Ibn Shoshan in heaven (*Tahkemoni,* p. 404) suggests that the latter did not actively support his son-in-law's polemical activity.

70. Marx, "Texts," pp. 414, 417.

71. See, e.g., G. Scholem, "Mi-Hoqer le-Mequbbal," *Tarbiz* 6 (1935): 90–98.

72. Brill, *Kitāb,* pp. 51–105. In this response Ramah also took the opportunity to correct some of R. Aaron's stylistic and grammatical errors (*Kitāb,* pp. 2, 97–102). But this was standard polemical sport in the Andalusian tradition; see Ibn Daud, *Sefer ha-Qabbalah,* p. 67; David Baneth, "Ta'uyot be-Shimush Leshon 'Arab," *Ozar Yehude Sefarad* 4 (1961): 14–15; Ashtor, *Sefarad ha-Muslamit,* II, 204; Chapter 4, n. 141; cf. Meshullam b. Kalonymous in Kobak, *Jeschurun,* VIII, 92–93. Ramah, with obvious relish, corrects Aaron's violation of a Maimonidean theological-linguistic principle; see *Kitāb,* p. 100; *MT, Yesode ha-Torah,* 2:10.

73. Brill, *Kitāb,* pp. 5–6.

74. Note that Ramah's second letter to Lunel seems to address itself to Sheshet's interpretation of *tehiyyat ha-metim;* see Brill, *Kitāb,* p. 65.

75. Brill, *Kitāb,* p. 6.

76. See Robert Chazan, *Medieval Jewry in Northern France* (Baltimore, 1973), pp. 97–98, who, however, generalizes too much in seeing this correspondence as the first evidence of substantial contact between the Jewries of southern Europe and northern France; for earlier contact between southern and northern France, see B. Z. Benedict, "Merkaz ha-Torah be-Provence," *Tarbiz* 22 (1951): 85–109.

77. Brill, *Kitāb,* pp. 3–4.

78. See Urbach, *Ba'ale ha-Tosafot,* pp. 219–283; on the Provençal contacts of Isaac b. Abraham, see ibid., pp. 221–222.

79. See Gross, "Etude sur Simson b. Abraham," *Revue des études juives* 7 (1883): 46; Urbach, *Ba'ale ha-Tosafot,* pp. 279–280.

80. Vol. 2, ed. M. Schlesinger (Berlin, 1902), p. 364; see Gross, "Simson b. Abraham," p. 47.

81. For a conjecture on David's identity, see Gross, "Simson b. Abraham," pp. 46–47.

82. Cf. Chapter 5.

83. See Chapter 4.

84. See Urbach, *Ba'ale ha-Tosafot,* pp. 201–202.

85. Brill, *Kitāb,* p. 106.

86. See Abraham b. Azriel, '*Arugat ha-Bosem,* ed. E. Urbach (Jerusalem, 1947), II, 259–262; Urbach, "Hakme Ashkenaz ve-Zarfat 'al ha-Rambam," *Zion* 12 (1947): 150–152. I cannot agree with Urbach's contention that Moses b. Hasdai was closer to Ramah than Eliezer Rokeah (who paraphrases Saadya in support of Ramah); when it comes to the question of rationalism, the same man, Saadya, is Ramah's hero and Moses b. Hasdai's villain; see Chapter 5.

87. Dan. 8:4–7.

88. Brill, *Kitāb,* pp. 107–108.

89. Tosefta, *Miqva'ot,* 8:6; *Sifre, Bamidbar,* ed. H. S. Horowitz (Jerusalem, 1966), pp. 158–159.

90. Brill, *Kitāb,* pp. 108–110, 134–137.

91. See Chapter 4.

92. Baer's explanation (*History,* I, 101) that the deteriorated political situation of the Jews in France may be responsible is unsatisfying, for the situation in France was no better thirty years later; see, e.g., Chazan, *Medieval Jewry,* pp. 100ff. It is interesting that persecution has been seen as both an inhibitor and the true cause of anti-rationalistic activity. For the second view, see Silver, *Maimonidean Criticism,* pp. 3ff.

93. Cf. Urbach, *Ba'ale ha-Tosafot,* pp. 226–227.

94. See below, n. 146.

95. For a hint at the role of philosophy, see Ramah's allusion (in Brill, *Kitāb,* p. 103) to Isa. 2:6; cf. Targum and Kimhi, ad loc.; cf. too Lichtenberg, *Qobez,* III, 6d, 8c; Kobak, *Jeschurun,* VIII, 27.

96. Brill, *Kitāb,* p. 131. This phrase was thrown back at the scholars of northern France during the controversy of the 1230s; see the letter of Samuel b. Abraham Saporta in Kobak, *Jeschurun,* VIII, 131. On R. Samson's final opinion of Maimonides, see Stern, "Rabbi Yehudah Alharizi be-Shebaho shel ha-Rambam," pp. 94–95.

97. See Alharizi, *Tahkemoni,* p. 403.

98. See Chapter 1; Chapter 2, n. 54; above, n. 60.

99. See the dialogue of body, soul, and intellect in Alharizi, *Tahkemoni,* chap. 13; cf. *Sanhedrin,* 91a–b; see especially *Tahkemoni,* p. 144: "So long as I dwell in the body I am counted dead therein, but when I go out I live." It must be conceded, however, that this poetic description of bodily death as initiating a *tehiyyat ha-metim* is a fairly common motif and is not necessarily proof of Alharizi's theological position.

100. See Chapter 1.

101. The manuscripts used by Brill for his edition have the introduction translated in Hebrew, though some editorial comments are still given in Arabic; see *Kitāb,* pp. 107, 137–138, 148–149; a fragment of *Kitāb al-Rasā'il,* including the Arabic original of the introduction, was published by D. Yellin in *Qiryat Sefer* 6 (1929): 139–144. The Cambridge manuscript of *Kitāb al-Rasā'il* also contains the Arabic original of Ramah's introduction. Note Ramah's reference to Maimonides in his introduction as still living (נר"ו); the preliminary edition of *Kitāb al-Rasā'il* thus predates the arrival of the northern French response; the latter, in addition to further exchanges between Ramah and R. Samson, was added subsequently.

102. For a critical edition of both the original Arabic and Ibn Tibbon's

translation, see Joshua Finkel, "Maimonides' Treatise on Resurrection," *Proceedings of the American Academy for Jewish Research* 9 (1939): 63–105, 1–42 (Heb. sec.); see too Finkel, "Maimonides' Treatise on Resurrection: A Comparative Study," in *Essays on Maimonides,* ed. S. Baron (New York, 1941), pp. 93–121.

103. Maimonides mentions misunderstanding of his position in Damascus, Yemen, and Baghdad; see Finkel, "Maimonides' Treatise on Resurrection," pp. 11–12 (Heb.). Ramah's later mention of Isfahan in this connection (*HRS,* 159b) is puzzling. There was some confusion in Europe about the location of the Messianic incident that prompted Maimonides' *Epistle to Yemen*—some locating it in Isfahan; see Halkin's appendix to his edition of *Iggeret Teman,* p. 108. Perhaps some lingering confusion on this score carried over to the *Treatise on Resurrection* and caused Ramah or a copyist inadvertently to mention Isfahan.

104. Steinschneider, *Die hebraeischen Uebersetzungen,* I, 431.

105. Besides, it is inconceivable that the *Treatise*—had it been known—would not have been quoted in a polemic over Maimonides' position on resurrection.

106. See *HRS,* 159a–162b.

107. See S. Z. Halberstam quoted by S. P. Rabinowitz in his edition of Graetz, *Dibre Yeme Yisrael,* V, 39 (who also corrects Graetz's characterization of Ramah as an obscurantist). Note, however, that in his first letter to Lunel, Ramah had already rejected the notion of a temporary resurrection followed by a second bodily death; see Brill, *Kitāb,* p. 14. It has been claimed that he was reacting to Maimonides' theory as put forward in the *Treatise;* see I. Zinberg, *Toledot Sifrut Yisrael,* ed. A. M. Habermann (Tel Aviv, 1959), I, 306; Finkel, "Maimonides' Treatise on Resurrection: A Comparative Study," p. 115. But this is contradicted by Ramah's own testimony that he had not seen the *Treatise* when writing to Lunel (*HRS,* 159). This is why temporary resurrection is mentioned in *Kitāb* as a possible, not definitive, Maimonidean position. Ramah may have known it from other sources, e.g., Ibn Ezra; see Finkel, "Maimonides' Treatise on Resurrection: A Comparative Study," pp. 98–99. For the reason that the *Treatise* nevertheless changed Ramah's mind, see Chapter 5, nn. 100–102.

108. *HRS,* 159b.

109. Maimonides is referred to as "רבי משה נ"ר בר' מיימון" "נ"ע" in *HRS,* 19b, 21b. "נ"ר" is omitted, ibid., 111b. In the discussion of resurrection he is mentioned first with "ז"ל" and then "נ"ר" (ibid., 159a, 159b). The latter reading is to be preferred since copyists are likely to change "נ"ר" to "ז"ל" but not vice versa.

110. See Brill, *Kitāb,* pp. 16–19; the criticisms of *Qiddush ha-Hodesh,* 4:2 and 4:16 relate to the leap year, relevant to *Sanhedrin,* chap. 1; cf. *HRS,* 23a; the criticism of *'Abodah Zarah,* 4:6 relates to *'ir ha-niddahat* relevant to the end of *Sanhedrin;* the criticisms of *"Abodah Zarah,* 2:7 relate to blasphemy relevant to *Sanhedrin,* chap. 7; cf. *HRS,* 107a; the criticism of *Mamrim,* 4:3 relates to the rebellious elder, relevant to *Sanhedrin,* chap. 10 (Ramah's comments on this chapter are missing). Ramah may have been commenting on the tractates of *Neziqin* in order, for his commentaries to *Horayot* and *Abot* were composed in 1207; see Chapter 1, n. 156. The *Treatise on Resurrection* was thus fresh in his mind; see Chapter 1, n. 93.

111. Quoted in Finkel, "Maimonides' Treatise on Resurrection," pp. 101–103.

112. See Steinschneider, *Die hebraeischen Uebersetzungen*, I, 420–421, 428–432; Schirmann, *Ha-Shirah ha-'Ibrit*, II, 97–98. Despite Schirmann's even-handed disapproval of the behavior of both Alharizi and Ibn Tibbon in this affair, Ibn Tibbon seems to me to have been fundamentally in the right; the philosophical glossary of Alharizi that Ibn Tibbon criticizes so intemperately is indeed a scandalous piece of work. Alharizi is a good example of someone for whom the heroic image of Maimonides is more important than a precise understanding of his philosophy.

Ibn Tibbon followed his father's method of literal translation; see Judah ibn Tibbon's introduction to his translation of *Hobot ha-Lebabot*. Maimonides himself had advised Ibn Tibbon against a literal, word-for-word approach and gave some interesting samples; see D. Baneth, "Ha-Rambam ke-Metargem Dibre Azmo," *Tarbiz* 23 (1951–52): 170–191; cf. too Moses ibn Ezra, *Kitāb al-Muhādara wal-Mudhākara*, ed. A. S. Halkin (Jerusalem, 1975), pp. 42–43. Can we perhaps speak of a Spanish versus a Provençal approach to translation?

113. This attitude would seem to have been foreign to Alharizi himself; see Abraham Halkin, "The Medieval Jewish Attitude Toward Hebrew," in *Biblical and Other Studies*, ed. Alexander Altmann (Cambridge, 1963), pp. 237–241.

114. Quoted in Finkel, "Maimonides' Treatise on Resurrection," p. 102.

115. See, e.g., ibid., pp. 79–84; Finkel even denies Alharizi's authorship of this introduction.

116. This would further support the conclusion of D. Z. Baneth, "R. Yehudah Alharizi ve-Shalshelet ha-Targumim shel Ma'amar Tehiyyat ha-Metim," *Tarbiz* 11 (1940): 260–270; Baneth, miraculously making sense out of some very strange and confused data, shows that Alharizi's story is indeed to be taken seriously. Baneth's conclusion has now been fully confirmed by A. David's discovery of the full text of Alharizi's rival translation; see A. H. Halkin, "Ma'mar Tehiyyat ha-Metim la-Rambam be-Targumo shel R. Yehudah Alharizi," *Qobez 'al Yad* 9 (1979): 131–150.

117. Cf. Baneth, "R. Yehudah Alharizi," pp. 268–269. Note that Joseph b. Joel seems to refer to Maimonides as still living; see ibid., p. 270. Moreover Alharizi's introduction begins with a poem in praise of Maimonides (Finkel, "Maimonides' Treatise on Resurrection," p. 101) which appears in Alharizi, *Tahkemoni*, p. 389, with the additional information that it was sent to Maimonides from Spain; this is further indication that the *Treatise* reached Europe before the death of Maimonides.

118. *Me'or 'Enayim*, ed. D. Cassel (Vilna, 1866), I, 92–93.

119. Alharizi, *Tahkemoni*, pp. 403–404. Ibn Shoshan's tombstone inscription in *Abne Zikkaron*, ed. S. D. Luzzatto (Prague, 1841), p. 65, gives the date of his death as "the end of Shevat." The date given by the editor of Ramah's *dīwān* is 7 Elul, 4965; Brody considers the latter date the correct one; see "Shirim," pp. 8–9. If so, it took five and a half to six and a half months for the news of Maimonides' death to reach Toledo, for Maimonides died 20 Tevet, 4965; see Joseph Sambari in Neubauer, *Medieval Jewish Chronicles* I, 133. This would support Stern, "Halifat ha-Miktabim ben ha-Rambam ve-Hakme Provence," *Zion* 16 (1951): 27, n. 23.

120. Brody, "Shirim," pp. 32–35, and "Qinat Ramah 'al ha-Rambam," *Tarbiz* 6 (1935): 1–9.

121. Brody, "Shirim," p. 33 and Brody's note; on Ramah's attitude to *Mishneh Torah*, see also Chapter 4.

122. Perhaps an allusion to Maimonides' metaphor for perception of the truth as lightning flashes in the darkness; see his introduction to the *Guide*.

123. For a different translation, see Silver, *Maimonidean Criticism*, p. 111.

124. Cf. the introduction to the *Guide*.

125. Brody, "Shirim," p. 33.

126. Ibid., p. 32.

127. For a conflicting appraisal of the *Guide* by Ramah, see Chapter 5.

128. Brody, "Shirim," p. 34.

129. See Ramah's introductory note to R. Samson's reply in Brill, *Kitāb*, p. 107. Silver (*Maimonidean Criticism*, p. 127) mistakes this note to mean that Ha-Yarhi is the author of a reply to Ramah from France and is puzzled that no such reply follows.

130. Brill, *Kitāb*, pp. 138–152.

131. Finkel, "Maimonides' Treatise on Resurrection," p. 19. The word "wicked" (*ra'*) intriguingly occurs only in the Hebrew translation.

132. Brody, "Shirim," p. 34.

133. See Brody's note, ibid.

134. Ps. 106:32.

135. Num. 27:14.

136. Lichtenberg, *Qobez*, III, 7a. Cf. Ramah's similar language in Brill, *Kitāb*, p. 104.

137. See Chapters 4 and 5.

138. *HRS*, 158b–162a.

139. Brill, *Kitāb*, p. 36.

140. Ibid., p. 53.

141. Ibid., pp. 56–57; *Emunot ve-De'ot*, 7:1 (ed. Kafih, pp. 219–220).

142. Brill, *Kitāb*, p. 136.

143. *HRS*, 158b.

144. Both factors are apparent in the letter of Sheshet Benveniste; see Marx, "Texts," pp. 418–426.

145. *HRS*, 160a.

146. *HRS*, 160a–b; for a similar attack on the elitist implications of the rationalistic interpretation of immortality, see Shimon b. Yosef, *Hoshen Mishpat* in *Zunz Jubelschrift* (Berlin, 1884), pp. 155–156 (Heb. sec.). On the conception of nature with which Ramah is operating here and its difference from the modern conception, see the clear formulation of Guttmann, *Philosophies of Judaism*, p. 140; see also Chapter 5. The notion that *'olam ha-ba* is a natural phenomenon is explicitly stated in the *Treatise on Resurrection* but not in Ramah's paraphrase thereof; see Finkel, "Maimonides' Treatise on Resurrection," p. 25; *HRS*, 159b–160a. Cf. Bahya ibn Paqudah, *Hobot ha-Lebabot*, 4:4 (ed. Kafih, pp. 229–230). According to Bahya, immortality is dependent on divine pleasure and grace. Although Bahya anticipates Maimonides' eschatological spirituality, he does not anticipate his eschatological naturalism.

IV. The Maimonidean Controversy

1. There is an extensive literature touching on the Maimonidean Controversy; for some important treatments see N. Brüll, "Die Polemik für und gegen Maimuni im dreizehnten Jahrhunderte," *Jahbücher für jüdische Geschichte und Literatur*, 4 (1879): 1–33; H. Graetz, *Dibre Yeme Yisrael*, trans. and annot. by S. P. Rabinowitz, with additional notes by A. Harkavy (Warsaw, 1897), V, 35–67, 349–352; Ze'ev Ya'vetz, *Toledot Yisrael* (Tel Aviv, 1963), pp. 68–80, 175–186; I. Zinberg, *Toledot Sifrut Yisrael*, ed. A. M. Habermann (Tel Aviv, 1959), I, 258–279; J. Sarachek, *Faith and Reason: The Conflict over the Rationalism of Maimonides* (New York, 1935); E. Urbach, "Helkam shel Hakme Ashkenaz ve-Zarfat ba-Pulmus 'al ha-Rambam," *Zion* 12 (1947): 149–159; Baer, *History*, I, 96–110; J. Rosenthal, *Mehqarim u-Meqorot* (Jerusalem, 1967), pp. 126–202; G. Scholem, *Ursprung und Anfänge der Kabbala* (Berlin, 1962), pp. 357–366; D. J. Silver, *Maimonidean Criticism and the Maimonidean Controversy* (Leiden, 1965); B. Z. Dinur, *Yisrael ba-Golah*, vol. II, bk. IV (Jerusalem, 1969), pp. 139–225; C. Touati, "Les deux conflits autour de Maïmonide et des études philosophiques et scientifiques," in *Juifs et judaïsme de Languedoc*, ed. M.-H. Vicaire and B. Blumenkranz (Toulouse, 1977), pp. 173–184. A very important advance has resulted from the new manuscript material brought to light and studied by J. Shatzmiller, "Le-Temunat ha-Mahaloqet ha-Rishonah 'al Kitbe ha-Rambam," *Zion* 34 (1969): 126–144. A good survey and reevaluation of the controversy, taking into account Shatzmiller's discoveries, is A. Shohet, "Berurim be-Parashat ha-Pulmus ha-Rishon 'al Sifre ha-Rambam," *Zion* 36 (1971): 27–60. Another important manuscript, as yet unpublished, is described by Shatzmiller, "Iggarto shel R. Asher b. Gershom le-Rabbane Zarfat" in *Mehqarim le-Zeker Zvi Avineri* (Tel Aviv, 1970), pp. 129–140. I have dealt with the controversy in Catalonia and related matters in "Ma'abaq 'al Shilton Zibburi be-Barcelona be-Tequfat ha-Pulmus 'al Sifre ha-Rambam," *Tarbiz* 42 (1973): 389–400 and in "Piety and Power in Thirteenth Century Catalonia" in *Studies in Medieval Jewish History and Literature*, ed. I. Twersky (Cambridge, 1979), pp. 197–230.

2. See Guttmann, *Philosophies of Judaism*, pp. 61–73.

3. Bahya ibn Paqudah, introduction to *Hobot ha-Lebabot*, ed. Kafih, p. 18; cf. Guttmann, *Philosophies of Judaism*, pp. 55–56; Yizhaq Heinemann, "Ha-Razionalism shel R. Saadya Gaon," in *Rab Saadya Gaon*, ed. Y. L. Fishman (Jerusalem, 1943), pp. 214ff.

4. *Emunot ve-De'ot*, introduction: 6 (ed. Kafih, pp. 23–24). Cf., however, H. Wolfson, *The Philosophy of the Kalam* (Cambridge, 1976), pp. 92–93.

5. See, e.g., J. Schirmann, "Solomon ibn Gabirol: Sa vie et son oeuvre poétique," *Revue des études juives* 131 (1972): 323–350.

6. See S. Assaf, ed., *Meqorot le-Toledot ha-Hinuk be-Yisrael* (Tel Aviv, 1931), II, 19–20; Wolfson, *Philosophy of the Kalam*, p. 93. Note too that there is anti-rationalistic polemic in the commentaries of Judah ibn Bal'am (d. circa 1080); see Ashtor, *Sefarad ha-Muslamit*, II, 293.

7. See, e.g., Chapter 3 on *'olam ha-ba*.

8. See Guttmann, *Philosophies of Judaism*, pp. 134–135.

9. See Baer, *History*, I, 67–77; Cohen, *Sefer ha-Qabbalah*, pp. 296–300.

10. See, e.g., Yizhaq Heinemann, "R. Yehudah Halevi—Ha-Ish ve-Hogeh ha-De'ot," in *Qobez R. Yehudah Halevi*, ed. Yisrael Zmora (Tel Aviv, 1950), pp. 131–165; Heinemann, "Ha-Filosof ha-Meshorer," in *Qobez R. Yehudah Halevi*, ed. Zmora, pp. 174–175; Eliezer Schweid, "Ha-Mibneh ha-Sifruti shel ha-Ma'amar ha-Rishon min ha-Kuzari," *Tarbiz* 30 (1961): 257–272; Schweid, *Ta'am ve-Haqashah* (Ramat Gan, 1970), pp. 37–79.

11. Apparently this was the view of Yedaya ha-Penini who (in arguing against anti-rationalism) gives Halevi a prominent place among the great scholars that put philosophy to the service of Torah; see his *Ktab ha-Hitnazlut*, in *She'elot u-Teshubot R. Shlomo b. Adret* (Benai Brak, 1958), I, 166, no. 418. It would seem that the contemporary movement away from neo-Platonism in the direction of a stricter Aristotelianism is even reflected in differences between the earlier and later sections of Halevi's *Kuzari*; see D. Baneth, "Le-Autografim shel Yehudah Halevi ule-Hithavut Sefer ha-Kuzari," *Tarbiz* 26 (1957): 300.

12. Judah b. Barzilai's *Perush Sefer Yezirah*, ed. S. Z. H. Halberstam (Berlin, 1885) is built on geonic material, especially that of Saadya; see the list of sources in Halberstam's introduction, pp. x–xv; on Bahya, see above, n. 3 and his glowing recommendation of Saadya's works *Hobot ha-Lebabot*, p. 42 (end of introduction).

13. See Guttmann, *Philosophies of Judaism*, pp. 134–143.

14. See Maimonides, *Guide of the Perplexed*, 1:71. I owe this formulation to Professor I. Twersky. That Maimonides is referring primarily to Saadya is pointed out in the commentary of Narboni, ad loc.

15. Maimonides, *Guide of the Perplexed*, 1:71.

16. Ibid.

17. By this time radical tendencies had received still further impetus through the influence of Averroës; see Guttmann, *Philosophies of Judaism*, pp. 195–196. Though Ramah was deeply influenced by Saadya's theological stance, there was no going back to Saadya's philosophical methods or his buoyant optimism on the concord of faith and reason. On Saadya's "double faith theory," see H. Wolfson, *Studies in the History of Philosophy and Religion*, I (Cambridge, 1973), pp. 583–618. But "reason" was not saying quite the same thing to Ramah as it had to Saadya.

A good sense of the shift in mood can be seen in Ramah's explanation of the following talmudic exegesis: " 'He who walks blamelessly (*holek tamim*)' (Ps. 25:2)—this is Abraham" (*Makkot*, 24a). According to Ramah *holek tamim* refers to Abraham "because he had faith (*he'emin*) in God and set aside his understanding and wisdom in favor of the Omnipresent as it is written . . . '[God said to Abraham]: abandon your astrology' (*Shabbat*,156a) and it is written: 'and he had faith in the Lord' (Gen. 15:6)" (quoted in Jacob ibn Habib, *'En Ya'aqob*, V, 249). For Ramah's opposition to scientific astrology (in which he was in agreement with Maimonides), see Chapter 5, n. 80. But here Abraham's abandonment of astrology simply provides an example of human reason set aside in favor of faith. This image of Abraham as a "knight of faith" and the accompanying interpretation of *Shabbat*, 156a, are indebted to Judah Halevi, *Kuzari*, 4:17—a crucial passage. It contrasts sharply with the "knight of reason" in

Maimonides, *MT, Abodah Zarah,* 1:3; cf. the revision of Maimonides' image of Abraham in Hasdai Crescas, *Or Ha-Shem,* I, 3, 6.

Ramah's anti-rationalistic understanding of the term *tamim* ("of simple faith") seems also indebted to Halevi; see his use of Deut. 18:13 in Schirmann, *Ha-Shirah ha-'Ibrit,* I, 519. Here too there is a counterinterpretation of *tamim* ("intellectually unblemished") in Maimonides, *MT, 'Abodah Zarah,* 11:16; cf. the commentaries of Rashi, Ibn Ezra, and Nahmanides to Deut. 18:13, and Ha-Yarhi, *Sefer ha-Manhig,* I, 17.

On Ramah's anti-rationalistic reading of Genesis 15:16, cf. H. Wolfson, *Philo* (Cambridge, 1962), I, pp. 151–152; cf. too Rom. 4:3 and Profiat Duran, "Iggeret Al Tehi ka-Aboteka" in *Ozar Vikkuhim,* ed. J. D. Eisenstein (New York, 1928), p. 95a (on Hab. 2:4—"and the righteous shall live by his faith [*be-emunato*]"). Duran sees the setting of "faith" (*emunah*) in opposition to reason as characteristic of Christian interpretation. But the original thrust of the Christian exegesis of Gen. 15:16 and Hab. 2:4 is the superiority of faith to *works;* see Rom. 1:17; Gal. 3:11. Ramah was doubtless aware of this interpretation and took pains to deny it possible talmudic support. The previously mentioned passage in *Makkot* 24a has the 613 commandments gradually reduced and concentrated until Habakkuk, in a final distillation, reduces them to "the righteous shall live by his faith." According to Ramah, "that does not mean that if one does this alone he achieves the life of *'olam ha-ba;* for if that were the case, punishment for sins and reward for *mizvot* would cease to exist" (quoted in Jacob ibn Habib, *'En Ya'aqob,* V, 249; Moses of Trani, *Bet Elohim* [reprint: New York, n.d.], "Sha'ar ha-Yesodot," chap. 34, p. 199). Ramah explains that what was reduced to faith was the precondition for obtaining divine aid in the struggle with the evil *yezer;* for the rabbinic doctrine of "grace" upon which this interpretation is based, see S. Schechter, *Aspects of Rabbinic Theology* (New York, 1961), pp. 278–292; cf., however, Maimonides, *MT, Teshubah,* 6:5. It is also possible that Ramah's concern, in this comment, was to remove potential support for rationalistic antinomianism; see, e.g., Chapter 5, n. 134 and Chapter 3, n. 146. But an anti-Christian motivation seems more likely, given Ramah's interpretation of *emunah.*

Consistent with Ramah's nonrationalistic conception of faith is his interpretation of the first of the Ten Commandments as "a positive commandment to accept Him upon us as Deity" (in Jacob ibn Habib, *'En Ya'aqob,* V, 249). This may have been intended to modify the more intellectualistic definition of Maimonides, *MT, Yesode ha-Torah,* 1:1–6; cf. Nahmanides, *Commentary on the Torah,* Ex. 10:2. Thus Ramah goes on to reject (implicitly) Maimonides' interpretation (*Guide,* II, 33) of the talmudic teaching that Israel heard the first two commandments "from the mouth of the Force," as referring to their rational comprehension.

18. See the surprisingly frank formulation of Abraham Maimonides, *Milhamot Hashem,.* in Lichtenberg, *Qobez,* III, 16c–d. Abraham's tradition-conscious Provençal correspondents must have winced at his praise of them for having abandoned their fathers' ways while he condemns the anti-rationalists for "remaining firm in the corrupt belief which they inherited from their fathers."

19. See *OZ*, pp. 149–153, no. 255; Halberstam in Kobak, *Jeschurun*, VIII, 113, n. 1; Ta-Shema, "R. Meir Abulafia," *Qiryat Sefer* 44 (1969): 429

20. See Urbach, *Ba'ale ha-Tosafot*, pp. 395–396.

21. See further Shohet, "Berurim," pp. 27–31.

22. See, e.g., *Qobez*, III, 1a, 1c, 5c–6b; *Zion* 34 (1969): 141–142.

23. See Chapter 5.

24. See Shohet, "Berurim," pp. 30–31.

25. Shatzmiller, "Le-Temunat ha-Mahaloqet," pp. 126–130, 137–139.

26. See the sources quoted by Twersky, "Provençal Jewry," p. 196.

27. See Urbach, *Ba'ale ha-Tosafot*, p. 94.

28. Kobak, *Jeschurun*, VIII, 845.

29. See Schirmann, *Ha-Shirah ha-'Ibrit*, I, 147–148 and II, 440. This motif and its relationship to geographical stereotypes requires further study.

30. See Twersky, "Provençal Jewry," p. 196. But twelfth-century Provençal scholars do not see themselves as residents of Zarfat; see, e.g., M. Guedemann, *Ha-Torah veha-Hayyim* (Tel Aviv, 1968), p. 6, n. 1; Twersky, *Rabad*, pp. 232–236. The usage seems restricted to Spaniards; see, e.g., Ibn Daud, *Sefer ha-Qabbalah*, p. 66 (Heb. text); Maimonides, "Letter on Astrology," ed. A. Marx, *Hebrew Union College Annual* 3 (1926): 358. Ramah may be one of the earliest Spaniards to use Zarfat in its more restricted sense.

31. Kobak, *Jeschurun*, VIII, 45; cf. too the polemical letter published in *Tarbiz* 42 (1973): 399. Note the clear differentiation between Zarfat and Provence in the letter of Abraham and Judah ibn Hasdai, *Jeschurun*, VIII, 49 and all other Spanish polemical writing of the 1230s. The poet, Meshullam da Piera of Gerona, is characterized as "shā'ir al-zarfatiyin," which has led to speculation about his possible French origins; see H. Brody, "Shire Meshullam b. Shelomoh da Piera," in *Yedi'ot ha-Makon le-Heqer ha-Shirah ha-'Ibrit*, 4 (1938): 4. More likely it means the poet who took the side of the French (in his polemical poetry); see, e.g., poems number 3, 11, 12, 15, 24, 40, 44, 48, 49.

32. Shatzmiller, "Le-Temunat ha-Mahaloqet," pp. 136–137, 142–144.

33. Ibid., p. 144.

34. Ibid., p. 140.

35. See ibid., pp. 142, 144; Lichtenberg, *Qobez*, III, 1a–c; on the moderate position of Meshullam b. Kalonymous, see below, n. 69.

36. See the letter of Samuel Saporta in Kobak, *Jeschurun*, VIII, 125–155.

37. The letter of Asher b. Gershom, Cambridge MS 507.1; for a description see Shatzmiller, "Iggarto shel R. Asher b. R. Gershom," pp. 129–140.

38. See Lichtenberg, *Qobez*, III, 1.

39. Ibid., p. 1c.

40. Ibid., pp. 5b–6b.

41. See Septimus, "Ma'abaq," pp. 389–400, and "Piety and Power," pp. 197–230.

42. Lichtenberg, *Qobez*, III, 4d–5b, 8–10; Kobak, *Jeschurun*, VIII, 102–103; Septimus, "Ma'abaq," pp. 394–395.

43. See Shohet, "Berurim," pp. 45–52.

44. See the letter of Hillel of Verona, in Lichtenberg, *Qobez*, III, 14b–c; on the tendentiousness of this report, see Baer, *History*, I, 401–402. But there may

be a kernel of truth to the reports of R. Jonah's repentance, for there was strong disapproval of the appeal to the Church even in anti-rationalist circles; see Joseph b. Todros in Kobak, *Jeschurun*, VIII, 42–43.

45. *Zion*, 34 (1969): 141–142.

46. Lichtenberg, *Qobez*, III, 6d.

47. Ibid., p. 6b.

48. See Chapter 5.

49. Lichtenberg, *Qobez,*, III, 6c; Kobak, *Jeschurun*, VIII, 99–101.

50. Lichtenberg, *Qobez,*, III, 6c–6d.

51. Ibid., p. 6d.

52. Ibid., pp. 6d–7a. Ramah's anti-rationalist activities are described as much more vigorous and effective by Meshullam da Piera (if the Meir he describes is in fact Ramah); see Brody, "Shire Meshullam da Piera," p. 33 and Brody's note; but Meshullam likes to exaggerate.

53. Lichtenberg, *Qobez*, III, 7a; see Chapter 5.

54. Dinur uses this estimate, in conjunction with the date of 1232 given in the Saragossa *herem* (Lichtenberg, *Qobez*, III, 5b), to date the Resurrection Controversy at approximately 1200; see his *Yisrael ba-Golah*, vol. II, bk. IV, 265. But it is quite possible that the controversy was an extended one and that Ramah's letter was written later in the decade; cf. the date in *Qobez*, III, 17a.

55. Lichtenberg, *Qobez,*, III, 7a.

56. See, e.g., Twersky, "Provençal Jewry," p. 207.

57. Lichtenberg, *Qobez*, III, 7a.

58. See Lichtenberg, *Qobez*, III, 7c.

59. *Zion* 34 (1969): 140–141.

60. See Chapter 1, n. 120.

61. Lichtenberg, *Qobez*, III, 1c–4d.

62. Ibid., pp. 1c–3b; Guttmann, *Philosophies of Judaism*, p. 186.

63. R. Asher b. Yehiel may have read Alfakar's letter after arriving in Toledo early in the fourteenth century; his anti-philosophical play on Deut. 13:3 seems to be borrowed from Alfakar; see Lichtenberg, *Qobez*, III, 1d and R. Asher's well-known responsum to R. Israel of Toledo in *Meqorot le-Toledot ha-Hinuk be-Yisrael*, ed. S. Assaf (Tel Aviv, 1930), II, 57.

64. Kobak, *Jeschurun*, VIII, 21–47.

65. Ibid., p. 41.

66. Ibid., p. 42.

67. Ibid., p. 40; for a conjecture on the identity of R. Nathan, see Kohen, *Ozar ha-Gedolim*, VII, 254. Kimhi did succeed in getting some signatures for the Provençal *herem* in Burgos; Joseph b. Todros dismisses these as insignificant and not representative of the community.

68. Kobak, *Jeschurun*, VIII, 98; see Chapter 5.

69. Kobak, *Jeschurun*, VIII, 91.

70. See Lichtenberg, *Qobez*, III, 1a–b; Kobak, *Jeschurun*, VIII, 103–120; Septimus, "Ma'abaq," pp. 390–393.

71. Kobak, *Jeschurun*, VIII, 117.

72. See Septimus, "Ma'abaq," p. 392, n. 21.

73. *Zion* 34 (1969): 140.

74. Montpellier, it should be remembered, was controlled by the Crown of Aragon until 1349.

75. See Septimus, "Ma'abaq," pp. 390–395.

76. The letter is published ibid., pp. 397–400.

77. Kobak, *Jeschurun*, VIII, 48–56.

78. See Septimus, "Ma'abaq," p. 395.

79. See ibid.

80. See ibid., pp. 395–396.

81. Lichtenberg, *Qobez*, III, 7b.

82. Ibid., p. 7c.

83. See Kobak, *Jeschurun*, VIII, 121.

84. *Zion* 24 (1969): 142. This appraisal may explain the confusion of the prorationalist editor whose introductory note to Nahmanides' circular to the communities of Spain (Lichtenberg, *Qobez*, III, 4d) characterizes it as a call for the excommunication of Solomon of Montpellier and his pupils.

85. See Septimus, "Ma'abaq," p. 396; on the ultimate victory of Nahmanides' circle in about 1241, see pp. 396–397. For more on the origin and development of the Catalonian conflict and its connection with the Provençal arena of the Maimonidean Controversy, see Septimus, "Piety and Power," pp. 197–230.

86. See above, n. 50; Kobak, *Jeschurun*, VIII, 41. Cohen (*Sefer ha-Qabbalah*, p. 302) notes the significance of Joseph's appeal to lineage (but inadvertently calls him a "pro-Maimunist"). For the possible influence of anti-rationalistic Jewish courtiers on the *Fuero Real* (c. 1255) of Alfonso X, see A. Castro, *The Spaniards* (Berkeley, 1971), pp. 546–547; J. N. Hillgarth, *The Spanish Kingdoms*, I (Oxford, 1976), 165.

87. Baer in his *History of the Jews in Christian Spain* sees a close relationship between rationalism and the Hispano-Jewish aristocracy; see the critical comments of Isaiah Sonne, "On Baer and His Philosophy of Jewish History," *Jewish Social Studies* 9 (1947): 61–80; on the need for a balanced reappraisal of Baer's thesis, see Twersky, "Provençal Jewry," p. 189. See also the judicious comments of H. H. Ben-Sasson, "Dor Gole Sefarad 'al 'Azmo," *Zion* 26 (1961): 28–34, 59–64. Baer, in line with his general tendency, portrayed Ramah in the 1230s as isolated and powerless in the face of "an aristocracy that cultivated philosophy . . . as a convenient rationalization for a life of pleasure" (*History*, I, 106–107). In light of the letter from Lunel, discovered by Shatzmiller (above, n. 59) this view can no longer be maintained. Though far from all-powerful, Ramah and Alfakar appear to have asserted effective leadership over the Toledo aristocracy during the Maimonidean controversy.

Ramah's writings also suggest qualification of Baer's close linkage of moral decay and aristocratic rationalism. Ramah was particularly sensitive to what he perceived as moral decay in the Jewish community; see Chapter 1, nn. 19 and 20; yet he passes up a perfect opportunity to link it with rationalism; see Chapter 5, n. 134.

It is interesting that the only group singled out for moral censure in Ramah's surviving works are certain *talmide hakamim!* See *OZ*, no. 248, p. 146; *YRB*, 1:82. The intensity of Ramah's feelings on this subject can be seen from a comment preserved in the commentary to *Baba Mezia* of Abraham b. Yom Tob of Tudela: "This exemption [of scholars from taxes] applies only to scholars who occupy themselves with [study of] the Torah as they should. But if . . . their reputation is hateful (*sanu shum'anayhu*) owing to persistent rumor we collect [taxes] from them *even by the scourge*" (Oxford MS 446/2, p. 183b). The expression *sanu shum'anayhu* suggests a particular concern with sexual impropriety; see, e.g., *Megillah*, 25b and Rashi ad loc.; cf. too Chapter 1, n. 19. The problem of corrupt scholars and religious leaders in early thirteenth century Spain is also discussed by R. Jonah ibn Bahlul in his *Minhat Qena'ot*, Oxford MS, Opp. Add. 4°, 19, p. 3a. The entire question requires separate treatment.

88. See I. Twersky, "The Beginnings of Mishneh Torah Criticism," in *Biblical and Other Studies*, ed. A. Altmann (Cambridge, 1963), pp. 178–182, and *Rabad of Posquières* (Cambridge, 1962), pp. 178–197.

89. Marx, "Texts," p. 426.

90. Oxford MS, Opp. Add. 4°1 19, p. 3a.

91. Ibid., p. 1b.

92. Ibid., pp. 6a–b.

93. *OZ*, p. 298, no. 258.

94. Ibid., p. 156, no. 259.

95. See Twersky, "Mishneh Torah Criticism," pp. 178–179.

96. See Brill, *Kitāb*, p. 138.

97. Lichtenberg, *Qobez*, III, 6d.

98. See Chapter 1, n. 146.

V. Varieties of Anti-rationalism

1. See the letter of the Lunel community published by Shatzmiller, "Le-Temunat ha-Mahaloqet," p. 142.

2. Ibid., pp. 140–141; partially translated in Chapter 4.

3. The problem is raised by Shatzmiller, "Le-Temunat ha-Mahaloqet," p. 132, n. 24.

4. Lichtenberg, *Qobez*, III, 7a; see Chapter 4.

5. *Moreh Nebukim* 1:59; see the commentary of Shem Tob, ad loc.; cf. Gershom Scholem, *Major Trends in Jewish Mysticism* (New York, 1954), pp. 30–32.

6. *Sanhedrin*, 97b.

7. *HRS*, 169a; see *Ta'anit*, 5a.

8. Cf. also Judah Halevi, *Kuzari*, 3:73 (end). On the problem of aggadah generally, see the discussion in M. Saperstein, *Decoding the Rabbis* (Cambridge, 1980), pp. 1–20.

9. See below, n. 55.

10. "qabbalah peshutah be-dibre hakamim"; cf. *HRS*, 158b.

11. See the sources collected in Azariah de Rossi, *Me'or 'Enayim*, I, 196–214; Z. H. Chajes, *Kol Kitbe Maharaz Hayot* (Jerusalem, 1958), I, 243–245; S. L. Rapoport, *Erek Millin* (Warsaw, 1914), p. 24; B. Z. Dinur, *Yisrael ba-Golah*, vol. I, bk. II (Jerusalem, 1962), pp. 260–261; *Ozar ha-Geonim*, *Berakot*, ed. B. M. Lewin, II, 91; ibid., *Hagigah*, pp. 4–5, 59–60; see too Judah b. Barzilai, *Perush*

Sefer Yezirah, pp. 41, 121. Considering the centrality of the issue of aggadah in the Provençal arena of the Maimonidean Controversy, it is worth noting that the geonic-Andalusian view had been adopted in Provence even before philosophical thinking made significant inroads; see Twersky, *Rabad*, pp. 270-271.

12. Samuel ha-Nagid, *Mebo ha-Talmud*, printed in the standard Vilna editions of the Talmud, *Berakot* s.v. *ve-haggadah*; the attribution of this work to the Spanish Nagid has been questioned by Mordecai Margaliyot, *Sefer Hilkot ha-Nagid* (Jerusalem, 1962), pp. 68-73.

13. Cf. Saadya Gaon, *Emunot ve-De'ot*, 7:4 (ed. Kafih, pp. 226-227).

14. *HRS*, 161a; cf. Ibn Ezra to Gen. 22:4.

15. See below, n. 62.

16. See, e.g., *Moreh*, III, 43.

17. See Ibn Ezra's introduction to his *Commentary on Lamentations*.

18. See Chapter 3, n. 66; cf. Judah b. Barzilai, *Perush Sefer Yezirah*, p. 41.

19. For a combination of the last two methods, see Abraham Maimonides, *Milhamot Hashem*, in Lichtenberg, *Qobez*, III, 18b-19a. On nonliteral exegesis, see, e.g., Judah Halevi, *Kuzari*, 3:73; Ibn Ezra, introduction to his *Commentary on the Torah*, s.v. *ha-derek ha-rebi'it* and his commentary on Exod. 20:1; *Mishnah 'im Perush R. Mosheh b. Maimon*, IV, 200-202 ("Introduction to Heleq"); Maimonides, introduction to the *Moreh*. The method of nonliteral exegesis has abundant geonic precedent, especially when used to avoid anthropomorphism; see, e.g., the sources quoted by Samuel Saporta in Kobak, *Jeschurun*, VIII, 132-139.

20. See below, n. 55.

21. See Samuel Saporta in Kobak, *Jeschurun*, VIII, 152; Asher b. Gershom, Cambridge MS 507.1, p. 10a.

22. *Sanhedrin*, 103a.

23. Rashi, ad loc.

24. *HRS*, 176a-b; on the authorship of the commentary to the last chapter of *Sanhedrin* attributed to Rashi, see J. Fraenkel, *Darko shel Rashi be-Perusho la-Talmud ha-Babli* (Jerusalem, 1975), pp. 304-305. Ramah consistently attributes material from this commentary to Rashi, according to Fraenkel, quite correctly.

25. *Sanhedrin*, 98b.

26. *HRS*, 170a-b; for Ramah's closing warning, see the *Commentary of R. Hananel, Sanhedrin*, 38b; cf. Ramah's comment ad loc. (*HRS*, 80a); see too *HRS*, 175a.

27. The formulation of E. M. Lifshutz, *Rashi* (Jerusalem, 1966), p. 187.

28. *Ktab Tamin*, ed. R. Kircheim, in *Ozar Nehmad* 3 (1860): 54-99.

29. See, e.g., R. Samuel b. Meir (Rashbam), *Perush ha-Torah*, ed. A. Bromberg (Tel Aviv, 1965), pp. 5-6 (on Gen. 1:26-27); Urbach, *Ba'ale ha- Tosafot*, p. 115 (on R. Joseph Bekor Shor); Joseph Dan, *Torat ha-Sod shel Hasidut Ashkenaz* (Jerusalem, 1968), pp. 31-35 (on the German pietists who were the immediate objects of Moses b. Hasdai's attack).

30. See Lichtenberg, *Qobez*, III, 9d-10b; Kobak, *Jeschurun*, VIII, 132-139; Asher b. Gershom, Cambridge MS 507.1, p. 7. Guedemann (*Ha-Torah veha-Hayyim*, p. 56) nevertheless maintains that the attribution of anthropomorphism to the northern French was the result of slanderous propaganda.

31. See further "Shire Meshullam da Piera," ed. Brody, pp. 34, 91, 102; Yedaya ha-Penini, *Ktab ha-Hitnazlut* in *Teshubot ha-Rashba*, I, 166–67, no. 418; Yom Tob b. Abraham al-Ishbili, *Sefer ha-Zikkaron*, ed. K. Kahana (Jerusalem, 1956), p. 32; E. Urbach, *'Arugat ha-Bosem* (Jerusalem, 1963), IV, 74–81; Dan, *Torat ha-Sod*, pp. 31–35; Twersky, *Rabad*, pp. 284–286.

32. Deut. 21:22.

33. *Sanhedrin*, 46b; *Ktab Tamim* in *Ozar Nehmad*, 3 (1860): 60.

34. *HRS*, 90b.

35. *MT, Yesode ha-Torah*, 4:8; *Moreh*, 1:1. Note that Ramah has chosen Maimonides' interpretation over that of Saadya, *Emunot ve-De'ot*, 2:9.

36. Cf. *HRS*, 7a, 171a, 179b.

37. *HRS*, 160b.

38. See *Mishnah 'im Perush R. Mosheh b. Maimon*, IV, 211 ("Introduction to Heleq"); *MT, Yesode ha-Torah*, 1:9, 12; *Moreh*, 1:26, 33, 46 and 3:13; cf. Abraham Maimonides in Lichtenberg, *Qobez*, III, 20c.

39. *Berakot*, p. 31b; *Masoret ha-Shas* and *Yefeh Enayim*, ad loc. provide additional references.

40. See Y. Heinemann, *Darke ha-Aggadah* (Jerusalem, 1954), p. 12; M. Kadushin, *The Rabbinic Mind* (New York, 1952), p. 321.

41. Lichtenberg, *Qobez*, III, 1d. See too Nahmanides, *Commentary on the Torah*, Gen. 6:6.

42. See, e.g., Lewin, *Ozar ha-Geonim, Berakot*, I, 131; ibid., *Hagigah*, p. 30; S. Abramson, *Rab Nissim Gaon* (Jerusalem, 1965), p. 281; Bahya ibn Paqudah, *Hobot ha-Lebabot*, 1:10 (ed. Kafih, p. 79); Judah Halevi, *Kuzari*, 5:27; Ibn Ezra, *Commentary on the Torah*, Gen. 6:6.

43. Lichtenberg, *Qobez*, III, 3:15a–21a.

44. See ibid., pp. 17a, 21a–d.

45. Lichtenberg, *Qobez*, III, 19c; cf., however, Kimhi in *Qobez*, III, 3c. Abraham Maimonides implies that their denial of corporeality is a recent concession: "baruk ha-shem . . . shehazeru mizeh ha-minut veha-kafranut." Anthropomorphism is explicitly rejected by Jonah Gerondi, *Commentary on Abot*, 2:1.

46. Lichtenberg, *Qobez*, III, 19c–20d; on the Throne of Glory, cf. Moses b. Hasdai, *Ktab Tamim* in *Ozar Nehmad*, 3 (1860): 60, 68, 85.

47. Lichtenberg, *Qobez*, III, 6c.

48. *HRS*, 80b; *Moreh*, 1:9.

49. *Sanhedrin*, 38b.

50. *HRS*, 80b; *Moreh*, 1:9.

51. *Sanhedrin*, 38b.

52. *HRS*, 80b (after transposing the words *al-'uqūl* which are misplaced in our edition); for another interpretation of aggadah using Arabic terminology of *hakme tushiyyah*, see ibid., 80a (for this equation of *golem* and *māddah* [matter], cf. *MT, Yesode ha-Torah*, 4:1). However, in *HRS*, 160a, Ramah refers to the *hakme ha-mehqar* among the geonim who supports his position on *'olam ha-ba*. This difference in terminology may be intentional, for Ibn Ezra explicitly distinguishes between the two groups; see M. Steinschneider, *Jewish Literature* (London, 1857), p. 296; see further Ibn Ezra's *Commentary on Psalms*, 104:30 where *anshe ha-mehqar* are said to affirm resurrection while *hakme ha-tushiyyah* deny it; the

former would seem to be *mutakallimun* and the latter philosophers; Ramah likely uses these terms in a similar sense; see too Ibn Ezra, *Yesod Mora* (Frankfort 1840), p. 11 (end chap. 1); such usage of *mehqar* is not general; see Steinschneider, *Jewish Literature*; cf. too Nahmanides, *Commentary on the Torah*, Gen. 2:7.

53. *Moreh*, 2:6.

54. The characterization of Nahmanides (Lichtenberg, *Qobez*, III, 9b). Cf. the contemporary German illustration in Bezalel Narkiss, *Hebrew Illuminated Manuscripts* (Jerusalem, 1969), p. 91.

55. *Zion* 34 (1969): 139.

56. *HRS*, 175b; cf. Abramson, *Rab Nissim Gaon*, p. 280, n. 227. Ramah's metaphorical interpretation of *gan 'eden* goes back to Saadya Gaon, *Emunot ve-De'ot*, 9:5 (ed. Kafih, p. 274). This interpretation differs from the one later developed by Nahmanides in his *Sha'ar ha-Gemul*. R. Mosheh Taku explicitly rejects Saadya's metaphorical interpretation of *gan 'eden*; see his *Ketab Tamim* in *Ozar Nehmad* 3 (1860): 93.

57. Ibid., 162a; cf. too ibid., 172b.

58. *Moreh*, 2:42; the phrase "mar'eh ha-nebu'ah" occurs in the Arabic original.

59. Lichtenberg, *Qobez*, III, 1c.

60. On talking animals in aggadah, see *HRS*, 183a–b; cf. Ibn Ezra, *Commentary on the Torah*, Gen. 3:1.

61. *Sanhedrin*, 63b.

62. *HRS*, 121b; see further 175b; a similar approach is attributed to the *geonim* in *Hiddushe ha-Ritba, Baba Batra*, ed. M. Blau (New York, 1954), II, 279; see further Z. H. Chajes, *Kol Kitbe Maharaz Hayot*, I, 336–337; Judah Halevi, *Kuzari*, 3:73; *Mishnah 'im Perush R. Mosheh b. Maimon*, IV, 209 ("Haqdamah le-Heleq"). For an assertion, by Ramah, that a biblical story occurred in *mar'eh ha-nebu'ah*, see *HRS*, 175b s.v. *ahar*.

63. See *Mishnah 'im Perush R. Mosheh b. Maimon*, IV, 207.

64. *HRS*, 81a.

65. Ibid., 163a–b; cf. the allusion to the commentary attributed to Rashi (ibid., 178a s.v. *va-tisa*); note that the latter's interpretation is based on the Talmud (*Yoma*, 20b).

66. *Sanhedrin*, 38b.

67. For this illustration, cf. Hai Gaon in *Teshubot Geonim*, ed. Y. Musafia (Lyck, 1864), no. 26.

68. *HRS*, 80a. For three different approaches to this problem see Simon Duran, *Magen Abot* (Leipzig, 1855), introduction; Eliyahu Mizrahi, *Commentary on Rashi*, Deut. 4:32; Azariah de Rossi, *Me'or Enayim*, 1:154ff.

69. See, e.g., *HRS*, 7a s.v. *ve-asiqna*; 53a s.v. *Rab Yehudah*; 88a s.v. *tahanunim*; 111a s.v. *ve-amar*; 165a s.v. *le-marbeh*; 166b s.v. *ba-yom*; 167a s.v. *amar R. Yohanan*; 170b s.v. *amar R. Yehudah*; 175a s.v.*va-yevaez*; 175b s.v. *ahar*; 176a s.v. *pisqa*; 176b s.v. *mai*; 178b s.v. *amar*; 179a s.v. *amar*; 179b s.v. *amar leh*; 182a–b.

70. See, e.g., *Sanhedrin*, 110a where sun and moon ascend to the upper heavens with an untimely complaint to God for which He shoots His arrows at them daily. Ramah (*HRS*, 184b) interprets this shooting of arrows as merely a

metaphor for punishment (which removes the problem of anthropomorphism) but retains the literal interpretation of the rest of the story! Apparently preserving God from anthropomorphism is an exegetical obligation; preserving the sun and moon is not.

Ramah was not even averse to ad hoc theological adaptation where necessary to remove anthropomorphism. See, e.g., *HRS*, 170b (top) where God's expression of wonder as to whether He can bring Himself to destroy Israel's enemies (*Sanhedrin*, 98b) gets the following preliminary explanation: "This does not mean that there is any doubt or wonder before Him. It rather refers to the attribute of His mercy . . . which would have it that the nations not be destroyed for Israel. And *this attribute is created* and is therefore susceptible to wonder as are all creatures." Now Ramah, like all geonic-Andalusian figures, generally denied the reality of divine attributes; see, e.g., H. Wolfson, *Repercussions of the Kalam in Jewish Philosophy* (Cambridge, 1979), pp. 1–74; Ramah "Shirim," pp. 79ff.; *HRS*, 182a (bottom). The notion of a real created attribute distinct from God is rare in the Muslim Kalam and can be found in Jewish sources only with the greatest difficulty; see, e.g., H. Wolfson, *The Philosophy of the Kalam* (Cambridge, 1976), pp. 136ff., and *Repercussions of the Kalam*, pp. 120ff. Ramah's use of it here is probably no more than a local solution to a particular problematic text and does not signify a radical new theory of attributes. It was perhaps suggested by similar geonic exegesis; see, e.g., R. Hai Gaon in *Ozar ha-Geonim, Berakot*, II, 93–94. This source suggests that Ramah may have had in mind a temporary "attribute" created for the occasion! In any case, Ramah himself goes on to offer a more satisfactory explanation of this text.

Cf. too *HRS*, 166b s.v. *ba-yom*, where a text describing how God "appeared to [Sennacherib] as an old man" (*Sanhedrin*, 98b) is interpreted to mean that "God prepared for him a certain old man or the *Sar ha-Madda'* [prepared for him] a certain old man." A reasonable guess is that the *Sar ha-Madda'* is something like the Active Intellect pressed into service here to create the necessary perceptions.

71. For an instructive sample, see *HRS*, 160b–161a; Ramah objects that if a certain aggadah was meant to be taken nonliterally, "Why did it use such obscure language; was its purpose to mislead people?" Yet he concludes that the aggadah in question is not authoritative.

72. *Zion* 34 (1969): 139; see *Baba Qamma*, p. 82b.

73. This is confirmed by our three surviving rebuttals of the northern French position; see Nahmanides in Lichtenberg, *Qobez*, III, 8c; Samuel Saporta in Kobak, *Jeschurun*, VIII, 143–144; Asher b. Gershom in Cambridge MS 507.1, p. 6a–b. Note, however, that this would not seem to have been the original Franco-German interpretation; see Rashi, *Baba Qamma*, 83a s.v. *hokmat yevanit; Tosafot, Abodah Zarah*, 10a s.v. *she-en*. This would confirm my contention (Chapter 3) that it was only through the Maimonidean Controversy that the northern French became conscious anti-rationalists.

74. See *Ozar ha-Geonim, Baba Qamma*, ed. B. M. Lewin (Jerusalem, 1943), I, 144.

75. *Mishnah 'im Perush R. Mosheh b. Maimon*, III, 277–278 (*Sotah*, 9:15).

76. Schirmann, *Ha-Shirah ha-'Ibrit*, I, 493; cf. too the critical comment of Alfakar in Lichtenberg, *Qobez*, III, 1b.

77. *Sefer ha-Qabbalah*, pp. 32, 80, 82, 87.

78. *Berakot*, 28b, following the interpretation of Hai Gaon; see Lewin, *Ozar ha-Geonim, Berakot*, II, 39.

79. Quoted in *Perushe R. Yizhaq b. R. Shlomo 'al Maseket Abot*, p. 75; Shmuel de Uceda, *Midrash Shmuel*, p. 42a (*Abot*, 2:16); see Saul Lieberman, *Hellenism in Jewish Palestine* (New York, 1962), pp. 100–105; cf. the similar interpretation in the slightly earlier *Malmad ha-Talmidim* of Jacob Anatoli quoted in Assaf, *Meqorot la-Toledot ha-Hinnuk be-Yisrael*, II, 45. Cf. too the somewhat different approach of Ha-Meiri in his *Bet ha-Behirah, Baba Qamma*, ed. K. Schlesinger (Jerusalem, 1950), p. 239, and his allusion to Maimonides, *MT, Yesode ha-Torah*, 4:13.

80. See Bezalel Ashkenazi, *Shittah Mequbbezet, Baba Qamma* (New York, 1953), p. 262 (to 83a); *HRS*, 95b.

81. Joseph b. Todros does seem to identify the banned *hokmah yevanit* with Greek philosophy; see Kobak, *Jeschurun*, VIII, 30; but later he justifies his own study of secular works (*sefarim hizonim*) on the grounds of his faithfulness to the words of the Sages; see ibid., p. 41. Cf. the approach of Nahmanides to the question of *hokmah yevanit* in Lichtenberg, *Qobez*, III, 8c–d.

82. Lichtenberg, *Qobez*, III, 3d; for Kimhi's use of "hokmah" here, cf. Twersky, "Non-Halakic Aspects of Mishneh Torah," pp. 99–102, 113–115.

82. Kobak, *Jeschurun*, VIII, 91.

84. On the title "master of the Name," see Gershom Scholem, *Kabbalah* (Jerusalem, 1974), pp. 310–311; for the master of the Name as a would-be prophet, see Judah Halevi, *Kuzari*, 3:53; on a contemporary French scholar who bore the title "prophet," see Urbach, *Ba'ale ha-Tosafot*, pp. 278–279. Note in this connection the significance of Asher b. Gershom's interpretation of the talmudic statement that prophecy has been given to the fools as a reference to would-be prophets; see *Baba Batra*, 12b; Cambridge MS 507.1, p. 6b.

85. *Zion*, 34 (1969): 143; cf. Jacob Anatoli, *Malmad ha-Talmidim*, quoted by B. Z. Dinur, *Yisrael ba-Golah*, vol. II, bk. V (Jerusalem, 1971), pp. 279–281; on these practices see Joshua Trachtenberg, *Jewish Magic and Superstition* (New York, 1939); H. J. Zimmels, *Ashkenazim and Sephardim* (London, 1950), pp. 246–249; for the attitude of Maimonides, see, e.g., *Mishnah 'im Perush R. Mosheh b. Maimon*, III, 267 (*Sotah*, 7:4); *MT, Abodah Zarah*, 12:16; *MT, Mezuzah*, 5:4; *Moreh*, 1:61; cf. too Halevi, *Kuzari*, 3:53; Judah b. Barzilai, *Perush Sefer Yezirah*, pp. 103–105 (quoting Hai Gaon).

86. *Sanhedrin*, 67b and Rashi ad loc.

87. Quoted in *She'elot u-Teshubot ha-Rashba*, I, no. 413 (p. 149); *She'elot u-Teshubot ha-Rashba ha-Meyuhasot la-Ramban* (Warsaw, 1883), no. 283 (p. 121).

88. *HRS*, 129b.

89. Nor did he deny, like Maimonides, the efficacy of magic—though he does limit it so that it does not impinge on divine omnipotence and justice; see ibid.

90. Ramah as quoted by Joseph ibn Habiba, *Nimuqe Yosef* to Alfasi, *Baba Qamma*, p. 9a; his probable source is Hai Gaon; see S. Abramson, *'Inyanot be-Sifrut ha-Geonim* (Jerusalem, 1974), p. 258.

91. See, e.g., Samuel Saporta in Kobak, *Jeschurun*, VIII, 143; Asher b.

Gershom, Cambridge MS 507.1, p. 10a; Kimhi in Lichtenberg, *Qobez*, III, 3d; Nahmanides in *Qobez*, III, 9d; Abraham Maimonides in *Qobez*, III, 15d (note his annexation of North Africa into Sefarad); cf. too Abramson, *R. Nissim Gaon*, p. 103); cf. too Yedaya ha-Penini, *Ktab ha-Hitnazlut*, in *She'elot u-Teshubot ha-Rashba*, I, no. 418 (p. 166).

92. *Zion*, 34 (1969): 139.

93. See his *Ktab Tamim* in *Ozar Nehmad*, 3 (1860): 68, 77; R. Moses is aware that Maimonides differs from Saadya on the question of bodily existence in *'olam ha-ba* (see ibid., p. 93) but apparently does not consider that difference crucial; see further Henry Malter, *Saadia Gaon: His Life and Works* (New York, 1926), pp. 282–283; earlier Tosafists speak highly of Saddya; see Malter, *Saadia Gaon*, p. 287; Brill, *Kitāb*, pp. 136–137.

94. Lichtenberg, *Qobez*, III, 15d.

95. See his *Yesod Mora*, p. 11 (end of chap. 1).

96. See *Moreh*, 1:71; see also Chapter 4.

97. Brill, *Kitāb*, pp. 36, 53ff.

98. *Moreh*, 2:22.

99. See Chapter 3.

100. *HRS*, 159a.

101. Finkel, "Maimonides' Treatise in Resurrection," pp. 16–19.

102. See *HRS*, 159a–162b.

103. Besides the instances noted above, see on free will and Divine foreknowledge, *HRS*, 179b–180a; *MT*, *Teshubah*, 5:5; *MT*, *Yesode ha-Torah*, 2:10; *Moreh*, 3:20–21.

104. *Sanhedrin*, 99a.

105. *HRS*, 171a; cf. Brody, "Shirim," p. 80 (top).

106. *MT*, *Yesode ha-Torah*, 1:7.

107. *Moreh*, 1:71; see Meir Simhah ha-Kohen, *Or Sameah* (Riga, 1926), 1:3; Joseph Rosin, *Zafnat Paneah* (Warsaw, 1902), p. 4a; cf. *Mishnah'im Perush R. Mosheh b. Maimon*, IV, 211–212 and Kafih's n. 34; see too the cryptic comment of Shem Tob Falaquera, *Moreh ha-Moreh* (Pressburg, 1837), p. 43.

108. For the Aristotelian origin and subsequent history of the argument for incorporeality used by Maimonides, see H. Davidson, "The Principle that a Finite Body Can Contain Only Finite Power," in *Studies in Jewish Religious and Intellectual History Presented to Alexander Altmann*, ed. S. Stein and R. Loewe (University of Alabama, 1979), pp. 75–92. Unlike the Aristotelian argument, Ramah's argument does not attempt demonstrative proof of incorporeality. It rather shows that given certain theological presuppositions—either that God maintains the universe while his power remains undiminished or that He created the world *ex nihilo*—incorporeality necessarily follows. Apparently, then, Ramah's argument is directed at those (standing outside the Andalusian tradition?) who can be expected to accept these presuppositions but still need to be convinced of incorporeality.

Ramah's argument for God's infinite power from the first presupposition is fairly clear: no finite power can remain undiminished after expenditure of some of that power. The argument for God's infinite power from creation *ex nihilo* is less clear—perhaps it is that since experience with finite forces shows them quite incapable of creating *ex nihilo*, any force which did so must be infinite; cf. Saadya Gaon, *Emunot ve-De'ot*, ed. Kafih, 2:4, p. 73 (top).

Hasdai Crescas later pointed out that Aristotle's reasoning establishes only that a finite body must contain power finite with respect to intensity, not power finite with respect to continuity, whereas his proof of incorporeality attempts to argue from the *continuous* motion imparted to the spheres; see Davidson, "Finite Body," pp. 85–89. It is therefore intriguing that both of Ramah's arguments are designed to establish God's infinite power with respect to *intensity*. But it seems unwise to press the hypothesis that this reflects anticipation of Crescas' point.

109. Lichtenberg, *Qobez*, III, 1c–3b; cf. too the lost polemical letter attacking *Moreh*, 3:15 cited by Mosheh Narboni, *Be'ur le-Sefer Moreh Nebukim* (Vienna, 1852), 3:15 (p. 53a).

110. Lichtenberg, *Qobez*, III, 2a.

111. Ibid.; see Guttman, *Philosophies of Judaism*, p. 186. Note, however, that Castilian anti-rationalists are not completely without reluctance to "lean on the miraculous"; see above, n. 7.

112. See Chapter 3.

113. Lichtenberg, *Qobez*, III, 2b; see the commentaries of Shem Tob and Narboni to *Moreh*, 1:42 and the indignant response of Abravanel, ad loc.; cf. *Iggeret ha-Teshubah* (attributed to Isaac ibn Latif), in *Qobez 'al Yad* 1 (1885): 54.

114. *Moreh*, 2:25.

115. Lichtenberg, *Qobez*, III, 1d; Moses b. Hasdai might have thought Maimonides' analogy more apt (though no less reprehensible); for he denies that either the biblical doctrine of God's unlikeness or the rabbinic teaching that "the Torah speaks in the language of men" rules out anthropomorphism; see his *Ktab Tamim* in *Ozar Nehmad*, 3 (1860): 61, 77.

116. For an early statement of this objection, see the responsum attributed to Hai Gaon in Lewin, *Ozar ha-Geonim, Hagigah*, pp. 65–66; T. Preschel, " 'Al Teshubah Ahat le-Rab Hai Gaon," *Sinai* 68 (1970): 180–181. Cf. *Moreh*, 3:51 and the commentary of Shem Tob, ad loc.

117. See Chapter 3; cf. too Chapter 6.

118. Lichtenberg, *Qobez*, III, 2c.

119. *MT, Yesode ha-Torah*, 4:13; on this passage and subsequent reaction to it, see Twersky, "Non-Halakic Aspects of Mishneh Torah," pp. 111–118 and *Introduction to the Code*, pp. 493–495.

120. Lichtenberg, *Qobez*, III, 3d.

121. Kimhi writes elsewhere that his main occupation has been teaching Talmud to boys; see the end of his *Sefer ha-Shorashim* (Berlin, 1847).

122. See Chapter 1.

123. Lichtenberg, *Qobez*, III, 2c.

124. Ibid., III, 3c–3d.

125. See Hai Gaon above, n. 116.

126. Kobak, *Jeschurun*, VIII, 123.

127. The "thousands" of Spanish Jews who, in 1236, accepted the commandments of *tefillin*, *mezuzah*, and *zizit* at the urging of the French halakist-preacher R. Moses of Coucy could not have all been repentant philosophers! See Moses of Coucy, *Sefer Mizvot Gadol* (Venice, 1547), II, 96d ('*aseh*, no. 3).

128. Kobak, *Jeschurun*, 8:44; cf. too ibid., p. 37: "u-peturin min ha-tefillah u-min ha-tefillin."

129. No such allowance is made by Baer, *History*, I, 108; cf. Kobak, *Jeschurun*, VIII, 28 where Joseph says that rationalistic heresy (unlike Karaism) cannot be recognized by its effect on performance of the commandments!

130. "latet ta'am lepegam"; a clever pun; see *'Abodah Zarah*, 39b; cf. the counter-pun in Menahem b. Zerah, *Zedah la-Derek*, p. 10.

131. See Mishnah, *Sheqalim*, 1:6–7; the agio ensures that payment of the half shekel is precise (see commentators, ad loc.); thus Ramah uses the phrase as a metaphor for punctilious discharge of religious obligations.

132. "va-niram abad heshbon"; for the translation given here, see *Baba Batra*, 78b.

133. Ramah was quite conscious of the implications of radical rationalistic body-soul dualism; see Chapter 3.

134. Lichtenberg, *Qobez*, III, 6c.

135. *Sanhedrin*, 26b.

136. *HRS*, 58a–b.

137. Chaps. 25–49; see Y. Heinemann, *Ta'ame ha-Mizvot be-Sifrut Yisrael* (Jerusalem, 1966), I, 79–97.

138. Kobak, *Jeschurun*, VIII, 36. On French anti-rationalist opposition to Maimonides' explanations for the commandments, see Abraham Maimonides in Lichtenberg, *Qobez*, III, 19a; Samuel Saporta in Kobak, *Jeschurun*, VIII, 145–148; Asher b. Gershom, Cambridge MS 507, pp. 8a–9a; from the latter two sources it would seem that the northern French scholars opposed any attempt to give reasons for the *mizvot*, but this is not entirely clear.

139. For an early formulation of the difference between Spanish and French anti-rationalism, see the interesting remarks of A. Geiger, *Qebuzat Ma'amarim*, ed. S. Poznanski (Warsaw, 1910), pp. 248–249. Having contrasted French and Castilian anti-rationalism, the important figure of Nahmanides remains unlocated. Nahmanides has significant points of contact with Ramah's circle: he too was no outsider to the geonic-Andalusian tradition; and his concerns as an anti-rationalist often dovetail with those of the Castilian anti-rationalists. There is a valid sense in which one can speak of a Spanish anti-rationalism within which both Ramah and Nahmanides are subsumed; but emphasis on Ramah's Castilian circle allows for a somewhat sharper focus. Nahmanides requires delicate, independent treatment: one must determine the way in which Franco-German learning, Provençal kabbalah, and Spanish culture were shaped and fused in his highly creative thought. Such a study is a major *desideratum*; see for the present Samuel Krauss, "Ha-Yihus ha-Mada'i ben ha-Ramban veha-Rambam," *Ha-Goren* 5 (1905): 78–114; see also Septimus, "Piety and Power," p. 213. It is hoped that some significant differences between Nahmanides and Ramah will emerge from the typological study in Chapter 6.

140. See Kobak, *Jeschurun*, VIII, 94–98.

141. See Chapter 3, n. 72.

142. Kobak, *Jeschurun*, VIII, 95; a pun.

143. Ibid., p. 97.

144. Ibid.; this theme is already present in his letter to Kimhi in Lichtenberg, *Qobez*, III, 3b.

145. Note the warning in his letter to Kimhi that the full implications of the adoption of philosophical rationalism in Provence will become apparent only in the future, when it will be too late; see ibid., p. 3a.

146. Ibid., pp. 3d–4a.

147. Kimhi and Ibn Tibbon, as sons of Spanish émigrés, were thoroughly trained in philosophy; see Judah ibn Tibbon's "will" in *Hebrew Ethical Wills,* trans. and ed. I. Abrahams (Philadelphia, 1926), I, 57. Note that Bernard Gui, who was well informed on matters Jewish, calls Kimhi a Spaniard; see Y. Yerushalmi, "The Inquisition and the Jews of France in the time of Bernard Gui," *Harvard Theological Review* 63 (1970): 353; see too Talmage, *David Kimhi,* p. 9.

148. A similar pattern can be seen in comparing the Provençal and northern French arenas: Solomon of Montpellier's surviving statement shows a sharper and more articulate awareness of the possibilities of philosophical rationalism than our surviving *Zarfati* letter (see Kobak, *Jeschurun,* VIII, 99–100; Guttmann, *Philosophies of Judaism,* pp. 185, 435, n. 138); for Solomon's anti-rationalism was forged in opposition to the nascent Provençal rationalism and even the mature rationalism of Samuel ibn Tibbon (see *Jeschurun,* VIII, 99–100); northern French rationalism hardly existed, if at all. In focusing on Ramah I have juxtaposed him to the French anti-rationalists, sometimes lumping the latter together for the sake of comparative perspective. In studying the French arena, one would want to pay closer attention to its complexity and heterogeneity; cf. too n. 29 above; Shatzmiller, "Iggarto shel R. Asher b. Gershom," p. 137. With regard to Solomon of Montpellier it should also be noted that he had close Catalonian contacts and may well have originated in Barcelona; see Septimus, "Piety and Power," pp. 210–211.

149. See Chapters 1 and 2.

150. *Midrash Hokmah,* Oxford MS, 1321, section on Proverbs. For Ibn Matka's attitude toward Aristotle, see Halevi, *Kuzari,* 1:36, 65, 4:16; for a later example, see Abba Mari Ha-Yarhi, *Minhat Qena'ot* (Pressburg, 1838), p. 15; contrast the hostile comments of Nahmanides, *Commentary on the Torah,* Lev. 16:8.

151. *Midrash Hokmah,* Oxford MS, 1321, section on Proverbs.

152. Ibid.

153. *Midrash Hokmah,* Parma MS 421, p. 37.

154. Ibid., p. 4b.

155. *Midrash Hokmah,* Oxford MS 1321, section on Proverbs.

156. *She'elot u-Teshubot ha-Ribash,* no. 157. See S. H. Wilensky, "Isaac ibn Latif—Philosopher or Kabbalist?" in *Jewish Medieval and Renaissance Studies,* ed. A. Altmann (Cambridge, 1967), pp. 185–223.

157. Introduction to *Sha'ar ha-Shamayim,* ed. Y. H. Schor, *He-Haluz* 13 (1881): 123.

158. Lichtenberg, *Qobez,* III, 8d. The meaning of "Sadducee" in this context is unclear; see the interpretation inserted into the text ibid. (by A Lichtenberg?). It is not impossible that the reference is to a contemporary Jew; see, e.g., on Nicholas Donin: Grayzel, *The Church and the Jews,* pp. 339–340; Urbach, *Ba'ale ha-Tosafot,* p. 373; cf. Ch. Merchavia, *Ha-Talmud be-Re'i ha-Nazrut* (Jerusa-

lem, 1970), pp. 229ff. On Franco-German use of *MT*, see Twersky, "Mishneh Torah Criticism," pp. 168–169; but it was not a central text for most of the Tosafists; otherwise the reckless evaluation quoted by Nahmanides would hardly have been possible. Reports are that some northern French scholars modified their original positions; see Shatzmiller, "Le-Temunat ha-Mahaloqet," pp. 132–133; this likely included revision of their image of Maimonides.

159. Kobak, *Jeschurun*, VIII, 100. The precise meaning is unclear. Can Maimonides' writing in Arabic have been the concealment and Ibn Tibbon's translation into Hebrew the revelation? More likely R. Solomon is referring to Ibn Tibbon's oral explication of difficult passages. "The translator" is probably used here as a fixed title for Ibn Tibbon, even when his translating activity is not under discussion. Shohet, "Berurim," pp. 30–31, n. 25 suggests that Solomon is alluding to Ibn Tibbon's *Ma'amar Yiqqavu ha-Mayim*.

160. Kobak, *Jeschurun*, VIII, 100.

161. Ibid., pp. 102–103.

162. Ibid., p. 23; see Chapter 3, n. 54.

163. Kobak, *Jeschurun*, VIII, 39.

164. Lichtenberg, *Qobez*, III, 2d.

165. There is, however, greater circumspection among the Castilian antirationalists in the 1230s in the use of rhetoric directed against Maimonides. Alfakar is generally sharper than Ramah or Joseph b. Todros.

166. Lichtenberg, *Qobez*, III, 9b–9d; Kobak *Jeschurun*, VIII, 24. Cf. too Brody, "Shire Meshullam da Piera," p. 34. Alfakar and Ramah simply contrast *Mishneh Torah* (as a whole) to the *Guide*; see *Qobez*, III, 2d, 6d.

167. Lichtenberg, *Qobez*, III, 2b.

168. See above, n. 114.

169. *'Amude Kesef u-Maskiyyot Kesef*, ed. S. Werbluner (Frankfort, 1848), pp. 99–101. For modern examples of this type of interpretation of the *Guide*, see Leo Strauss, *Persecution and the Art of Writing* (Glencoe, 1952), pp. 38–94; Shlomo Pines, "The Philosophic Sources of the Guide of the Perplexed," in his translation of Maimonides' *Guide of the Perplexed* (Chicago, 1963), pp. lvi–cxxxiv. See the survey of G. Vajda, "Les études de philosophie juive du Moyen Age depuis la synthèse de Julius Guttmann," *Hebrew Union College Annual* 45 (1974): 209–225.

170. Lichtenberg, *Qobez*, III, 2d.

171. Kobak, *Jeschurun*, VIII, 29.

172. See Chapter 3.

173. Lichtenberg, *Qobez*, III, 6d.

174. H. Brody, "Qinat Ramah 'al ha-Rambam," *Tarbiz* 6 (1935): 4–5.

175. Perhaps an allusion to Isa. 26:2, the invocation to *Moreh Nebukim*, bk. 1 (which would explain why it was an act of boldness).

176. See Prov. 9:5; cf. the invocation to the introduction to the *Moreh*, quoting Prov. 8:4.

177. For this metaphor, cf. n. 134 above and Chapter 3, n. 28.

178. Lichtenberg, *Qobez*, III, 6d.

179. See, e.g., *'Abodah Zarah*, 17a on Prov. 5:8; cf. Rashi, Prov. 2:12 and 6:29.

180. Ramah's last sentence is unclear; but it is presented as an explanation for the previous sentence; it would, therefore, seem to mean that the *Guide*, because of its obscurity, is subject to misinterpretation; and so Maimonides may be innocent of the views of which he is suspected; hence the allusion to Num. 14:24.

VI. Anti-rationalism and Mysticism

1. See G. Scholem, *Reshit ha-Kabbalah* (Tel Aviv, 1948), pp. 127–161; *Ursprung und Anfänge der Kabbala* (Berlin, 1962), pp. 324–420; *Ha-Kabbalah be-Gerona* (Jerusalem, 1969); *Kabbalah* (Jerusalem, 1974), pp. 48–57.

2. See G. Scholem, "Te'udah Hadashah le-Toledot Reshit ha-Kabbalah," in *Sefer Bialik* (Tel Aviv, 1934), pp. 141–162.

3. Spanish kabbalah went from nonexistence to maturity and immense influence within two generations—an almost astounding speed for so revolutionary and profound a religous-intellectual transformation. Contrast thirteenth-century Ashkenazic Jewry among whom the impact of kabbalah was much more modest; see Y. Dan, *Torat ha-Sod shel Haside Ashkenaz* (Jerusalem, 1968), pp. 128–129, 252–262. Even more striking is the rapidity with which Spanish kabbalah eclipsed its Provençal mother. I. Twersky, "R. Yedaya ha-Penini u-Perusho le-Aggadah," in *Studies in Jewish Religious and Intellectual History* (University of Alabama, 1979), pp. 80–81 (Heb. sec.), n. 79, alludes to this development in passing. In fact, at precisely the moment when important elements of the Hispano-Jewish leadership were converting to kabbalah, part of the Provençal leadership was uniting to suppress kabbalah; see Scholem, n. 2 above, and *Ursprug und Anfänge*, pp. 349–357; see further n. 4 below.

4. Scholem, in the works cited in n. 1 above, calls attention to the complex relationship of kabbalah to philosophy: early interest, parallel themes and trends, borrowings and transformations, occasional consciousness of common ground—with a sense of strong opposition developing among some kabbalists only in the period of the Maimonidean Controversy. For the earlier Provençal period see also Twersky, *Rabad*, pp. 258–300. A good sense of the complex relationship of thirteenth-century Spanish kabbalah to philosophy and the rivalry between them emerges from some of the topical introductions in I. Tishby, *Mishnat ha-Zohar*, I (Jerusalem, 1971) and II (Jerusalem, 1961). Also very useful on the relationship of kabbalah to philosophy are some of the studies in E. Gottlieb, *Mehqarim be-Sifrut ha-Kabbalah* (Tel Aviv, 1976) and G. Vajda, *Recherches sur la philosophie et la kabbale dans la pensée juive du moyen age* (Paris, 1962).

The earliest work of kabbalistic anti-rationalism is Jacob b. Sheshet's *Meshib Debarim Nekohim*, ed. G. Vajda (Jerusalem, 1968), probably composed about 1240; see Vajda, *Recherches sur la philosophie et la kabbale*, pp. 33–113. But a sense of sharp opposition is already explicit in the polemical poems of Meshullam da Piera, some of which are still earlier; see "Shire Meshullam da Piera," ed. Brody, nos. 3, 11, 12, 15, 24, 40, 44, 48, 49. Particularly interesting is no. 48, an autobiographical poem in which Meshullam demands of kabbalists that they come forward and rescue him from rationalistic heresy. They do.

Scholem has argued that the anti-rationalist party in the Maimonidean

Controversy was closely connected with kabbalah; see, e.g., *Ursprung und Anfänge*, pp. 357–363. But this connection should not be exaggerated; see the remainder of Chapter 6 on Ramah and Castilian anti-rationalism. The letter of the Lunel rationalists in which Nahmanides is praised to the skies (Chapter 4, n. 84) would seem to indicate that in *their* minds kabbalah and anti-rationalism were at most peripherally linked. A closer linkage does appear only a few years later in a struggle between rationalists and kabbalists for communal leadership in Catalonia; see Septimus, "Ma'abaq," pp. 393–394; and "Piety and Power," pp. 201–215.

This increased hostility is perhaps related to a contemporary Provençal campaign against kabbalah; see n. 3 above. According to Scholem, this campaign reflects the opposition not of rationalists but of traditional talmudists; see, e.g. *Ursprung und Anfänge*, p. 352; *Ha-Kabbalah be-Gerona*, pp. 46, 99. In fact, the director of the antikabbalistic campaign, Meshullam b. Mosheh of Beziers, was a very prominent member of the Maimonidean camp; see, e.g., Septimus "Piety and Power," pp. 200–211; Saperstein, *Decoding the Rabbis*, p. 179. Note too that the author of this campaign's surviving antikabbalistic polemic, Meshullam's nephew Meir b. Simon of Narbonne, occasionally uses philosophical argumentation in his anti-Christian polemics; see D. Lasker, *Jewish Philosophical Polemics against Christianity in the Middle Ages* (New York, 1977), pp. 66, 86, 116. It may well be that steadily increasing philosophical sophistication coupled with the increasing pressure of Christian polemic contributed to a conviction, in Provençal circles, that the doctrine of the *sefirot* was inconsistent with the doctrine of the pure unity of God. (Even in the fourteenth century this sort of objection to the *sefirot* is identified with rationalism; see Isaac b. Sheshet Perfet, *She'elot u-Teshubot*, no.157.) In reading Meir b. Simon's polemic—both anti-Christian and anti-kabbalist—it should be remembered that, at this juncture in Provence, even Maimonideans should not be expected to write like dyed-in-the-wool philosophical rationalists; see Chapter 5. It is therefore quite possible that the Provençal proponents of Maimonides and opponents of kabbalah were roughly the same group. This group apparently constituted the bulk of the communal leadership of Provence; see Chapter 4. Their determined efforts at suppression may have been a factor in the sudden decline of Provençal kabbalah. The entire question requires further study.

5. *Ozar ha-Kabod* (Warsaw, 1879), p. 32b. On the term "internal" (*penimit*), see Twersky, *Rabad*, p. 243, n. 16. Scholem (*Ursprung und Anfänge*, p. 359) considers this a reliable tradition and views Ramah as an instance of the confluence of kabbalah and anti-rationalism, but observes that *HRS*, despite numerous opportunities, gives no evidence of kabbalah. On Todros b. Joseph Abulafia, see Scholem in the *Encyclopaedia Judaica* (Jerusalem, 1972), II, 194–195.

Ramah's occasional use, in his halakic writings of the geonic formula "as we have been shown by Heaven" (*OZ*, p. 185; *HRS*, 180b), is not to be taken literally and is irrelevant to the question of his relationship to kabbalah; see Twersky, *Rabad*, pp. 291–299. Alharizi could playfully apply this formula to his poetry (*Tahkemoni*, p. 28)—a variation on his very frequent poetry-prophecy motif; see, on this association, the sources in J. Kugel, *The Idea of Biblical Poetry* (New Haven, 1981), p. 182. (Correct on this point S. Spiegel, "On Medieval

Hebrew Poetry," in *The Jews: Their Religion and Culture*, ed. L. Finkelstein [New York, 1971], pp. 84–85) For a similar formula, standardly applied to a business judgment, see Goitein, *A Mediterranean Society*, I, 168. Elsewhere, playing on the geonic formula, Ramah writes of "what my intellect has shown me from the Lord's Torah" (*OZ*, p. 148).

6. The equation of moon to rainbow is presumably based on the fact that both are symbols for Shekinah; see, e.g., Tishby, *Mishnat ha-Zohar*, I, 476, 489–490. For a halakist of Ramah's classical sensibilities to invent a completely new norm on kabbalistic grounds seems completely out of character. Moreover, propagation of such a ruling through "many warnings" implies an abandonment of esotericism—which would make Ramah's literary silence on kabbalah harder to understand. Note that it is possible to read Todros as *inferring* that Ramah was a kabbalist from this reported ruling.

7. See G. Scholem, "Mi-Hoqer le-Mequbbal," *Tarbiz* 6 (1935): 90–95. R. Todros' report may be responsible for the attribution of pseudepigraphic kabbalistic works to Ramah; see the commentary of Moses Botarel to *Sefer Yezirah* (Jerusalem, 1965), p. 33; Yedidyah Norzi, introduction to *Minhat Shai*, p. 13, in *Ozar Perushim 'al ha-Torah* (New York, 1950); see too E. Gottlieb, *Mehqarim be-Sifrut ha-Kabbalah* (Tel Aviv, 1976), pp. 477–478, 483 n. 18.

8. In the following analysis I will attempt whenever possible to compare Ramah to Nahmanides. Nahmanides was a central figure in thirteenth-century Hispano-Jewish culture. He was also in contact with Ramah and shared many of the latter's anti-rationalistic concerns and positions. Moreover, Nahmanides shared Ramah's expertise in and deep commitment to talmudic studies; see J. Katz, "Halakah ve-Kabbalah—Maga'im Rishonim," *Zion* 44 (1979): 171. Differences between Ramah and Nahmanides should thus be particularly telling.

9. See Chapter 5, nn. 23 and 24.

10. *HRS*, 176b (top).

11. See, e.g., Tishby, *Mishnat ha-Zohar*, II, 737–738, 752. The term *middah*, used by Ramah for "attribute," is also used by kabbalists as one of many synonyms of *sefirah*. The "attribute of justice" could refer to the "lower attribute of justice," the last *sefirah* which is the least "profound and hidden." The reader unfamiliar with the doctrine of the *sefirot* may consult Scholem, *Kabbalah*, pp. 87ff.

12. See, e.g., Nahmanides' *Commentary on Job* in *Kitbe ha-Ramban*, ed. Chavel, I, 88ff.; Ezra b. Solomon, *Commentary on Song of Songs* in *Kitbe ha-Ramban*, II, 483. It is not impossible that Ramah intended an oblique allusion to "binah," an antecedent of this phrase in Job 28:20; but such a technical hint seems unlikely here.

13. An early Toledo kabbalist whose name has come down to us is R. Judah ibn Ziza; see the very interesting document published by Scholem in "Iqbotav shel Gabirol ba-Kabbalah," in *Meassef Sofre Erez Yisrael*, ed. A. Kabak and A. Steinman (Tel Aviv, 1940), pp. 175–176 and n. 77; see too *Ursprung und Anfänge*, pp. 199–200, 347. Ha-Yarhi was also familiar with kabbalah. Note too Ramah's close Catalonian and Provençal contacts, discussed in Chapter 2.

14. Crucial here is that the *sefirot* are *not* viewed as created beings separate and distinct from the realm of Divinity; see, e.g., Scholem, *Kabbalah*, pp. 96ff. I

would not exclude the possibility that Ramah understood and accepted the *sefirot* in some other sense—in which they are identified with the attributes or separate intelligences of philosophy. Such an interpretation appears already in the early Provençal document mentioned in n. 13 above. Thus the tenth *sefirah* is identified with Maimonides' tenth, intelligence, which communicates to the prophets. The author views this *sefirah* as an angel which speaks in God's name "as an agent speaks in the name of his principal." (The text is corrupt here and can be better understood with the help of MS. Mantua 8, 7886, photographed in Dinur, *Yisrael ba-Golah*, vol. II, bk. IV, opposite p. 325.) For this formula see, e.g., Ibn Ezra's *Short Commentary* to Exod. 3:6. This *sefirah* is thus viewed as an angel—quite distinct from the Divinity. See Halevi's poetic formulation of Ibn Ezra's formula in Schirmann, *Ha-Shirah ha-'Ibrit*, I, 534, ll. 31–32 and Nahmanides' objection, qua kabbalist, in Chavel, *Kitbe ha-Ramban*, I, 148; see too his *Commentary* to Exod. 23:20 (Chavel, ed., I, 442, ll. 22–23). Cf. S. Heller-Wilensky, "Isaac ibn Latif," in *Jewish Medieval and Renaissance Studies*, ed. A. Altmann, pp. 213–214.

15. See, e.g., Scholem, *Pirqe Yesod be-Habanat ha-Kabbalah u-Semaleha* (Jerusalem, 1976), pp. 259–307.

16. *Commentary on the Torah*, ed. Chavel, I, 250 (to Gen. 46:1). Nahmanides identifies this view with Maimonides. Perhaps he did not want to accentuate his divergence from the geonic-Andalusian tradition as a whole. For the origins of this doctrine of "created Glory" see A. Altmann, "Saadya's Theory of Revelation," in *Saadya Studies*, ed. E. Rosenthal (Manchester, 1953), pp. 4–25. See too Scholem, *Pirqe Yesod*, p. 271, and the references in Wolfson, *Studies in the History of Philosophy and Religion*, II, 93. Actually, Maimonides himself sometimes departs from this theory (see, e.g., *MT, Teshubah*, 8:2) but for reasons quite different from those of Nahmanides.

17. Lichtenberg, *Qobez*, III, 1d.

18. See, e.g., *HRS*, s.v. *amar*. Ramah's exegesis of Num. 14:14 may have been suggested by Ibn Ezra, *ad loc.* or Halevi, *Kuzari*, 5:23 and 3:19 (end); see too *HRS*, 163b s.v. *'ula*. Ramah's description of the grades of *visio beatifica* shows the influence of R. Hai Gaon; see *Ozar ha-Geonim, Yebamot*, ed. B. M. Lewin (Jerusalem, 1936), I, pp. 124–125. See too *HRS*, 175b s.v. *ahar*; 176b s.v. *arba'*; 183b l. 10; 185b s.v. *amar*. Nahmanides, *Hiddushe ha-Ramban* (Jerusalem, 1938), I, to *Yebamot*, 49b, juxtaposes to the geonic-Andalusian theory "the interpretation which is true (*emet*)" and suggests an alternative (kabbalistic) interpretation to Num. 14:14, repeated in his *Commentary on the Torah, ad loc.*; on "emet," see below, n. 21.

Note too Ramah's assumption that Metatron "whose name is the same as his Master's" (*Sanhedrin*, 38b) is an angel plain and simple (*HRS*, 80b)—rather than Shekinah, as in kabbalistic doctrine. Nahmanides' sharp rejection (in his *Commentary* to Exod. 24:1) of Rashi's comments on Metatron applies equally to Ramah, who follows Rashi though—typically—in a manner more theologically fastidious. Where Rashi merely says of Metatron "that he has no power to pardon our sins," Ramah says "that he has no power to do anything without the permission of his Master."

19. It should be recalled, in this connection, that Ramah was not averse

to ad hoc theological adaptation for the sake of removing anthropomorphism; see Chapter 5, n. 70.

20. G. Scholem, *Major Trends in Jewish Mysticism* (New York, 1954), p. 32.

21. *HRS*, 169a; see Chapter 5. Cf. Nahmanides for whom "truth" (*emet*) has become a synonym for kabbalah; see, e.g., Scholem, *Ursprung und Anfänge*, p. 340.

22. See, e.g., in Chavel, *Kitbe ha-Ramban*, I, 424–425; *Ma'areket ha-Elohut* (Jerusalem, 1963), 152b; Scholem, *Pirqe Yesod*, 285. Scholem (*Ursprung und Anfänge*, p. 359, n. 85) already noted that Ramah's expression of perplexity over the celestial Jerusalem is hard to understand in the mouth of a possessor of esoteric wisdom. Scholem (*Ursprung und Anfänge*, p. 359) sees Ramah's formulation of the proof for God's incorporeality from his infinite power (*HRS*, 171a) as consistent with kabbalah. I have tried to show that this is a conservative reworking of a Maimonidean proof; see Chapter 5.

23. *Sanhedrin*, 99b.

24. See, e.g., Scholem, *Major Trends in Jewish Mysticism*, pp. 29–30.

25. See, e.g., *Zohar*, III, 14b.

26. *HRS*, 172a; for the expression *nahat ruah*, see *Sifra*, ed. I. Weiss (New York, 1946), 7c (to Lev. 1:9), where the tendency is somewhat akin to Ramah's.

27. G. Scholem, *On the Kabbalah and its Symbolism* (New York, 1965), p. 40.

28. Quoted in *Perush R. Yizhaq b. R. Shlomoh 'al Maseket Abot*, ed. Kasher and Blochrowitz, p. 110.

29. Ramah, in Brody, "Shirim," p. 76, l. 9; see too Judah b. Barzilai, *Perush Sefer Yezirah*, p. 85; Wolfson, *Repercussions of the Kalam in Jewish Philosophy*, p. 123. For an early poetic formulation, see Ibn Gabirol's *Keter Malkut* in Schirmann, *Ha-Shirah ha-'Ibrit*, I, p. 262, l. 80. Here the argument is more complex since Ibn Gabirol, in context, has just introduced his preexistent Wisdom. He was obviously aware of the problem addressed by Ramah's *Abot* commentary—the tension between the notion of a preexistent Torah through which the world is created and the notion that God creates without an instrument, and wished to preserve both.

30. Ramah's position is akin to that of Saadya, who denies the antemundane creation of the Torah and explains the talmudic passage (*Pesahim* 54a) in which the Torah is said to be one of the seven things created prior to the creation of the world as meaning, figuratively, that it is because of them that all things have been created; see Wolfson, *Repercussions of the Kalam in Jewish Philosophy*, pp. 92–93. Halevi too (*Kuzari*, 3:73) takes this position, comparing the talmudic passage to the Aristotelian teaching that "the original thought [corresponds to] the final execution"; on this formula see the note of F. Rosenthal in his edition of Ibn Khaldun, *The Muqaddimah* (Princeton, 1967), II, 415. Thus even conservative elements in the geonic-Andalusian tradition had no use for a mystical conception of the Torah and gave talmudic sources pointing in that direction a teleological twist. For subsequent use of the Aristotelian formula, see, e.g., S. Abramson's introduction to the reprint of Joshua ibn Shu'ib, *Derashot 'al ha-Torah* (Jerusalem, 1969). p. 35.

31. See Chapter 3 for the dating of *Perate-Sanhedrin* and *Perate-Abot*.

32. See Chapter 2, n. 89.

33. *Masoret Seyag la-Torah*, p. 3b. Even the occasional explanations that Ramah *did* include, according to his introduction, are missing from the published version; cf. Kimhi to Gen. 24:39.

34. See Nahmanides' introduction to his *Commentary on the Torah* (ed. Chavel, I, 6–7); Tishby, *Mishnat ha-Zohar*, II, 366; Scholem, *On the Kabbalah and Its Symbolism*, pp. 37ff. The early Gerona kabbalist Ezra b. Solomon, in his *Commentary on Song of Songs* (in Chavel, *Kitbe ha-Ramban*, II, 548), sees this view of the text of the Torah as analogous to the linkage of the 613 commandments with the 613 human limbs and sinews. Here too every single commandment is indispensable to the total person. (For further development of this correspondence in later sources, see, e.g., Meir ibn Gabbai, *Abodat ha-Qodesh* [Warsaw, 1843], 2:16, p. 70.) But Ramah characterized the rabbinic parallel between human limbs and positive commandments (*Makkot*, 23b) as *simana be-'alma* (a mere sign); see Jacob in Habib, *'En Ya'aqob* (Jerusalem, 1961), V, 248, quoting the lost *Perate-Makkot*. Ramah thus made a point of denying any intrinsic relationship between the two. This would not, in itself, constitute evidence that he was not a kabbalist. (Nahmanides could ascribe a somewhat similar position to the author of *Halakot Gedolot*, though for nontheological reasons; see his first gloss to Maimonides' *Sefer ha-Mizvot* [Jerusalem, 1959], p. 2.) But it does fit well the nonmystical picture of Ramah's view of the Torah that emerges from other sources.

35. For example, *'Erubin*, 13a. (The comments of Rashi and Tosafot ad loc. also testify to their distance from a mystical conception of the Torah); see Tishby, *Mishnat ha-Zohar* II, 366, n. 26.

36. *Masoret Seyag la-Torah*, p. 3b. Note Ramah's allusion to Isa. 29:14: "And the wisdom of their wise men shall perish . . ." Maimonides also used this verse to explain current inability to explain aggadah; see *Mishnah 'im Perush R. Mosheh b. Maimon*, I, 38. But the rationalistic twist in Maimonides' interpretation is missing here; cf. too the *Guide*, II, 11.

37. See, e.g., *HRS*. 158b. Scholem (*Ursprung und Anfänge*, p. 359, n. 85) already noted that Ramah's use of "qabbalah" was the very opposite of the esoteric sense given it by the kabbalists.

38. Association of the Merkabah tradition with kabbalah is fundamental in *Sefer ha-Bahir*—even before the technical term "kabbalah" came into use; see Scholem, *Ursprung und Anfänge*, p. 53. Maimonides' identification of the Merkabah tradition and "the secrets of the Torah" with philosophy is well known; see, e.g., Twersky, "Non-Halakic Aspects of Mishneh Torah," pp. 111ff.; S. Klein-Braslavy, *Perush ha-Rambam le-Sippur Beri'at ha-'Olam* (Jerusalem, 1978), pp. 22–34.

39. Lichtenberg, *Qobez*, III, 4b, 6c.

40. Joseph (in Kobak, *Jeschurun*, VIII, 28) seems to identify the talmudic *pardes* with philosophy, an impossible position for a kabbalist. Cf. Scholem, *Ursprung und Anfänge*, p. 359.

41. *HRS*, 158b.

42. There is no evidence that any of Ramah's remarks were intentionally directed against kabbalah. But if we are correct in assuming that Ramah was familiar with kabbalah, this possibility cannot be discounted.

43. See Scholem, *Ursprung und Anfänge,* pp. 324ff.; Septimus, "Piety and Power," pp. 201–221.

44. See, e.g., Isaac b. Sheshet Perfet, *She'elot u-Teshubot,* nos. 45, 157.

45. See n. 4 above and I. Twersky, "Religion and Law," in *Religion in a Religious Age,* ed. S. D. Goitein (Cambridge, 1974), pp. 69–82.

46. See Nahmanides, *Commentary on the Torah,* introductory poem, on his relationship to Ibn Ezra.

47. See Chapter 5.

48. After confessing perplexity about the "heavenly Jerusalem," Ramah prays for divine help in interpreting "the plain sense of this dictum" (*HRS,* 169a). The implication is that interpretations that depart from the plain sense are available without prayer—but are unattractive.

49. See I. Tishby, "Aggadah ve-Kabbalah be-Perushe ha-Aggadot shel R. 'Ezra ve-R. 'Azriel me-Gerona," in *Minhah le-Yehudah* (Jerusalem, 1950), pp. 170ff.

50. See, e.g., S. Klein-Braslavy, *Perush ha-Rambam le-Sippur Beri'at ha-'Olam,* pp. 47–51.

51. The context of Ramah's restraint and conservatism in aggadic exegesis should be seen as historical as well as typological. In the generation after Ramah a more ambitious and extended type of aggadic exegesis began to flower, at least in part in response to a new use of aggadah in Christian polemic. On this development and the problem of aggadic interpretation generally, see I. Twersky, "R. Yedayah ha-Penini u-Perusho la-Aggadah," in *Studies in Jewish Religious and Intellectual History Presented to Alexander Altmann,* pp. 63–82 (Heb. sec.), and M. Saperstein *Decoding the Rabbis,* pp. 1–78.

52. See Chapter 5.

53. *Kitbe ha-Ramban,* I, 153; for parallel passages see the editor's n. 34; on this passage see Baer, *History,* I, 245, who tends to overemphasize the hostility between kabbalah and rationalism.

54. The whole question of Nahmanides' theory of "hidden miracles" requires separate treatment. For a brief but useful formulation of the distinction between Nahmanides' position and a strict occasionalism, see Gottlieb, *Mehqarim be-Sifrut ha-Kabbalah,* p. 266.

55. See Chapter 5.

56. See his *Commentary* to Exod. 6:2 and Lev. 26:12. Note that in this last passage the soul's reward "in 'olam ha-ba after resurrection" is also subsumed under the natural.

57. *Kitbe ha-Ramban,* I, 191. Not only is the naturalism striking here but also the soteriological centrality of knowledge; cf. *Kitbe ha-Ramban,* II, 281; Vajda, *Recherches sur la philosophie et la kabbale,* pp. 373, 376. It is interesting that Hasdai Crescas returns to Ramah's position, denying a natural immortality; see *Or Hashem,* II:2:1, II:5:5, and II:6:1; E. Schweid, *Ta'am ve-Haqashah* (Ramat Gan, 1970), pp. 200–201 (but the suggestion that this reflects Nahmanides' influence requires qualification).

58. See his *Commentary* to Gen. 17:1, Gen. 46:15, Exod. 6:2, Exod. 23:25, Lev. 26:12.

59. *'Abodat ha-Qodesh* (Warsaw, 1883), 2:17, p. 72b.

60. Ibn Gabbai's perception of Nahmanides' "art of writing" brings the method of kabbalistic esotericism very close to its philosophical counterpart: not just silence but intentionally misleading statements are addressed to those outside the elite. Cf. too Scholem, *Kabbalah*, 94–95. But I am not at all sure that Ibn Gabbai has got Nahmanides right on this score; see n. 61 below.

61. See *'Abodat ha-Qodesh*, 2:17, p. 72a–b. Nahmanides himself probably meant the term "nature" (*teba'*) in its scientific sense. More than a concession to ordinary usage, this nature plays a role in Nahmanides' kabbalah; see, e.g., *Ma'areket ha-Elohut*, pp. 70b–71a. I doubt, therefore, that Nahmanides was really guilty of inconsistency. Ibn Gabbai's value for us is heuristic. The kabbalistic "naturalism" to which Ibn Gabbai calls attention goes beyond providence and extends to other religious phenomena—perhaps even creation and miracle itself! Particularly helpful on this whole question are some of the studies of E. Gottlieb in *Mehqarim be-Sifrut ha-Kabbalah*; see, e.g., pp. 11–37, 263ff. Gottlieb has already called attention to the usefulness of Ibn Gabbai.

62. See Twersky, n. 45 above.

63. See Chapter 3.

64. See, e.g., Scholem, *Kabbalah*, p. 336.

65. *Kitbe ha-Ramban*, II, 264–311; a careful study of *Sha'ar ha-Gemul* remains a desideratum.

66. Published by G. Scholem, "Kabbalat R. Ya'aqob ve-R. Yizhaq," in *Mada'e ha-Yahadut*, I (Jerusalem, 1926), 237–238 and later identified by him as R. Azriel's letter to Burgos; see "Seridim Hadashim me-Kitbe R. Azriel me-Gerona," in *Sefer Zikkaron le-Asher Gulak ule-Shmuel Klein* (Jerusalem, 1942), p. 202, n. 2.; *Ursprung und Anfänge*, pp. 330–331. I would like to acknowledge the help of Professor I. Tishby in locating and interpreting this source.

67. See Chapter 3.

68. The identification of *tehiyyat ha-metim* with *gilgul* is made in several thirteenth-century works; see E. Gottlieb, *Ha-Kabbalah be-Kitbe R. Bahya b. Asher* (Jerusalem, 1970), p. 145; see too Bahya b. Asher's *Commentary* to Gen. 3:19. Bahya knew and borrowed from the letter of R. Azriel; see Gottlieb, *Ha-Kabbalah*, p. 82. (Note, however, that Bahya also explicitly takes the position of Ramah and Nahmanides on resurrection; see his *Commentary* to Deut. 30:15.) Analogy (but not identification) between transmigration and resurrection is frequent in patristic writings; see H. Wolfson, *Religious Philosophy* (New York, 1965), pp. 75–76. Whether there is any connection between R. Azriel's ideas and Christian sources, I do not know. (It is interesting that Abarbanel argued that Nahmanides' view of a spiritualized body in the period after resurrection reflects Christian influence; see *Nahalat Abot* [New York, 1953], end of chap. 4, pp. 289–293.)

69. Cf. Scholem, *Ursprung und Anfänge*, p. 358. R. Azriel was writing fairly closely in time and place, to R. Sheshet and may well have been acquainted with his letter to Lunel. Sheshet's argument that physical resurrection would be a terrible "comedown" could be quite troublesome to members of the Gerona circle; see Brody, "Shire Meshullam da Piera," p. 18, ll. 43–50. Meshullam indicates that there is a kabbalistic solution to this problem but gives no hint as to what it might be.

70. Lichtenberg, *Qobez*, III, 6c.

71. See Chapter 5, nn. 56 and 57.

72. See *OZ*, pp. 145–146, no. 248; *YRB*, 1:82. For Maimonides' position, see *Mishnah 'im Perush R. Mosheh b. Maimon*, IV, 441–446 (to *Abot*, 4:7); *MT*, *Talmud Torah*, 3:10–11.

73. See, e.g., the quotation in Samuel de Uceda, *Midrash Shmuel* (Jerusalem, 1960), p. 108a (to *Abot* 5:13); see too *Perushe R. Yonah 'al Maseket Abot*, ed. M. Kasher and Y. Blochrovitz (Jerusalem, 1966), p. 30 (to *Abot* 2:13).

74. See in de Uceda, *Midrash Shmuel*, p. 111b (to *Abot*, 5:17); *Mishnah 'im Perush R. Mosheh b. Maimon*, IV, pp. 461ff. Ramah's definition of *hasid* and the doctrine of the mean upon which it is based are borrowed from Maimonides.

75. See *Perush R. Yonah 'al Maseket Abot*, p. 35; *Perush R. Yizhaq b. R. Shelomoh 'al Maseket Abot*, p. 72 (to 2:12).

76. *HRS*, 185 s.v. *amar*; cf. *Mishnah 'im Perush R. Mosheh b. Maimon*, IV, 391–393 (*Shemonah Perqim*, 6). Ramah's comments may reflect a different solution to the problems of aggadic interpretation raised by Maimonides.

77. See de Uceda, *Midrash Shmuel*, 7a (to *Abot*, 1:3); see too *YRB*, 1:130. Cf. *Mishnah 'im Perush R. Mosheh b. Maimon*, IV, 199–200, 409; *MT, Teshubah*, chap. 10.

78. *Perush R. Yizhaq b. R. Shelomoh 'al Maseket Abot*, p. 108.

79. See Chapter 5, nn. 34 and 35.

80. Ramah might also have had in mind the striking passage in which Jonah ibn Janah interprets the concluding verses of Ecclesiastes as a warning against absorption in metaphysical speculation; see the quotation in Wolfson, *The Philosophy of the Kalam*, p. 93; cf. Maimonides' interpretation of Eccles. 12:13 in the introduction to his Mishnah commentary (*Mishnah 'im Perush R. Mosheh b. Maimon*, I, 45).

81. See too the sources cited above, n. 77. Ramah, in his *Abot* commentary, eliminated every trace of the intellectualism so prominent in Maimonides' conception of love. He also strove to maintain fear as a high religious attainment without compromising purity of motivation. It seems likely that, for Ramah, Talmud, if anything, was "queen of the sciences"; see Chapter 1. But there is no trace of a direct soteriological function for knowledge *of any kind* in Ramah's thought. In fact, the view that knowledge of the right sort is a direct cause of salvation is usually a concomitant of the sort of eschatological naturalism that Ramah so roundly rejected. Cf., however, the formulation of Profiat Duran, *Ma'aseh Efod* (Vienna, 1865), pp. 4–6; see on this source Twersky, n. 45 above.

82. Brill, *Kitāb*, p. 58.

83. Brill, *Kitāb*, pp. 37–38, 58–59.

84. *HRS*, 158b s.v. *kol*; "lo . . . lahaqor ahar ha-nistarot asher . . . en lanu 'eseq bahen"; see *Hagigah*, 13a.

85. Ed. Chavel, I, 8.

86. In the midst of his warning Nahmanides adds that God "will show those whom he favors wondrous things from his Torah." There are encouraging comments sprinkled throughout the *Commentary*; e.g., on Lev. 25:2: "Here [the rabbis] have called our attention to one of the great secrets of the Torah . . .

incline your ear to listen to what I am permitted to let you hear ot it . . . and if you are found worthy you will understand." See too on Gen. 4:1 (ed. Chavel, I, 14–15), Gen. 1:14, Lev. 18:25, and elsewhere. On occasion Nahmanides indicates that he is going beyond appropriate bounds in order to respond to rationalistic disparagement of aggadah; see on Gen. 1:1 (ed. Chavel, I, 11) and Gen. 24:1 (ed. Chavel, I, 134).

87. See n. 84 above; cf. Halevi's *Dīwān*, ed. Brody, III, 232, ll. 32–33 and his poem in Schirmann, *Ha-Shirah ha-'Ibrit*, I, 519, ll. 27–29. Ramah's use of Ben Sira is anticipated and rejected in the *Guide*, I:32. For a kabbalistic parallel to Maimonides' interpretation of Ben Sira as a warning to the adept not to reach beyond human capability, see, e.g., *Ma'areket ha-Elohut*, pp. 82b–83b, based on *Sefer ha-Bahir*, ed. R. Margoliyot (Jerusalem, 1951), p. 23, no. 49. Note, however, that the interpretation of Ben Sira as a warning to the adept against overreaching, rather than as a universal renunciation of the esoteric, is already implicit in its use in *Hagigah*, 13a.

88. Brody, "Shirim," p. 67. Here too Ramah is alluding to Ben Sira's warning, in the versions of the Palestinian Talmud and Genesis Rabba; see Brody's note. Ramah's second line is based on Ps. 131:1; see Ibn Ezra to Ps. 131:2. To Ramah's poetic interpretation of the sin of the Tree of Knowledge, contrast the *Guide*, I:2; see L. Berman, "Maimonides on the Fall of Man," *AJS Review* 5 (1980): 1–15. Ramah's understanding of the prohibition against eating of the Tree of Knowledge is similar to that of L. Strauss, *Persecution and the Art of Writing*, p. 20.

Cf. also the contrast between Ramah's image of Abraham and that of Maimonides (Chapter 4, n. 17). The kabbalistic view of Abraham, as a possessor of the secrets of Creation, based on the conclusion to *Sefer Yezirah*, parallels Maimonides' image; see, e.g., Ibn Gabbai, *'Abodat ha-Qodesh*, 3:21, pp. 165–167, for a kabbalistic critique of Maimonides' image of Abraham that nevertheless (when compared to Ramah's image) reveals the parallelism of the rationalistic and kabbalistic views. Ramah's interpretation of Gen. 15:6 (Chapter 4, n. 17) is diametrically opposed to the interpretation given at the end of *Sefer Yezirah* according to which Abraham's *emunah* consisted of esoteric wisdom. This sense of "emunah" becomes standard in kabbalah; see, e.g., Nahmanides in Chavel, *Kitbe ha-Ramban*, II, 297, l. 18.

89. As a final footnote to the career and controversies of Ramah, it is perhaps fitting to mention the long poetic inscription on his tombstone which once stood in the Jewish cemetery of Toledo. The tombstone is no longer extant. Its inscription was copied anonymously at the end of the fifteenth or beginning of the sixteenth century along with those of seventy-five other Toledan scholars and communal leaders; see *Abne Zikkaron*, ed. Yosef Almanzi and S. D. Luzzatto (Prague, 1841), pp. 1–3, 18–19; F. Cantera and J. M. Millas, *Las inscripciones hebraicas de España* (Madrid, 1956), pp. 36–37, 74–76. The copyist knew the rabbinic history of Toledo well and was particularly interested in the Abulafia, Ibn Shoshan, and Alfakar families (including a possible but doubtful son of Ramah; see Cantera and Millas, *Las inscripciones*, p. 76.) His brief introduction permits us to imagine a son of the Toledo Jewish community at about the time of the Expulsion or somewhat later (if he was living as a *converso*) searching out

and copying tombstone inscriptions before taking final leave of his native city. Perhaps in this way he could preserve for "the generation to come" something of the memory of "the scholars, nobles and great men . . . of Toledo, the once acclaimed city." Prominent among the inscriptions that he chose is the one that testifies to the immense scholarship and spiritual stature of "the prince over the princes of the Levites, R. Meir Halevi, may the memory of the righteous and holy be for a blessing."

Index

Aaron b. Meshullam (of Lunel), 5, 12; position in Resurrection Controversy, 43–52, 57, 59, 89, 113; on Maimonides, 45–46, 47–48, 63, 100; Spanish epistolary style, 133n34

Abarbanel, Isaac, 114, 171n68

Abba Mari of Lunel, 114

Abraham, image of, 148n17, 173n88

Abraham b. Moses (of Carcassonne), 30

Abraham b. Nathan Ha-Yarhi (*Sefer ha-Manhig*), 10, 32–35, 41, 48, 55

Abraham of Toques, 49

Abulafia, Joseph b. Meir (Ramah's uncle), 5, 28

Abulafia, Joseph b. Todros (Ramah's brother), 7, 9; anti-rationalism, 62; defense of *Zarfatim*, 64; role in Maimonidean Controversy, 69, 72, 94–96 (passim); on antinomianism, 94; on Maimonides, 100–101; and kabbalah, 109

Abulafia, Judah b. Meir (Ramah's son), 38

Abulafia, Judah b. Meir (Ramah's uncle), 5, 29

Abulafia, Meir (Ramah's grandfather), 5

Abulafia, Meir b. Judah (Ramah's cousin), 29

Abulafia, Samuel (Ramah's brother), 29, 133n27

Abulafia, Todros b. Joseph (Ramah's nephew), 105

Abulafia, Todros b. Judah, 64, 127n103, 135n52, 135n72

Abulafia, Todros b. Meir (Ramah's father), 5–9

Abulafia, Todros b. Zerahyah (Ramah's cousin), 119n26

Abulafia, Zerahyah b. Meir (Ramah's uncle), 5

Aggadah: nonliteral interpretation, 57–58, 78–85, 110; naturalistic reinterpretation, 59, 92; problem of, 76–78, 109–110; authority, 77, 84; as repository of secret wisdom, 110; and kabbalah, 106–108, 109–110

Albalia, Baruk b. Isaac, 24

Albalia, Isaac b. Baruk, 24

Alfakar, Abraham, 5, 17–18, 33, 37

Alfakar, Joseph, 17, 69

Alfakar, Judah b. Joseph, 18; anti-rationalism, 62; role in Maimonidean Controversy, 68–69, 71, 75, 95–96; critique of rationalism, 69, 91–92, 93; use of Maimonidean formula, 80; philosophical study, 86; on Maimonides, 100–101; and kabbalah, 106, 109, 114

Alfasi, Isaac (*Halakot*), 24, 30, 74; exclusive study of, 20; translation of Arabic works, 23, 29; on love poetry, 33

Alfonso VII (of Castile), 2

Alfonso VIII (of Castile), 6, 7

Alfonso X (of Castile), 152n86

Alharizi, Judah: on Spain and Toledo, 2–3, 10, 32; on Ramah, 3, 4, 32, 44; poetry, 16, 136n76; contrasted to Ha-Yarhi, 32; on *Mishneh Torah*, 40; and Resurrection Controversy, 51; translation of *Treatise on Resurrection*, 53–54; poem sent to Maimonides, 138n4

Almohades, 2, 13–14, 123n66; Spanish-Provençal contact accelerated by, 29

Almoravids, 1

Anatoli, Jacob, 158n79

Andalusian tradition: political, 2, 11, 17; cultural, 2, 14–15, 16; talmudic, 23–25;

influence in Provence, 29, 30, 64–65.
See also Arabic; Aristocracy; Geonic-
Andalusian tradition
Anthropomorphism, 78–81, 92, 106,
157n70. *See also* Incorporeality of God
Antinomianism, 59, 93–95, 149n17
Anti-rationalism, periodization, 61–63
Arabic: knowledge and use of, 15, 17–18,
27, 32, 52, 53–54, 81, 95–96, 126n99,
155n52; competition with, 16
Aragon, 27, 33, 65, 72
Arama, Isaac, 114
Aramaic, 15, 25
Aristocracy (Hispano-Jewish): in Toledo,
2–4, 11, 17; in Burgos, 6; in Barcelona,
28, 65, 70–72, 93; and Maimonidean
Controversy, 62, 65, 66, 68, 70–72,
93–94; and religious-moral decay,
93–94, 152n87; and kabbalah, 104, 109.
See also Nesi'im
Aristotelianism, 18–20, 55, 62, 89–92,
97–98, 101
Aristotle, 20, 97, 160n108
Asher b. Gershom, 150n37, 158n84
Asher b. Yehiel, 13, 138n6, 151n63
Astrology, 86, 148n17
Attribute (*middah*): and *sefirah*, 105–106;
created, 157n71
Averroës, 18, 19, 20, 148n17
Azriel of Gerona, 112

Bahya b. Asher, 171n68
Barcelona, 27–29; during Maimonidean
Controversy, 65, 70–72; socioreligious
controversy, 70–72, 93
Bar Hiyya, Abraham, 64
Ben Asher codex, 38
Ben Sira, 114
Benveniste, Isaac (Barcelona *nasi*), 9, 28,
123n66
Benveniste, Samuel b. Sheshet, 28
Benveniste, Sheshet b. Isaac, 28; position
in Resurrection Controversy, 46–48,
49–56 (passim), 57–60; spirituality, 47,
49, 58, 112; on Maimonides, 47–48; on
critics of *Mishneh Torah*, 73–74
Beziers, 28
Biblical studies, 15–16. *See also* Masorah
Burgos: Ramah's origins, 4–9; Ramah's
ties with, 16, 22, 37–38; kabbalah in,
30, 112; during Maimonidean Controversy, 68, 69

Catalonia, 27–29, 30, 65, 72, 109
Christianity and Christians, 6, 9–11,
13–14, 149n17, 165n4
Commandments: reasons for, 95; and
human limbs, 169n34
Convivencia, 122n66
Córdoba, 24
Crescas, Hasdai, 114, 149n17, 160n108,
170n57
Cuenca, 22
Custom (*minhag*), 32–33, 34–35

David b. Joseph (of Narbonne), 29
David b. Saul, 80–81
David of Chateau Thierry, 49
Death, 42. *See also* Spirituality
De'ot, 112
Donin, Nicholas, 162n158
Duran, Profiat, 172n81

Edom, 14
Eliezer b. Aaron (of Bourgogne), 49
Eliezer Rokeah, 49
Emunah, 148n17, 173n88
Eschatology, 40–60 (passim), 81–82,
110–112. *See also* '*Olam ha-ba*; Resurrec-
tion Controversy; *Tehiyyat ha-metim*;
Wisdom
Estella, 22
Eternity of the world, 91, 97, 101
Ethical theory, 112–113
Ezra b. Solomon (of Gerona), 169n34

Fourth Lateran Council, 123n66
Franco-German tradition: image of Maimonides, 49, 99; emergence of anti-rationalism, 50–51, 59, 63, 157n73; and
Moses b. Hasdai, 79; and geonic-Andalusian tradition, 85, 95; and Castilian
anti-rationalism, 95. *See also* Aggadah;
Anthropomorphism; Rashi; Superstition; Tosafists
Fredrick II, 19, 27

Geonic-Andalusian tradition: and ratio-
nalism, 80, 85–89, 92, 95, 100–101; and
Franco-German tradition, 88; differing
perceptions of, 88–89; and mysticism,
106, 108, 109, 114, 168n30
German pietists, 49, 87, 154n29
Germany (Ashkenaz), 37, 49, 85, 87
Gerona, 22, 27, 28, 35, 65, 112

Ghazzali, 18
Granada, 24

Hai Gaon, 157n70, 158n78, 158n90,
  160n116, 167n18
Halevi, Judah (*Kuzari*): rejects Spain for
  Land of Israel, 2, 11, 118n16; letter to
  Moses ibn Ezra, 15; and David Nar-
  boni, 29; philosophical anti-ratio-
  nalism, 62; on Greek wisdom, 85; on
  Muslim and Christian Spain, 117n10;
  on Messianic Sabbath, 125n92; on
  Abraham, 148n17; on prophecy
  through angels, 167n14; denies preexis-
  tent Torah, 168n30
Hebrew: study of and style, 15–16; unify-
  ing role, 27; style in translations,
  53–54; polemical corrections of errors,
  142n72
Hillel of Verona, 150n44
Hokmah, 86
Hokmah yevanit (Greek wisdom), 85–86
Honorious III, 123n66

Ibn Bahlul, Jonah, 12, 20, 73–74, 153n87
Ibn Bal'am, Judah, 147n6
Ibn Chiquitilla, Moses, 29
Ibn Daud, Abraham, 5; on transfer to
  Christian Spain, 2, 26, 33; response to
  Halevi, 11; Aristotelianism, 18, 62; *hok-
  mah yevanit*, 86; *Zikron Dibre Romi*,
  128n136
Ibn Ezra, Abraham, 88, 89, 155n52; and
  R. Tam, 64; on temporary resurrection,
  144n107; on prophecy through angels,
  167n14
Ibn Ezra, Judah, 2, 11
Ibn Ezra, Moses: letter from Halevi, 15;
  poetic canons, 16; perception of Chris-
  tian Spain, 118n16; philosophical
  poem, 129n41; eschatological poem,
  139n18
Ibn Gabbai, Meir, 110–111
Ibn Gabirol, Solomon, 61, 139n16,
  168n29
Ibn Giat, Isaac, 24
Ibn Giat, Judah, 29
Ibn Hasdai, Abraham, 70–72
Ibn Hasdai, Judah, 70–71
Ibn Janah, Jonah, 61, 172n80
Ibn Kaspi, Joseph, 101
Ibn Latif, Isaac, 97–99

Ibn Matkah, Judah: *Midrash Hokmah*,
  19–20, 27; philosophical anti-ratio-
  nalism, 62, 97–98; on Maimonides, 98,
  101
Ibn Megash, Isaac b. Meir, 23, 24
Ibn Megash, Joseph, 2, 13, 24, 25, 30, 37
Ibn Megash, Meir, 2, 23
Ibn Paqudah, Bahya, 20, 62, 129n141,
  146n146
Ibn Sahl, Joseph (d. *1123*), 23
Ibn Sahl, Joseph (d. *1207*), 23–24
Ibn Shabbetai, Judah, 5–7, 16
Ibn Shoshan, Isaac, 32
Ibn Shoshan, Joseph, 7, 27, 47, 55;
  synagogue, 10; elegy for, 10–11;
  opposition to, 17; and Ha-Yarhi, 32,
  33, 34
Ibn Shoshan, Solomon, 32, 47
Ibn Tibbon, Judah, 118n10, 162n147;
  "Will," 133n34; translation method,
  145n112
Ibn Tibbon, Samuel, 14, 96, 99; Spanish
  connections, 29–30, 39; translation of
  Treatise on Resurrection, 52–53
Ibn Ziza, Judah, 30, 166n13
Incorporeality of God, 78–81, 90–92,
  159n108. *See also* Anthropomorphism
Innocent III, 6
Inquisition (in Montpellier), 66
Intelligences, separate, 81
Isaac (author of *Women's Aid*), 5
Isaac b. Abraham (of Dampierre), 49
Isaac b. Samuel (of Dampierre), 49
Isfahan, 144n103
Islam, 1–2, 13–14
Islamic religion, Ramah's knowledge of,
  126n99
Israeli, Israel (of Toledo), 85

Jacob b. Asher (*Turim*), 22
Jacob b. El'azar (*Kitāb al-Kāmil*), 15, 16
Jacob b. Meir (R. Tam), 64
Jacob b. Sheshet, 164n4
Jerusalem, celestial, 76–77, 106
Jonah b. Abraham (of Gerona), 118n20,
  155n45; role in Maimonidean Contro-
  versy, 63–64, 69–70; in Barcelona, 70;
  alleged repentance, 151n44
Jonathan ha-Kohen (of Lunel), 39, 42–44,
  46
Joseph b. Israel (of Toledo), 29
Joseph b. Joel (translator), 53–54

Joseph ha-Nagid, 24
Judah b. Barzilai, 30, 62

Kabbalah, 30, 32, 104–114
Kabod, 106
Kalonymous b. Todros (Provençal *nasi*),
    5, 29
Karaism, 7, 17
Kimhi, David, 27; role in Maimonidean
    Controversy, 65–66, 68–69, 86, 93; in-
    tellectual isolation, 96

Las Navas de Tolosa (battle), 13–14
Latin, 18
Lucena, 24, 29
Lunel, 28, 29, 39; during Resurrection
    Controversy, 42–56 (passim); during
    Maimonidean Controversy, 64, 75, 88

Ma'arab, 15, 37
Maimonides, Abraham, 80–81, 89,
    149n18
Maimonides, Moses: images of, 3, 45–46,
    47–48, 49, 60, 63–64, 88, 97–103; *Guide
    of the Perplexed*, 18, 55, 63–64, 66, 72,
    81, 82, 91, 92, 95, 96, 98–102; *Mishneh
    Torah*, 36, 38, 39–44, 47, 49, 55, 56, 57,
    73, 74, 102; *responsa* to Lunel, 39, 43;
    Ramah on, 39–40, 42–43, 45, 55–56,
    72–74, 101–103; *Sefer ha-Madda'*, 40–42,
    63–64, 66, 72, 74, 82, 90, 93, 98–101;
    Treatise on Resurrection, 52–56, 90, 92
Mar'eh ha-nebu'ah, 83
Marseilles, 29, 39
Masorah, 15, 21; *Masoret Seyag la-Torah*,
    35–38; and kabbalah, 108
Master of the Name, 86, 158n84
Mehqar, 155n52
Meir b. Simon (of Narbonne), 165n4
Meir ha-Kohen (of Saragossa), 27
Meiri, Menahem b. Solomon, 26, 37,
    158n79
Menahem b. Zerah, 20, 161n130
Meshullam b. Kalonymous (Provençal
    nasi), 65, 69, 86
Meshullam b. Mosheh (of Beziers),
    69–70, 165n4
Meshullam da Piera, 139n19, 150n31,
    151n52, 164n4, 171n69
Messiah and messianism, 4, 125n92,
    137n111
Metatron, 167n18

Molina, 20
Monarchy, 10–13
Montpellier, 28, 63, 152n74
Moses b. Hasdai (Taku), 79, 88, 143n86,
    156n56, 160n115
Moses of Coucy, 160n27
Mozarabs, 126n99
Muqammis, David al-), 139n18
Musar (adab), 17

Nahmanides, Moses, 139n16, 156n56,
    165n4; and Ramah, 15, 28, 35, 66–68,
    69, 72; role in Maimonidean Contro-
    versy, 63–72 (passim), 75–76, 79,
    99–102 (passim); on German demonol-
    ogy, 87; on Barcelona nesi'im, 93; on
    Maimonides, 99–100; on Shekinah,
    106; compared to Ramah, 109,
    110–111, 114, 161n139, 166n8
Narbonne, 28, 29, 35, 142n63; during
    Maimonidean Controversy, 64, 86
Nathan (father-in-law of Joseph b.
    Todros), 69
Naturalism, 58, 59, 89–92, 146n146; and
    kabbalah, 110–111
Neoplatonism, 61, 148n11
Nesi'im: of Toledo, 3, 11; of Barcelona, 9,
    65, 70–72; illegitimate use of title,
    119n20
Nissim Gerondi, 114
North Africa, 37, 159n91
Northern France: new ties with, 31, 48;
    and Resurrection Controversy, 48–50;
    and Maimonidean Controversy, 63–67
    (passim), 70, 75, 76, 82. See also Franco-
    German tradition; Zarfat; Zarfati

'Olam ha-ba, 40–60 (passim), 82, 85, 90, 112

Pardes, 169n40
Perpignan, 37
Philosophy: study of, 18–20, 51. See also
    Hokmah yevanit; Wisdom
Poetry: quotations from Ramah's, 8, 9,
    11, 14, 24, 38, 55, 56, 114, 125; in To-
    ledo, 15, 16–17; philosophical, 19;
    Spanish influence in Provence, 30; on
    taxes, 33; opposition to, 33–34;
    Ramah's *dīwān*, 119n23, 121n37; and
    history, 135n52
Provençal rationalists: image of Maimon-
    ides, 45–46, 63, 88; role in Maimoni-

dean Controversy, 63–70 (passim), 75, 86, 88; and geonic-Andalusian tradition, 88; philosophical sophistication, 96; and kabbalah, 165n4. *See also* Aaron b. Meshullam; Kimhi, David

Provence: and Catalonia, 28, 46; Spanish influence, 29, 30, 64, 65; and Spain, 29–32; ties with Maimonides, 39, 42, 54; Kimhi's eulogy, 83

Qabbalah peshutah, 77, 108

Rabad (Abraham b. David), 28, 43–44, 133n33

Ramah: name, 3, 5; dates, 5, 7; origins and family, 4–10; mother, 120n31; career in Toledo, 10–25; economic and political activity, 11–12; communal authority, 12; social and religious criticism, 4, 118n20, 152n87; books, 21, 24–25, 37; travel, 31; alleged pride, 3, 44; humor, 4, 34, 142n72, 161n30; conservative temper, 16, 19, 22; death of son, 38; nephew's impression, 105; on medicine, 131n172; tombstone, 173n89

Rashi (Solomon b. Isaac), 25, 27, 31, 87; aggadic exegesis, 76–79, 105; commentary to Heleq, 154n24

Reconquista (Christian Reconquest of Spain): and transfer of Spanish Jewry, 1, 13–14; impact on position of Jews, 10–13

Resurrection Controversy, 39–60; related to other topics: 67, 74, 75, 81, 90, 92, 100, 111; date, 151n54

Ribash (Isaac b. Sheshet Perfet), 22, 98, 114

Romance (*la'az*), 15, 18, 27

Rossi, Azariah de, 54

Saadya Gaon, 18, 88, 89, 156n56; Ramah's relation to, 19, 41, 148n17; eschatology, 41, 44, 59; nonliteral exegesis, 57; *Book of Doctrines and Beliefs*, 61; decline in influence, 61–62; and mysticism, 109, 168n30

Samson b. Abraham (of Sens): and Resurrection Controversy, 49–59 (passim); textualism of, 57–58, 78

Samson of Corbeil, 49

Samuel ha-Nagid, 24, 64, 154n12

Samuel ha-Sardi, 65–66, 70

Saragossa, 27, 61

Sar ha-Madda', 157n70

Scholars: self-supporting, 12, 112; self-serving and corrupt, 73, 152n87

Sefarim hizonim, 158n81

Sefer ha-Bahir, 169n38, 173n87

Sefer Yezirah, 173n88

Sefirot, 106

Seville, 24

Shekinah, 106

Shem Tob b. Shem Tob, 141n53

Solomon b. Abraham (of Montpellier), 28; role in Maimonidean Controversy, 63–72 (passim), 75, 93, 99, 162n148; literalism, 80, 82; Castilian anti-rationalists on, 81, 96; on Maimonides, 99, 100

Solomon b. Judah (of Dreux), 49

Spain (Sefarad), images of, 2–4, 26, 64–65, 86, 117n10, 118n16, 119n20, 158n91

Spanish, *see* Romance

Spirituality, 47, 58, 94, 104, 111–113

Superstition and demonology, 86–87

Talmudic studies: Ramah and revival of, 3, 20–25; communal function, 12–13, 22; curricular primacy, 15–16, 20–21, 93, 172n81; *Peratim*, 21–22; *responsa*, 22; originality and independence, 22, 165n5; teachers and colleagues, 23–24, 32–35; ties with northern halakah, 28–29, 30–32, 34–35; authorities quoted, 31; attitude to *Mishneh Torah*, 39–40, 72–74; in *Kitāb al-Rasā'il*, 43, 53, 55–56

Tamim ("of simple faith"), 149n17

Taxation, 12–13, 33, 124n83, 153n87

Tehiyyat ha-metim, 47, 52, 85, 112, 139n18

Throne of Glory, 81

Toledo: before Almohades, 1, 10; as refuge from Almohades, 2–3; as Jerusalem, 3, 137n111; as new Andalusia, 15; and Burgos, 7; political and economic life, 10–14; cultural life, 14–25; northern ties, 26–32; northerner in, 32–35; during Maimonidean Controversy, 66–69; tombstones copied, 173n89

Torah, mystical conception of, 107–108

Tosafists, 22, 31, 48–59 (passim), 64

Translators and translations (Arabic to Hebrew), 18, 23, 27, 29, 32, 52–54, 133n32

Translators and translations (Christian), 14, 18–19
Transmigration, 112
Tree of Knowledge, 114
Tudela, 22
Tushiyyah, 81, 155n52

Wisdom: soteriological function, 59, 92–93, 110, 113, 114, 172n84; quest for divine, 97–98, 104, 108–109, 110–111, 113–115. *See also Hokmah yevanit*

Yedaya ha-Penini, 148n11
Yizhaq b. Abba Mari (*'Ittur Soferim*), 134n45

Zacuto, Abraham (*Sefer Yuhasin*), 28, 47
Zarfat, 48, 64, 66–67, 70, 76, 85, 99; changing Spanish usage, 65, 132n22
Zarfati: image of, 64–65, 75, 86
Zerahyah Halevi (of Gerona), 28, 35, 120n26

HARVARD JUDAIC MONOGRAPHS

1. *David Kimhi: The Man and the Commentaries,* by Frank Talmage

2. *Studies in Medieval Jewish History and Literature,* edited by Isadore Twersky

3. *Decoding the Rabbis: A Thirteenth-Century Commentary on the Aggadah,* by Marc Saperstein

4. *Hispano-Jewish Culture in Transition: The Career and Controversies of Ramah,* by Bernard Septimus